THE
BREAKING

THE BREAKING

Gabriel Jacob Israel

THE BREAKING by Gabriel Jacob Israel
Published by Creation House Press
A Charisma Media Company
600 Rinehart Road
Lake Mary, Florida 32746
www.charismamedia.com

Design Director: Justin Evans
Cover design by Nathan Morgan

Library of Congress Cataloging-in-Publication Data: 2015944002
International Standard Book Number: 978-1-62998-472-8
E-book International Standard Book Number: 978-1-62998-473-5

Some names have been changed to protect the privacy of the individuals involved.

While the author has made every effort to provide accurate telephone numbers and Internet addresses at the time of publication, neither the publisher nor the author assumes any responsibility for errors or for changes that occur after publication.

First edition

15 16 17 18 19 — 987654321
Printed in the United States of America

You were taught, with regard to your former way of life, to put off your old self, which is being corrupted by its deceitful desires; to be made new in the attitude of your minds; and to put on the new self, created to be like God in true righteousness and holiness.

—Ephesians 4:22–24

I dedicate this book to the One who inspired me to write it—the love of my life and my one true Savior, Jesus Christ! Thine be *all* the glory! Without You, I would not be alive and well today! Hosanna! I love You and forever will! I can't wait to continue to worship You in heaven for all eternity! I pray that my life is a pleasing sacrifice to You.

Amen

SURROUNDED BY THE empty, oppressive silence of the night, I sat in my despair and looked up into the night sky. "God, there are so many questions I have for You. So many parts of my life are in a mess. But if there was one question I could have You answer out of all these, it would be this: What are You going to do about my broken heart?"

Without a pause, I heard the Lord say, "I'm going to break it open so wide that it will have nothing left to do but to come back together whole."

—SEPTEMBER 2013

CHAPTER 1

THE PHONE RANG, and one of the girls up at the front of the store answered it. "James…it's your brother." He never looked over in her direction; he was sure he already knew what this call was about. It was the middle of the day and he was swamped at work. As he continued to fill in a pharmacy label on the computer, he put the phone on his shoulder, holding it in place by tilting his head. "All right?"

"They're at your house right now," said the voice on the other end. "James, you can't just keep ignoring this. You need to go do something about it, today." My father came to a stopping point and decided to go ahead and leave work for a bit. He took the time to finish up what he was doing and then calmly headed outside to get into his truck.

His demeanor was as cool as a cucumber when he arrived at the house and walked through the door. From a distance he saw my mother standing in the kitchen next to another man. He then started to walk toward them, walking through the den and up the steps that led into a large open area where the kitchen was. He stood in front of them and extended his arm to shake the man's hand. "My name is James Pearson, and this is my wife. You need to get out of my house." Not a word was said as the

1

man stepped around my father and then made his way toward the door. My dad turned to watch the man until he was gone.

A car was parked on the street waiting for David to get into his own car and drive away. He would then be followed until he was clear outside the city limits to make sure he was good and gone. My father had surveillance following David and my mom for months now—phone calls, recordings, photos, you name it. He had known about the affair but never let on to my mother that he knew about anything.

I can't say I could blame him, due to recent events. I can see why my father would be satisfied to just leave things well enough alone. My sister, his daughter, had lost her lifelong battle with cancer less than a year earlier at the tender age of fourteen. After this, Dad spent most nights alone in the garage or downstairs in the den drinking his blues away. He was doing his best to just let these wounds heal, much less add to them. Denial is supposed to be a beautiful thing, but unfortunately for my father, ignoring my mother's infidelity didn't make it disappear.

I was nine at the time, and I can't tell you how confusing this all was for me as well. I had just lost my big sister, the family unit was falling apart, and now I was being dragged along with my mother to go see this other man. My mother would try to convince me how great this David was, even convincing me to join in with her as we drove back home, crying because she didn't want to go back home without him. I felt so much guilt having to walk back in the house and look at my daddy's face—I knew that he knew where we had been, and I felt awful being dragged along in this lie. My mom also had the audacity to have her boyfriend at our house when my dad was at work.

One afternoon, my best friend came over to play. My friend spotted my mom sitting in the den kissing this other man. "Gabriel, who's that?" she asked.

I tried to brush it off by saying, "Oh, it's just one of Mom's friends."

My friend stood there for a minute and watched them interact, then said, "No . . . Gabriel, I don't think that's her friend."

After David was evicted from the house, my dad had to go back to work. He didn't even look over at Linda before heading out the door. She ran after him. He had almost made it to the end of the garage when she called out, "What about Gabriel?"

He stopped midstride. He turned, shrugged his shoulders, and answered, "What about her?"

━ ━ ━ ━ ━ ━ ━

By the time I was eleven years old, my parents were divorced. My mother decided that she and I should move to Nashville, her reason being that if we didn't get out of Murfreesboro, someone was going to end up dead. After the divorce, my mother rented a house right around the corner from our old home, where my dad still lived. Life now consisted of late night drive-bys with my mom trying to see what my dad was up to, and my mother standing outside her house screaming and throwing things at him in her driveway when he would drop me off after having me for the weekend.

My dad bought me a pair of in-line skates for Christmas that year. One day after school, David came to the house to see my mom. When I saw him I gave it my all to smile the way I would if I wanted him there. But I didn't. I was sick of all this. I strapped on my new skates and barreled out the front door. A little angry in-line skating should do the trick to let out the rage!

I headed down the street, pushing my legs harder and harder to gain some speed on the bumpy pavement. I made a quick left and went up a steep hill. This was good! The fight to climb the hill was great for my frustrations! When I made it to the top, I headed down the other side. I had never gone *down* this hill before. As I gained momentum and started to lose control, I tried to turn my body to the left. Not able to gain control at this speed, I tripped over my feet and flipped once, landing on my back. I sat up, both legs stretched out in a V. I slumped my torso over and started to cry. I felt defeated—not just by the hill, but by life itself. I felt no need to try to pick myself up.

A neighbor spotted me and waited to see if I was OK. I just continued to sit there, hanging my head. She walked over and put one of my arms over her shoulder. She helped me to stand and walked me slowly back to my house. I felt stupid. All that for nothing! Now I had a rip in the knee of the jogging suit my daddy had bought for me too. Little did I know at the time, this scenario would be but a preview of how the next twenty-five years of my life would go.

━ ━ ━ ━ ━ ━ ━

After moving to Nashville, one night in a drunken rage my mother declared to me that she planned to get in the car, drive to Murfreesboro, and drive her minivan through my father's house. Not being able to stop her from getting into her car and divert her plan, I saw no other option but to get in the car with her. I didn't want her to hurt my dad. Before I could call my father to warn him, my mother was already out the door and getting into her car. I was also afraid for my mother's safety. She was way too drunk to be driving. I was doing the best I knew how to keep an eye on her and protect them both.

I hesitated before getting into the car; she could have killed us both. She had driven for almost fifteen minutes, ranting and raving, when we finally reached the exit that would put us on the interstate and take us to Murfreesboro. Fortunately, before she made the turn to veer onto the ramp, she changed her mind.

She then turned the car around, and by the grace of God, we returned safely home.

A lot of these things I kept to myself; I didn't even tell my dad. Every other weekend he would drive from Murfreesboro to Nashville to pick me up from my mom's. I loved being with my dad. He was my knight in shining armor. I was full of joy every time I got to go with him. It gave me a break from my mom's house, if only for a couple days. I didn't care what he and I did, I was just happy to be with him. I felt safe. I put all the thoughts of what went on at my mom's house in the back of my mind, until that dreaded time would come on Sunday when it was time for me to go back home.

I never told my dad what living with my mom was like. I never let on that her home was a torture chamber, my very own private hell. I didn't tell him about the angst I felt as I tried to prepare myself mentally to be left alone with her. I would start to feel homesick for him before we would even pull into her driveway.

If he only knew what was really going on behind that closed door as he walked away. As soon as the door was shut, Mom would come after me in her rage and take her war out on me. I did my best to deal or run from her to get away. In my mind I would think about my dad driving back to Nashville, unaware that he had dropped me off and left me in this kind of situation. In my mind I would call out for him: "Daddy, come back! Daddy, please come get me!" If he had only known he had left me somewhere that wasn't safe, he would have never taken me there. The notion made me sick—to think that someone was hurting his girl and he had no idea at all. It also made me sad to think of him driving back home alone. I didn't want him to be sad or lonely. I felt lonely too. My want for my dad increased; I ached when we were apart. I felt trapped in a world I didn't want to be a part of. I withheld these thoughts and how much I needed him.

I looked forward to seeing him until it was time for him to pick me up again for the weekend. Then the cycle would continue—he would drop me off at Mom's, and I would once again have to deal with the feelings of losing him. I would quietly and internally accept my fate and prepare my mind every time I walked into her home. The only thing that got me through was knowing my dad would be back in two weeks.

My mother would spend hours berating me with questions about what my father and I had done that weekend. She would demand answers.

"I don't know!" I would say.

"What do you mean you don't know?" She was relentless.

After doing this with her for months, I started to play the "I have no memory" card, because I never knew what information was going to set her off more and make things worse. So all I knew to say was, "I don't know." She wouldn't take that for an answer, though. If my answers did not appease her, or if she felt I was withholding information (which was usually the case), she would resort to physical means and violence to try to get me to talk. She would beat me, hit me, bite me, pull my hair, spit in my face, sit on me, block me from getting into my bedroom, hold me up against a wall—whatever it took to try to pry information out of me—information that I didn't have, because I never knew what the right answer would be.

She interrogated me like I was a suspect on trial for murder, only those people get treated nicer. Sometimes I really didn't have any news to tell her—this only provoked her anger. No matter what I answered, it always seemed to make it worse. This would go on all night until she would either pass out or get her fill of taking it out on me. The look in her eyes said, "There's no coming back from this!" It was complete mania. It was terrifying for me. Fear, panic, always being on guard, screaming, and confusion became my new norm.

The following week I went to school with kids and people I didn't know. I was in sixth grade. Not only had my life around me changed, but I was also going through puberty. There were things going on with me, on the inside and out, that were confusing enough on their own. I didn't have anyone to explain to me what was going on with my body, and I didn't talk to anyone about what was going on at home. My life was a war zone in all areas, inside of my head and in the world around me. I was caught in the line of fire on a battlefield, suffering the effects of a war that I didn't start and didn't belong to. Looking back on it now, even though I've never fought for my country, at the age of twelve, I'm sure I could have been diagnosed with Post-Traumatic Stress Disorder (PTSD).

One evening I heard bloodcurdling screams coming from my mom's room. I ran down the hall as a hot flash of terror penetrated my body. Fear consumed me as I got closer and closer to where the screams were coming from. What was I about to walk into? What was I about to see? Was my mom OK? I ran through the doorway and turned to see my mother standing in front of her toilet in the bathroom. She was standing in a puddle of water as water gushed out and over the bowl. I took a moment to let my brain process what I was seeing. Where was all the blood? Where was the horror? Was all that screaming and drama really necessary for just this?

She screamed at me, "Well, don't just stand there!" She was still panic stricken, and her voice sounded shrill. She turned something as simple as a toilet bowl flooding into a nightmare. The way she carried on made my heart race and sent me into a panic too. I still wasn't certain why, but her mania made me feel as though our lives were in danger. I did as I was told and ran to get her some towels. I ran through the house like it was on fire.

After we turned off the water behind the toilet and cleaned up all the water on the floor, I still wondered where that terrifying threat was that she called out to me to save her from. Everything was OK; it was no big deal. Unfortunately, though, it wasn't. The role reversal had begun. Instead of her being the one in charge with a level head, I was slowly slipping into the roles of her mother, her boyfriend, her husband, and her savior. Little did she know—and much to her dismay—I was ill equipped.

━ ━ ━ ━ ━ ━ ━

By the time I was in middle school, my mother moved us again to another home, this time in Brentwood. I would start yet another school my seventh grade year. All the friendships that I had tried to make in the past year were gone too. I would be starting all over again.

At this age, you try your best just to figure yourself out as your body changes. Everything changes; even the way you perceive the world around you begins to shift. Even at home back in Murfreesboro, with all of my friends I had grown up with, this puberty thing would have been tricky. But I knew those girls all my life; at least we could share in our experiences and give validity to the weird ways we felt about what was happening to us.

I had just started at a new school. It was hard enough trying to figure out how to fit in, get people to like me, and build new relationships. Who was I supposed to talk to and confide in about anything? I stayed trapped inside my mind trying to figure out things on my own. I couldn't talk to my mother—she made me feel strange and shameful about sexuality.

One night I tried on a tank top she bought me and went into the living room to model it for her. I stretched out both arms before doing a turn to proudly display how awesome I looked. I thought my mom would say how cute I looked, but instead she let out a horrific scream. "Oh my gosh! You've got arm hair!" I looked at my armpit and there was a tuft of red hair there. I had never noticed it before. How had…when did it…what do I do about… No one had ever told me this would happen. I put my arms down and ran out of the room, mortified. We didn't speak of it again.

I had heard that some girls my age were starting their periods; I dreaded the day it would happen to me. I checked my panties, my sheets, and the toilet paper after I would use the bathroom. I wanted to catch it before it caught me unexpectedly. I knew my mother wasn't going to take this well, so I didn't want her to see the evidence on my pants or anything else before I did. I didn't want her to know at all, let alone first. I just knew she wasn't going to take my new "state of being" well and somehow she would make me pay.

She would call me names a lot, and would scream at me and ask me if I let boys touch me. I didn't want her to think that I had my period. All I knew was that when you got your period, it meant that you were able to have babies. I didn't want my mom to know that my body was able to do this, giving her further reason to suspect I was promiscuous.

I was thirteen and still didn't know a thing about sex. I wasn't even sure why or how people did it. All I knew, from being around my mom, was that it was dirty and shameful. I wanted no part in it. I had no interest in asking questions or learning anything more about it. I did my best not to even let thoughts of it enter my mind.

▬ ▬ ▬ ▬ ▬ ▬ ▬

My dad dated a lot after the divorce and eventually met the woman he would marry. Her name was Gloria. She had two children of her own—a daughter named Rebecca and a son named Jackson, both of whom were a few years older than me. When Dad first started seeing Gloria, he told her that if I liked her and if his mother liked her, then she could stick around. After she became a part of his life, things started to shift. Two years later, my dad would look at me and say, "Gloria is first, then God, then my mother! If you think you come even close to being next in line, you are sadly mistaken!"

Until my dad met Gloria, I always slept in his bed. I never thought anything of it. Sometimes we would go spend the weekend with his parents and stay in the guest house. There was only one bed in this house, so the notion that we were to share the same bed seemed like a no-brainer. I never thought of it as a bad thing. It never occurred to me that I might need to consider sleeping somewhere else.

Before crawling into bed one night, he stood on the other side of the bed with a pillow in his hand, like he was about to tell me something about it. I waited to hear what he had to say before getting under the sheets. He said to me, "From now on, we must sleep with this in between us." Not sure why, all I could do was say, "OK."

We got in the bed, and he wedged the pillow between us. I turned on my side and faced away from him, I felt mortified, but I'm still not sure why. I didn't know what the pillow was for and if I had done something wrong to cause it. Had something happened that I didn't know about? There was literally a wedge between us now. He had put it in front of our private parts. I guess he didn't want them to come near each other for some reason. I tried to make sense of it all in my little mind. And what would happen if the pillow wasn't there? I felt ashamed of myself, but I wasn't sure why.

One Sunday night, after returning home from my dad's, I walked downstairs to go to the kitchen. I was a little older than thirteen at the time. My mom was on one of her tears, but by this time it had become my new norm. Her being "in a mood" was just a part of life now living in the same house with her. Just before I reached the kitchen, she stepped in front of me with an almost empty bottle of wine in her hand, blocking my path. I waited to hear what was about to come out of her mouth. She started bouncing up and down, making obscene motions and noises, then asked me in a whiny voice if that was how it sounded when my dad and Gloria had sex. I had no idea what sex looked or sounded like, but now I kind of did. Her crash course disgusted me, as did the sound of her voice and the look on her face as she demonstrated. I started to cry. I couldn't care less now about what I was going to the kitchen for, so I turned and ran back up the stairs into my room, closing the door behind me.

━ ━ ━ ━ ━ ━ ━

My mom got drunk one Christmas Eve and passed out right next to the Christmas tree. I was up in my bedroom when I heard the doorbell ring. I went downstairs, and that's when I saw my mom lying facedown next to an empty wine bottle. I wasn't sure who was at the door; all I knew was that I had to keep them from coming into the house. I walked past my mom and quickly moved to the door. I cracked the door open and saw my neighbor standing there. She said she had Christmas presents for us and asked if she could come in. I can't remember what I said to keep her from coming inside, but I thanked her, accepted the gifts, and closed the door before she could ask me anything else.

I set the presents on the dining room table, passed by my mom again, and then headed back up to my room. I sat on my bed and started watching TV again. Then the phone rang. It was my neighbor, asking if everything was OK over here. I thought to myself, how could she know something was up? I brushed her off as best I could and hurried to get off the phone. Then I went back to watching TV until it was time for me to go to bed.

How lonely that must have been for me—to walk down the stairs and see my mom lying facedown on the floor, and then having to answer the door and cover up for her, only to walk by her again and then go back up to my room. What's also disturbing is how normal this was for me. I didn't flinch when I saw her, and I didn't even check to make sure she was alive. I just went on about my life as though there was nothing going on around me. Her antics had become so commonplace that I was desensitized to them. She was "filler" in the house, like furniture or particles of dust in the atmosphere.

How awful and strange for a child to lose it all suddenly (home, family, sister, security, friends, someone to talk to); to be torn from a really good life only to land here. Not knowing how to deal, I did the best I could to just cope and survive. I stuffed all my emotions and thoughts down—I kept it all in and told no one what my life was like. In the mind of a child, I also believed I needed to protect my parents; to never let anyone find out what kind of people they were behind closed doors—a classic case of Stockholm syndrome. In my mind I believed that whatever they did had to be right because they were my parents, even when what they did was wrong. I didn't know that I had the right to be treated with respect, just like any other human being.

▬ ▬ ▬ ▬ ▬ ▬ ▬

Weeks later, in the middle of the night, my mom woke me up and dragged me out of bed. The bright light coming from the lamp on my nightstand made me squint my eyes as I tried to gather my thoughts. She pulled me by my arm, and before I could brace myself, my body hit the floor. I did all I could to pull myself backward across the floor until my back hit the wall. She straddled me and screamed words belligerently as she hit me over and over again. Her face was so close to mine that I turned my head to the side as she continued to violently scream at the side of my face and into my ear.

I cried out, yelling, "Mama, please stop! Mama, please..." All of a sudden she abruptly stopped yelling and hitting me. Then I stopped screaming too. The room became silent, but only for a few seconds. "Shh," she commanded. She leaned in and whispered in my ear, "Be quiet, the neighbors can hear you." Then she went right back to what she was doing before. With both hands she violently punched me over and over again. I did as I was told. I sat still, never making a sound. I just took it until she was done.

— — — — — — —

At school, I would test the waters to see if anyone would help me out. I mentioned to a group of kids that I had a cigarette burn on my shoulder. I was hoping the right person would catch wind of it if one of those kids went home and mentioned it to one of their parents. And then hopefully that parent would do something, like send for help and come to my rescue.

Every time I tried to reach out and tell anyone, in any form or fashion, it always seemed to backfire on me. Most adults would respond by "threatening" to call the cops. I didn't want them to do that, though. I didn't want my mom to get into trouble; I just wanted out. More often than not, I would backtrack on my story, negating it, and then I would just tell them to forget it. I would convince them to drop the conversation and never bring it back up again by telling them that it was all a lie and that I had made up the entire story.

By the end of that week, after I had thrown the fact that my mom had burned me out to a couple kids, I got a bite. Mom received a call from a local judge saying that he had received a call from a concerned parent. He just wanted to give her a ring and make sure that everything was all right and find out if there was, in fact, any reason for them to investigate further. My mother politely told the judge that everything was fine and that there was no need for concern.

About that same time, I came down the stairs, not aware of what was happening. My mother then turned toward me and stood there with tears in her eyes. When I saw her face, I stopped almost at the bottom, at the third or fourth stair. She said, "That was a judge calling because he heard that I was abusing you." At that moment, I was suddenly filled with regret. My face flushed bright red and my body temperature rose as I stood there feeling completely embarrassed for what I had done to my mother.

I plopped down and sat right there on the staircase. I couldn't even look at her face when I said, "Oh, Mama, I am so sorry." I started to cry, and my mother did too as she walked toward me. She sat down on the step right below mine, in between my legs, facing away from me. I put both of my arms around her and pulled her in close to me. She turned her body sideways so that she could lean her head up against my chest and wrap her arms around me. I did my best to comfort her and let her know that everything was going to be OK. "It's OK," I said as I continued to hold her, rocking ever so gently from side to side. "I won't ever do that again...I promise."

— — — — — — —

My self-worth rapidly dissipated with every day that passed. With no solid ground to stand on, living one day to the next not knowing what the day might bring, I lost all confidence and became very insecure. My little mind needed to make sense of what was going on around me. The only thing I could come up with was that my parents treated me the way they did because I didn't have any worth or value. I turned the tables and blamed myself for their poor behavior. I figured that if my dad was slowly pushing me out of his life and my mom was taking everything out on me, then it had to be something about me personally that was making the two people that are supposed to love me the most suddenly treat me no better than a common dog.

One evening, I sat in the den with my mom, watching a little TV before bed. She sat in a recliner, kind of behind me and over to my right. The TV was in the top left-hand corner of the room; when I sat facing it, I could barely see my mom, only slightly in my peripheral view. All of a sudden, my head was being pulled over toward my mother. She had a handful of my hair in her fist. She continued to pull it toward her as I started to lose my balance, catching myself to keep from falling off the couch. I extended my arm and placed my right hand down on the couch to balance myself.

I looked over at my mom to see what the matter was. This sudden outburst seemed to appear out of nowhere. I wasn't even aware that there might be some kind of problem, because for the most part, before now, it had been a relatively quiet night. Her face looked evil as she began to speak through gritted teeth: "You're so ugly! Look at you! Your hair is ugly! Your face is so ugly!"

She let go of my hair, and I resumed my position, sitting Indian style on the couch. I was mortified as this new revelation started to register in my mind. Tears rolled down my cheeks as

I started to cry quietly, trying to not make it so obvious to my mom and just play it off like nothing happened. One minute I was sitting on the couch watching TV, not really thinking about anything in particular; just another school night at home, a place where you are supposed to feel the safest. Then, all of a sudden, my mom was pulling my hair and telling me how awful I looked. I had never been told that before. It must be really bad, though, if someone sitting next to me could have that kind of reaction by just looking at me.

I had naturally curly red hair. Since I came out of the womb, people would always stop us wherever we were and compliment me on having the most gorgeous hair they had ever seen. I didn't think much of it because it was mine and I saw it every day. Even though people told me how lucky I was to have hair like that, most days I still felt a little out of place. I never saw a lot of redheads, nor did I ever see a lot of girls with thick, curly hair. I always felt a bit odd since I didn't really look like the people around me at school. Due to the fact that people took the time to say how fortunate I was to have it, though, I figured the best thing to do was to just go with it; there must be something good about it.

Until this moment I had never had anyone call me out and say the words out loud that I questioned on the inside every time I looked in the mirror. I would spend the next twenty years of my life doing all I could to cover up my hair and change it by coloring it and straightening it. I did my best to cover my freckles on my face with makeup. I did my best to make myself look like anyone else but me. Obviously my authentic self was no good, so I put her away.

As my appearance started to gradually change, so did I. The harder I tried to appear appealing to anyone, the sexier my image became as I began to blossom into a little young lady.

By this time, Gloria was living in my dad's house with him. She and her daughter both wore lots of makeup and tight clothes, and carried themselves and moved their bodies and mannerisms in such a way that screamed to any and every man, "You know you want it! Come hither!" They were sexy, and my dad liked it, so I jumped in there and quickly learned how to do my makeup and hair like they did—"Va-va-voom" it. I was desperate for my daddy to want me again too. As soon as he had an option other than me, he dropped me like a bad habit and gave his life and attention over to them.

My plan worked. I was now getting a piece of the action, but not all of it—I had to squeeze in where I could just to get the spotlight to shine on me too. When my dad was very pleased with me, he would walk past me and discreetly grab a handful of my rear end. Sometimes he would give me the "silent nod" and take a more gentle approach by sliding his open palm from one side of my rear end to the other. It was his way of letting me know that he found me to be pleasing in his sight.

When that moment would come, I would smile with delight, filled with joy, knowing my daddy found me acceptable. I would think to myself, "See...he does love me!" I wanted his attention so badly that I would take it—be it good or bad, I didn't care; just as long as I was being shown that something, anything about me had worth and value. Even if that something was sex appeal and the way I looked; it mattered not to me.

When the other two ladies were nowhere near us, Dad would sometimes compliment me on the way my body made my clothes fit so well. He had me try on an off-the-shoulder top at a women's boutique. Since I had never owned such a thing before, I felt shy as he handed me the blouse to try on.

When I stepped out of the dressing room, he was delighted at the sight of me in clothing that showed more skin. He put one hand on my shoulder and slid his fingertips from my collarbone to the very edge of my shoulder. "I love this on you," he said. "You look so sexy with your shoulders out." I felt embarrassed and pulled my shoulder away from him. I wanted his attention, but sometimes it could be more than I bargained for, making me feel uncomfortable rather than validated. I quickly stepped back into the dressing room and shut the door, putting a barrier between the two of us.

However uncomfortable this kind of affection might have made me feel at times, it was worth it to me. I had finally found something that might make my dad want to keep me around a bit longer. Anything would suffice at this point. Whatever the circumstances, anything was better compared to what went on at home with my mom. All I had was two unhealthy environments that this Russian roulette game called life had dealt me. So I chose to go with the better option of the two. What I had to endure at my dad's seemed like an episode of *Leave It to Beaver* compared to what went on at my mom's house.

Just before my fourteenth birthday, I had returned back home to my mother's house after spending another great weekend at my dad's. It was a typical Sunday evening; my mom and I were in my bedroom. My back was propped up against my bed, my suitcase sitting there next to me on the floor. My mom sat on top of my lap, straddling both of her legs over me. It was the usual game she liked to play after I got home, where she prodded me for information about what my dad was doing and what we had done that weekend.

I sat there expressionless, not saying a word as she screamed in my face and hit me, trying to force me to talk. I was used to it by now. I usually just sat there and waited for her to tire out and give up until she was ready for another round. Never once, after all these years, after day upon day of running from my mother and being attacked by her, had I ever tried to defend myself by pushing her off of me or trying to fight back to at least keep her off of me. It just never even crossed my mind to do so; I never thought of it as an option. But on this night, as I sat there being tormented by her, it crossed my mind that I sure would like to be doing something other than sitting here with this lady on top of me. By this time, I guess her little show had become old news to me. I remember my right hand suddenly, as if out of nowhere, punched her in the chest. It shocked both of us.

She stopped hitting me, and we looked at each other with our eyes wide, stunned by what had just taken place. I waited for her reaction, not sure what it would be, not even sure what I should do next. And the strangest thing happened, the last thing I ever expected. My mother started sobbing like a little kid that had just fallen off of a swing in the middle of the playground.

I kept watching this scene unfold right in front of me, rendered speechless, intrigued by this odd thing that was happening. My mother cried, "You hit me!" She sobbed a bit harder. "Oh my gosh...I can't believe you hit me!" My mouth dropped open. I was so confused by all this. She turned her head over to the side, looking down at the floor beside us as she continued to wail, sticking out her bottom lip. "You hit me," she muttered once more before standing up and running out of my bedroom.

All of a sudden, it was over. I thought, "Just a moment ago, she was screaming and sitting on top of me, and now...I'm sitting alone in my room. She's not on me anymore. It's quiet again...peaceful. *Wow.*" I sat there for a good while trying to process what had just taken place. I lifted my right hand and balled it up into a fist, holding it close to my face. I held it there for a bit, taking it in, and thought, "*This* is what did it. This thing, this thing that I have in my possession, is what stopped it." In that moment I realized that what I had been desperately searching for had always been with me; I held the power. This was my answer. This is what would rescue me. All of a sudden, and just that quickly, the power in that home shifted. That was the last time Linda ever sat on top of me.

This is when I became what people looking in from the outside considered a "problem child"; the black sheep, damaged, a troubled teen, a harlot, the bad one—the list goes on. But whatever people called me, I didn't care. No one knew what went on at either one of my parents' homes during those years; I never told a soul. People just began pointing the finger and blaming me for everyone's problems. I never tried to defend myself, though. I still protected my parents and kept their secrets safe with me.

Away I went, like a hurricane, looking for something and someone to demolish. I didn't care anymore. I didn't care about—nor did I respect—either of my parents or their rules. My thinking was, "They didn't care about me or my feelings all those years, so why should they suddenly start to become parents now? Why should I care about how they feel?" Their ploys seemed too little too late to me.

I gave them both an extremely hard time from that day forward. And I liked it. I enjoyed watching them suffer like they had made me suffer. It was payback to the ninth degree. This would also be the driving force behind many of the decisions I made later on in life, when I was of legal age to move out of the house, and on into my twenties. I did things for money and trashed my body because no one ever thought it had much worth. I continued to believe this for years and years to come; I didn't think I was worth much more than the garbage left on the side of highways.

To this day I am surprised that I made it out alive. Many times I put myself in dangerous situations that should have killed me. I think I did it on purpose. I think I wanted to get killed. I think I wanted people to hurt me. I hated myself and thought I deserved it. I wanted people to treat me badly. I'd spent years wanting to escape my reality when I was a child— I would then spend years as an adult trying to recreate those scenes by dating men who treated me deplorably. It's funny how that happens, isn't it? Not so much funny as it is sad; we humans will look for situations that recreate our family of origin. No matter how unhealthy the situation, it is what we "know." It is our "normal." Besides, how can you be a good partner, parent, friend, or lover—or even sustain a healthy living environment, for that matter—if you have never seen an example of one or experienced it for yourself?

━━ ━━ ━━ ━━ ━━ ━━ ━━

One day, my stepbrother came over for a visit. He stayed in a small RV parked in the backyard of my dad's house during his visit.

I remember one night a group of his friends, my stepsister, and I all cooked out and enjoyed an evening goofing off and getting into the hot tub. After everyone had left for the evening, my stepsister went inside to go to bed. I stayed out in the camper with Jackson. He was sweet and had a charisma about him that could draw anybody in. The family always used to laugh and say that Jackson was loved by all, especially old people and puppies. I thought nothing of being out there with him by myself. He was older than me, nineteen at the time. I felt safe and wanted around him. After all the turmoil and the separation of the family unit, it made me feel good to be amongst Jackson, Rebecca, and their friends. I felt I was a part of something, like I was included.

Jackson invited me to sleep out there with him instead of going back inside. I didn't think twice about it. He was my brother now; there was nothing sexual about it. That's what you do if you're a family—or so I assumed. We lay next to each other; he was the big spoon, I was the little. Just as I was falling asleep, I felt his hand go over my boxers and into the front opening. I grabbed his hand and said, "No, Jackson, don't do that." I didn't know what else to do, so I hopped up and went inside the house and got in my own bed.

The next morning Rebecca and I were sitting in the den, and I told her what happened with Jackson the night before. Angrily she said, "Well, you shouldn't have been out there with him in the first place!" That was not at all the reaction I had expected. Before we could say anything else, my dad, Gloria, and Jackson walked into the room. Rebecca looked at me as if to say, "Not another word about this." And it was never brought up again.

━━ ━━ ━━ ━━ ━━ ━━ ━━

Over the years, I would continue to bounce back and forth between both parents' houses. I would stay with one until I felt I couldn't tolerate it anymore, then move back again until I had my fill of the other. Before the beginning of my freshman year, I moved back to Murfreesboro to stay at my dad's. After the first day of school, the phone rang off the hook. The boys had noticed me that day at school. They called my father's house phone back to back asking me if they could be my boyfriend. I was surprised by all the attention, and flattered, but I still turned all of them down. Of course, I thanked them for calling.

Not too long after, I had my first official boyfriend. I was only fifteen. The girls at school terrorized me and threatened to beat me up. I was called names like "whore" and "slut." I didn't understand the reason for the attacks or why they would call me such names. I had never had sex before, so why would they call me those names?

I didn't have anyone to talk to or some sort of mentor to explain that they were only bullying me because they were jealous and wanted to tear me down. I decided that if they were going to call me those names anyway, I might as well give them a reason to and give my torture some validation. I decided that I might as well be what they said I was. What was all the hoopla about, anyway? I decided to have sex and find out.

I had sex with my boyfriend for the very first time. Wide-eyed, disgusted, shocked, and in pain as he lay on top of me, I pushed him up and away from me. *This is what sex is? I had no idea that's how you went about it.* I wasn't thrilled after this epiphany, but still curious about this thing called sex, I let go of him. *Ouch.* It hurt. I closed my eyes and closed them tight, grimacing in pain. It felt awful, and I squirmed a bit uncomfortably. *This is what people are so crazy about, some people risking their very lives just to do it? This is the wonderful thing that people write songs about? No way, no how!* I was so disappointed. I was convinced that there would forever be this huge void in my life because I would spend my life hating what other people loved. That would soon change, as things do.

I found out that my boyfriend and my best friend were having a relationship behind my back. This was my first dose of reality in the love game. I was humiliated. On top of that, the girl was pudgy in comparison to me, and she had a lazy eye! I dealt with the rejection like any other confused fifteen-year-old would: I slept with anyone who would have me.

Now I loved sex. I had spent years between two homes where love and feelings of acceptance were absent. Sex with "randoms" was just what the doctor ordered. The seal had been broken, so to speak. It was like breaking the floodgate. Pandora's Box was open. It didn't matter if I had just met the guy, if he was a one-night stand, or if I would never see the guy again. Sex became a drug. It made me feel good, if only for a fleeting moment.

I was love starved. I had finally found a way to have intimacy with another human being. After years of being verbally abused by my mom and rejected by my dad, I had found my temporary fix. The very idea that someone would find me worthy or valuable enough to have sex with me gave me feelings of worth and value, even if just for a moment. I finally gave my bullies and naysayers a reason to call me those names. I gave them a reason to hunt me down that I could understand.

▬ ▬ ▬ ▬ ▬ ▬ ▬

I was seventeen when my stepsister got married. I was a part of her wedding party. I watched my dad walk her down the aisle and give her away.

I returned to Nashville after the wedding because I was living with my mom at the time. Upon my arrival, my mom flew into one of her fits of rage and jealousy. I picked up the house phone and called my dad for help. By this time, he didn't take my call seriously. He brushed me off like the little boy who cried wolf.

My mother hounded me for information and stormed behind me through the house with every step I took. I was fed up and sick of her antics. I gathered a few things and headed toward the garage to put them in my car. Staying on my heels, still prodding, she angrily spit out words—meaningless banter, it seemed. I opened the trunk of my car to throw my bags in as she screamed at the side of my face. I placed my hand on the top of my trunk to close it, but before I did, Mom threw her arm underneath it and screamed, "Just do it! Just slam it on my arm!" I let out a sigh from exhaustion. I'd had enough of this woman. It was time for me to go. "But where?" I thought to myself. I hadn't a clue. But this was over; it had gone on long enough.

I spent a few nights with a friend from high school, but I knew I needed something more permanent. I had a feeling this wouldn't last too long. Sure, these people let me stay the night and they fed me; but what would happen when these nights turned into a month? I knew they wouldn't go for that. I already knew I shouldn't try to explain to my friend's parents what life was like for me at home; they would never understand.

Before long I found myself in a very bad part of town with a friend of a friend that I had met out at a club. These people understood what my home life was like; I didn't even have to bring it up. It was not a safe place for me to be, but it was somewhere I could stay indefinitely until I figured out something else.

I returned to my mom's house a couple of weeks later to get some of my things. She'd had the locks changed after convincing herself and others that I was a threat. I was no longer allowed in her house. Always eager to fit in with the crowd, she had also found a way to become confidants with Gloria and Dad. The three of them joined forces and teamed up against me. It's always good to have something in common if you want to belong to something, don't you agree? The victim role she loved so much also worked in her best interest, because then the tables were turned over at me. By pointing a finger at me she discredited anything I had to say about her actions. Her secrets were safe; they stayed just that—secrets.

Mom told me that if I wanted to get my things out of her home, I would have to agree to her terms. "Sure, whatever" was my attitude about her little show. At the time she had assigned, I met her at her home. I walked in the back door and saw two of her female middle-aged neighbors sitting on the living room couch staring me down as I walked in. They seemed to be her bodyguards, ready to pounce if I were to suddenly lunge at my mother without warning. My mother took a seat in her recliner next to them. I looked back at her and shook my head. I stared into her eyes for a brief moment, as if to say, "You know you're wrong for this." I looked at her in disgust but decided to say nothing. Saying something would do me no good anyway. "Whatever," I said.

She had turned me into the bad guy. I was frustrated and angry at my mother's audacity to turn this all around on me while she sat there with a sad, pouty face and a halo over her head. I had a half-empty soda can in my hand, and with no other resolve, I tossed it behind me as I walked up the stairs. I heard the women gasp as soda spattered everywhere. This out-burst was exactly what my mom needed to justify her motives. Regretting my actions, I turned back to look at their faces. They looked at my mom sympathetically. She ate it up with a look that said, "Do you see how mean she is to me? See what she puts me through?" I continued up the stairs, got what I could gather in one trip, and then headed out the back door.

Several months later, my mother told me that after months of not hearing from me, she took one of my senior pictures to a police department in an area known for prostitution. She said one of the officers took a look at my photo and said, "It's such a shame for a kid like that to be out here on these streets." I guess my mom got a kick out of this. She was a hero out there looking for her child. I'm sure she liked all the sympathy she got too. Poor Linda. We have a passive-aggressive saying in the South for people like her: "Bless her heart."

I spent months on the streets, jumping from place to place, sleeping anywhere people would let me stay for a night. I dodged pimps, was beaten up and raped, and survived death several times. After finally having enough of it all, I called my dad from a pay phone. It was the first time he had heard from me in months: "Daddy, I want to come home." Without hesitation he said, "Come on, baby. Come home! We'll be here waiting for you!"

I returned to his home in Murfreesboro. I felt safe there. After my dose of reality out on the streets, I was willing to do whatever was necessary to turn my life around. My father's open arms welcoming me home made me feel like I was where I was supposed to be. Surely after going through all that—after not hearing from me and finding out I'd been living on the streets—they would be supportive and love me through this, right?

After the third day, I sat in my bedroom talking to my dad about my experiences and what my life had been like since the last time he saw me before I "ran away." We heard footsteps pound closer to my bedroom door. My stepmother appeared in the doorway with a bar of soap in her hand. *"My bathtub?"* she screamed. She threw the bar of soap at me and continued to yell. "Out of *all* the bathtubs in this house, you have to use *my* bathtub?" She stormed away.

I looked over at my dad like, *What?* Then I looked away and down at the floor because I knew what was coming next. If it was between me and her, I already knew which one would have to leave. I didn't even wait for him to tell me I had to go. I knew he wanted to say the words but didn't know how, so I just took it upon myself to do it for him. "It's forty dollars to get a room for the night. If you will at least give me that much, then I'll have somewhere to go."

He pulled his wallet out and handed me two twenty-dollar bills. I grabbed my bags and headed out the door, then got in my car and hit the highway back to Nashville.

━━ ━━ ━━ ━━ ━━ ━━ ━━

During the brief time I spent at my daddy's house, Jackson stopped by the house to use the computer. No one was there, just he and I alone. I walked into my dad's office to ask him a question, and then went back to my bathroom to take a shower. Afterward, I opened my bathroom door to walk into my bedroom. I saw Jackson sitting on the couch in my room gesturing inappropriately. "Come on," he said. "No one has to know." Sickened by all of this, I ran out of my room.

My dad returned home shortly after and asked me to accompany him while he ran some errands. I got in the truck with him without saying a word. As he backed the truck out of the driveway, I scooted up on the edge of my seat and started punching the dashboard. I hit it hard three or four times in a fit of rage.

My dad turned his head to look at me and asked, "What's wrong with you?" He stopped the truck for a moment and waited for my reply.

I wasn't sure if I should tell him or not. I felt so embarrassed to say it out loud. I hung my head down and angrily admitted to him, "Jackson just tried to make me have sex with him." I waited to hear my father's response.

Quickly he replied, "Well, let's not tell Gloria about this. I don't want it to upset her." He continued backing the truck out of the drive, and not another word was said.

— — — — — — —

My stepsister got pregnant at a young age. My dad and Gloria got her an apartment; they made sure she had everything she needed. Since this was done for her, I didn't think it would be much different if they got me an apartment too. I thought that if my dad got me a place, at least I wouldn't be in his house and

I would have somewhere to go. It seemed like a win-win for both of us.

The night I moved into my new place, I stood and watched from my back door as my dad and Gloria walked down the stoop and out the drive to get in his truck. I thought everything was fine and on the up and up, so I was smiling and felt good inside. My father turned his head toward his wife as they walked, and I heard him say, "I bet she won't make it one night." He cut his eyes up and over at me and then back at Gloria, and they both started to laugh.

Suddenly I stopped smiling. I let go of the screen door and let it fall to close in front of me. In one brief moment, I went from feeling good and feeling included to feeling embarrassed. They smiled in my face, but it wasn't real; they still didn't like me. There was a year lease on the apartment, and in a year's time they never dropped by again to see me, even though they lived only a few short blocks away.

▬ ▬ ▬ ▬ ▬ ▬ ▬

Several months after I moved in, I had been dancing for a couple months or so and had become self-sufficient. I didn't need to call my dad for anything. I was proud of that accomplishment; I thought for sure *this* would make them like me—if not all the way, at least just a little.

One day, I stopped by my dad's house. I had made three thousand dollars in a couple of days. I told him I needed somewhere to put it, so I asked if he could put it in his safe. Truthfully, I didn't need somewhere to put it; I just wanted him to see it.

He let me come inside, and I followed him through the house to his bedroom. We walked by Gloria, who was playing on the floor with Jackson's infant son. She looked up at my dad in disapproval. He reassured her, "We're making a deposit, not a withdrawal!" I looked at Gloria and smiled and nodded in agreement. She went back to what she was doing as if to give us the "go ahead." I felt a knot in my throat like I wanted to cry. It was like being kicked in the stomach. What was I to these people? I should have left the house, but I went ahead and followed my dad to put the money away.

My stepsister had a habit of going over to Dad and Gloria's house to wash her clothes and get food, toilet paper, or whatever she needed. So I assumed this rule would apply to me too. I stopped by their house one day while they were at work to borrow some cleaning supplies to use at my house. Gloria walked in on her lunch break and was angry as soon as she saw me. "I don't want you in my house by yourself!" she yelled at me.

I looked at her, dumbfounded by her warm welcome, and said, "This is my dad's house." If it wasn't for my father, she wouldn't have anything.

With one hand on her hip, she answered fervently, "This is *my* house!" She then made me put down the bottle of cleaner and told me to leave.

CHAPTER 2

Y EARS LATER, I walked into my daddy's shop to spend some time with him. He was sitting in a chair, smoking a cigarette, and watching a movie on the small TV mounted up on the wall. He acknowledged my presence as I walked by him, grabbed another old wooden chair, unfolded it, and took a seat right next to his. He continued to watch the movie as he took a drag from his cigarette.

I looked up at the TV for a moment, and then my eyes started to wander around at the things placed on the two tall cabinets beneath it. There on one of them was a framed picture of me. I asked, "Daddy, what's that doing there?"

He looked in the direction where I was pointing and saw the picture. He looked back at the TV and took another puff of his cigarette. Never looking away, he said, "Sometimes I sit out here and I talk to you."

I turned my body forward and slid back to prop my back against the chair. I blinked a couple of times and tried to gather my thoughts at the gravity of how much this meant to me.

My dad and I never really talked. We didn't spend a lot of time together like we used to, just he and I. The presence, the matriarch that was up the hill inside of his home, had driven a wedge between us. I was not even "allowed" to sit on a chair next to my dad, let alone on his knee, nor were we able to touch or hug each other since Gloria had imposed these rules. I never assumed my father missed that connection with me. I knew I did. I wished he would talk to me, though, instead of that picture. We didn't say another word and finished watching the movie.

CHAPTER 3

AT THE AGE of eighteen, I started stripping and made a career of it. I continued to do so for ten years, until I was twenty-eight years old. At this time in my life, I also had a long-term boyfriend named Ethan. We started to date when we were both twenty-one. Somehow I tried to juggle a boyfriend in the "real world" and a job lying to men in exchange for sexual favors.

One night at work, I stepped out onto the floor to make my rounds. I walked around sizing up the men to shake 'em down for everything they had in their pockets. Unfortunately, this was no easy task because I drank too much before leaving the dressing room—so much so, I couldn't see. Everything was a blur, which made it impossible to see anything around me. I hated being in the club so much that I didn't want to work without being totally drunk. Ecstasy used to be my nightly drug of choice, so this seemed tamer—a step up in the right direction, you could say.

I finally came to the conclusion that this evening might be a lost cause; I was too drunk to work. Just as I was about to give up and head back to the dressing room, seemingly out of nowhere (I couldn't see anything out of my peripheral anyway) a tall, stocky man bumped into me. His body language seemed so awkward, like he had done it on purpose.

I tried my best to focus in on him and pull it together. I didn't want him to see how drunk I was. This could be the moment that sealed my fate, either to make or break my night.

He said, "I've been looking for you!" and I answered, "Oh. OK!" In my head I was thinking, "Great! I'm glad you're going to make this night easy for me!" I took him by the hand and said, "Let's go back to the VIP room," leading him toward the back of the club.

We entered the room where the dancers did lap dances for about forty dollars a pop. After an hour, between dances, I sat straddling his large lap. He told me that he had tried to contact me recently by phone. (According to him, we had met before and I had given him my number. I have no idea. I can't remember.) He said he had just returned from overseas. He wanted to offer me twenty thousand dollars to go with him, but he could never reach me. I suggested, "Well, since you didn't get the chance to do that, why don't we just leave the club now, and you can pay me three thousand dollars to meet you at a hotel?" He agreed that this sounded like a great idea.

Later that night I met him at his hotel room near the airport, where he was staying for the week. We had sex, and before I left, he bent over and unzipped a large duffel bag. I stood right beside him and watched him count out three grand from a sizable amount of cash inside the bag. With a smile on his face, he handed me the cash. Knowing that this guy had plenty more where that came from and seemed eager to give it away, I made about twelve thousand dollars more during that week. Afterward, as soon as he returned overseas, I convinced him to wire another twelve thousand dollars back to the states. It was wired to a Cadillac dealership for a down payment on a brand-new Escalade.

He became my "means to a way out." I was sick of working at the strip club, but I didn't have any skills to go out and get a job that would pay enough to support me. I registered for classes for the following semester at U of M. I had no idea how to make ends meet with a real job anyway. All I knew was fast money. All I knew was the hustle.

I had always been so amazed and curious about how people could take care of themselves, not even mentioning those with kids, with a job or even jobs for that matter only receiving minimum wage. Even living on ten to fifteen dollars per hour boggled my mind! The thought of trying to make that work without ending up in a homeless shelter terrified me. So until I could figure out how it all worked in the real world, I continued on and kept what I understood as a safety net. Robert wired an "allowance" to my bank account every month. This allowed me the opportunity to stop working in the club, giving me some time while I figured out the next step. I hoped to eventually be self-sufficient, away from the game, and making an honest living.

I spent a couple semesters at U of M. I had three more to go to receive my bachelor's degree in marketing. However, I still found myself having no direction, not knowing what kind of job to get after I graduated. It was during the recession, and most college grads I spoke to were either out of work or working lower-paying jobs that had nothing to do with their degrees. I also found that many people left college only to find out that there were just no jobs available. People weren't hiring.

I had to do something and quick. I couldn't let this thing with Robert drag out any further than I had to. I needed a career where I could go to school for two years or less; a trade that would always be in demand, recession or not, and one in which

I could find a job right away and start making decent money—at least enough money to get me away from Robert.

I felt bound. I didn't even like this guy. I only had to see him once a year. He would fly me to Mexico with him for a week. (He said if he stayed out of the states during his time off he wouldn't have to pay taxes. I'm still not sure of the "whats" and "whys." I didn't really care; it had nothing to do with me, as long as I got my money and my bills were paid.) That career that could help me get out of this situation, I decided, was cosmetology. Now all that was left to decide was which school I would attend.

CHAPTER 4

There's *Gold* in Them Thar Hills! Drive West, 'Lil One!

ETERMINED TO TURN my life around—this is how I ended up in Los Angeles at one of the most prestigious cosmetology schools in the country. I wanted more than anything to work hard, earn my own money, and have a career I could be proud of. Since I was "changing careers" so late in the game—I would be turning thirty that year—I decided to go big or go home. I decided to go somewhere I could get the best training possible. Hair was taken very seriously in LA. If I was going to do this, I wanted to be among the best of the best.

— — — — — — —

It was summertime, and something in me told me it was time to leave. Looking back on it, it seems as though I should have spent more time weighing out my options. But I just knew like I knew like I knew (exhale...breathe) that I was to pack up what I could in my pearl white Escalade and forgo the rest. I needed a goal to work toward once I got there; I chose cosmetology school as my excuse to abruptly "jump ship."

Like someone covering her eyes and spinning a globe on a pedestal, then placing an extended pointed finger on the spinning ball (remember the mother from the movie *Mermaids*? Yeah, like that) and uncovering her eyes to see where her extremity had landed, choosing her next move by wherever her finger had landed on the spinning globe—like a roll of the dice, I googled "cosmetology schools" and chose the first one that appeared. I proceeded with whatever steps were needed for enrollment. Before I knew it I was enlisted to start school in Los Angeles that September: September 9, to be exact.

I gave away everything I owned to goodwill or friends and neighbors who were willing to come get it. I packed my truck with mostly clothes, pictures—anything of sentimental value. And last but not least, my mini dachshund, Reese.

The best decision I made before departing for LA was buying a GPS for the trip. I knew nothing at all about where I was going. I knew nothing about LA. I didn't even know the right roads to take to get me from here in Tennessee out to California. When it was time to set sail to La-La Land, I entered "LA" into the device and it told me to drive west for 1,800 miles then turn left. Piece of cake!

A month before I set sail, I told my sugar daddy some ridiculous lie about needing money to pay tuition for a school there in Nashville: five thousand dollars, to be exact. He would have never gone for it if I told him I needed the money to move cross country. In his need to control me—and he had done a great job at it since he was the one holding the purse strings—he wanted me to stay in Nashville so it wouldn't be far for him to travel to come find me if he was ever to return home. He wired the cash to my bank account days before I left on my road trip. I'd have to figure out the details later, when he was to return home for Christmas and I wasn't in Nashville.

A week before leaving, I went around to say my good-byes to people. I journeyed to my father's house in Murfreesboro. I wanted to say good-bye to him in person.

After a short visit with Dad and his family, he walked me out to my truck. He turned to look back at his house, as if to make sure no one was looking—his wife didn't like when he gave me money—and then dropped a folded check down my shirt. I looked down at my shirt and back up at him, and opened my mouth to reject his contribution. Before I could even say a word, he beat me to it: "I'm not going in there to retrieve that!"

Sincerely I said, "But Daddy, you don't have to do that. I don't need it, really."

He leaned in to me and said, "If you think I'm just going to let my daughter drive all the way across country without giving her anything at all to help her out, then you're crazy!"

I thanked my daddy, hugged his neck, and said good-bye for now.

I didn't reach into my shirt to look at the check until I was well on my way back to Nashville. When I did, I was flattered by my dad's good graces. The check was for two thousand dollars. Adding this to the pot of the sum total that Robert had wired previously, I now had a grand total of seven thousand dollars for the journey.

I sometimes wonder if this healthy nest egg was part of my reason for lacking a generous dose of fear of driving out into the great unknown. Most people that jump ship and bail for the greater state of Cali leave on a wing and a prayer with barely more than the clothes that they have on their backs. I had a stack of cash to get me started when it was time to find a place to live, money for food, a down payment of one thousand dollars for school, and plenty left over to replace any odds and ends for the house. And let's not forget the big, comfy Escalade that would carry me across the states. The pilot chairs were great for long-distance drives.

But still, this was scary. I was heading out there by myself, dachshund in tow, and I didn't know yet if this was going to be a grand mistake or the best decision I'd ever made. All I could do was just step out and try. I didn't want to get to the end of my life and wonder, *What if?*

— — — — — — —

Ethan caught wind of my plans to depart. Since we were from a small city (and some of it being strategically sent through the grapevine through no intended "fault" of my own, of course), it was almost impossible that he wouldn't find out.

He showed up on "accident" to my going-away party at a popular night spot. I saw him at the bar and squeezed next to him to order a drink. "Good luck," he sputtered awkwardly. It was as though he couldn't get the broken words out of his mouth.

I grabbed my drinks, looking up at him as I turned away from the bar. "Thanks," I said in a cool, confident manner. I walked back over to my friends. Then I scanned the room for his whereabouts, and somehow he had disappeared amongst the crowd. I wasn't able to leave well enough alone, so I reached for my phone to text him. "Are you OK?"

He responded almost right away: "How could you tell that there was something wrong?" I sensed his frustration in those words, as though he was really saying, "You're the only person who knows me that well! How did you know that something was wrong?"

Long story short: Later that night, after I returned home to my loft downtown, he e-mailed me a letter. It was romantic and heart wrenching, to say the least. He said all the right things;

all the things I had so desperately been hoping, waiting, and dreaming that he would say:

> I remember the first time I saw you. You were wearing jeans and a cream-colored top, and you came walking up to the bar with this [hostile] look on your face. It was right after I moved back to Nashville from Los Angeles, so I was already mad, and when I saw you walking up to the bar I was like oh great another [jerk], and then not only were you nice to me but you tipped me as well. Then I started seeing you more, and I developed a crush on you. I remember when you gave me your number, and then almost every week after that I would call and ask if you were coming up and if you needed anything. I remember when I finally worked the nerve up to ask you out on a date, and I remember how happy I was when you said yes. I remember how much fun we had on our ten-hour date, and I remember everything we did and where we went. What happened to us?
>
> I know I'm not perfect by any means. I have said and done things that have hurt you and I will regret them the rest of my life. In retrospect, we should have gone to Hoffman together—at that point I thought it was all you, but I was wrong, it was both of us. I was so mad at you for the first year or so we were together and what you put me through. I thought that you were the messed up one and not me, but I realize that as a result I was just as much to blame for things going wrong, and for that I am so very sorry.
>
> Gabriel, you have been such a big part of my life. You have been there through pretty much every major event in my life. You know me better than anyone, and probably better than myself. Tonight is a perfect example. I tried to mask the fact that I'm not doing very well, and I thought I did, but you knew I wasn't. Honestly I was surprised you sent me a text asking if I was OK. Anyway, my

41

point is, how can two people that love each other as much as we do, understand each other like we do, and have such amazing times like we do end up like this? How do we go from one day cooking dinner and laughing and talking about getting married, to the next day fighting and putting our hands on each other? For the life of me I don't understand it and I don't think I ever will. I know we both had equal parts in everything, but still I can't fathom how someone I consider to be my best friend, my confidant, my love, and my future, can also be the person I'm fighting with, saying hurtful words to, and putting my hands on. I will always feel [terrible] for putting my hands on you—granted it wasn't just me, but I should have either done something different or just walked away and I didn't, and that will always make me feel like a [dirtbag].

So here we are. Earlier this year we were talking about getting married, you pinned my blue infantry cord on me at graduation (by the way, I still can't look at my class A uniform), and now you're moving within a few days and I am either going to Afghanistan or Monterrey. In case I do not see you again, my mentor and pretty much the reason I joined the army is dead—he was killed last month, along with three other guys in my unit, and it really [messed] me up, so I feel like I owe it to him to go to Afghanistan. On the flipside, though, revenge is never a good motive, as I have come to find out, so I don't know what to do. Of course I don't really have a say so in where I go, nor do I have a for-sure date, which is horrible because basically I am just in limbo. All I got was a call from my unit saying get your [stuff] ready, you're either going here or here. Wherever I go, and whatever the case may be, know this, Gabriel...I love you, and I always will, and I hate every single bad thing that happened between us. I would give anything to take it all back. It's not fair that we love each other so much and yet we still have the same problems. I have never hated you, and no matter how mad I get at you,

I can never truly hate you or stay mad at you, because I love you. I am truly sorry for everything I have done, and I hope you forgive me one day. It just kills me that my future won't be with you like I want it to be.

Love Always

I had been waiting almost ten years for him to say all this to me. We spent the next few days cleaning my home and packing my things so I could leave for California, but we would take breaks here and there to have sex after catching that "certain look" in each other's eyes.

The entire experience of us being there together felt perfect, innocent; like sweet love. We had a passion for each other that could only be expressed through physical means. As our bodies tangled around each other's and then finally came together to become one, it was as though the switch had been flipped to release the pressure valve. All the sadness and stress of being apart from each other seemed to disappear, replacing the bad memories for good. It was the kind of love when you still love each other amidst all the hurt and sordid history, and you somehow still find your way back together again; all that "stuff" just isn't that important anymore. All you see, feel, or think about is this love. It's hard to resist that pull, that tie that seems to continually draw you and keep you bound together, no matter what. This was what I wanted, what I wished for above everything else in life. I had my answer, my peace. He was there and we were there, back together in love and in harmony.

However, I still knew in my inner being that I was to continue on and follow through with the plan to leave Nashville. *Do not pass go, do not collect two hundred dollars.* How could this be? All I wanted, for my life to be complete and for me to feel "whole" again, was to be with him. How in the world could I still consider leaving? *Leave him behind, only for me to step out into the abyss of the unknown? Madness!* This didn't make sense. But I didn't think too much about the details; I just kept moving forward with my plan to get out of the city.

Ethan even agreed that I couldn't stay because of him. I had a plan and I was to stick with it. It was like I was moving around on autopilot. I just "knew like I knew" that this was what I was supposed to do, so despite how I felt or how illogical it sounded to my former common sense, I pushed through and stuck to the plan. Ethan reassured me by reminding me that I could always return home after school was over and he would be there. You know that old saying, "You can never return home again"? Yeah—but we'll talk more about that later.

I dragged my feet as long as I could. When school was about to start and it was finally impossible for me to put off leaving another day, I hopped in my truck and pointed it west. Through tears, Ethan and I said our farewells to one another. As I pulled away from my building, I looked to my left to look at Ethan one more time. His car faced the opposite direction; both of our driver's doors faced each other. I looked at his face and was shocked to see that he was crying like a baby. I was blown away that he would let me see him this way. I was unaware that he cared that much for me.

I was also taken aback that I had the strength to drive away from him. In times gone by, if he had ever tried to walk away from me, I would have held on to his leg as he slowly dragged me along. A couple of months ago—or a few years, for that matter—nothing could have kept me away from him. *How am I so OK with this?* I was driving away from the man I wanted more than life itself. For years, he was the very air I breathed. He was all that mattered; my everything. Now this man, my life support, was sitting in front of my home sobbing because I was leaving. *And I'm driving away from him?* And yet I knew I was to keep going. So I did. And I drove away.

— — — — — — —

I left for LA with only three days remaining before the first day of school. I made it there just in time. It took me all three days to get across the states. It was a beautiful drive. I was in awe. I had never seen countryside like this before in my life. It was beautiful! Especially when you start getting further over to the west into the desert-like terrain. I'm not knocking my beautiful land around me in the South, but this is the first time I had seen this side of the country in person. It's breathtaking! New Mexico will make you cry the first time you see it—or every time, for that matter. I remember trying to drive and take this all in at the same time. I could have stopped and looked at every inch of it for days. I remember thinking to myself, *Seeing this will make you believe for sure that God is real.* The open road made me want to put "drive across the country on motorcycle" on my bucket list. If you've never driven across the country before, make it a priority to do so before you die.

I didn't have a place to live yet, so when I arrived in California, I found the nicest hotel I could in Pasadena that allowed dogs. It was more money than I should have spent at the time (about two hundred dollars a night), and since I knew very little about the value of a dollar at the time, I stayed there for a little over a week. I needed some time to look for a place and a safe place to leave my truck (in a secured garage), and I didn't want to worry about Reese while I was at school.

I landed in school on the first day of class, early the next morning. I looked as fresh off the boat as I felt. At this point I couldn't have given a care, truthfully; I was exhausted from the haul.

When we were packing up all my belongings in Nashville, I forgot to set aside clothes to wear on the first day. By the time I got to Cali and realized I needed something appropriate to wear, I found that all my desirable clothes were packed tightly under and amidst boxes and large garbage bags heavy with stuff— so heavy and packed so tightly that it seemed a lost cause to drudge it all out and then have to pack it back into my vehicle. Considering how tired I was and how big of a hurry I was in just to make it to class on time, the cons outweighed the pros. It seemed like too much work to dig out an outfit that would "wow" my new peers on the first day of class. At this point, I was just happy to be there. I would have strolled into class barefoot and mismatched if I had to. *Take it or leave it, new people! You get what you get. I have arrived!*

At the beginning of class, our teacher told us to stand up one at a time and introduce ourselves, including a little something about ourselves, so we could get to know one another better. I was the second person to say hello. I stood up and looked amongst the class of over thirty people and enthusiastically announced to all, "Hi, y'all! My name is Gabriel!" My Southern accent and that undeniable twang enveloped the room, and in those brief seconds I had the entire room's undivided attention. There was a look of interest and wonder on the people's faces. Like people gawking at the lonely gorilla at the zoo, their eyes looked upon me in curiosity, and some might say horror, as they eagerly waited for what would come out of my mouth next.

I continued, "I just got to LA last night. I've been driving the last three days all the way from Nashville, Tennessee. I drove across the country with just me, my dog, and my truck." I laughed a little, looked over at my teacher, and went on to say, "It sounds like the perfect country song, doesn't it?" She paused a moment in her disbelief, and replied, "Uh...yeah," agreeing wholeheartedly. At this point, every jaw in the room had hit the floor. I guess they were waiting for the hidden camera crew to walk in any moment (this *is* LA, by the way) and tell them that this was all a joke. The door to the classroom didn't swing open, no camera crews; this is real, people.

I went on to say, "I got rid of everything I own, and right now my dog and I are living in a hotel room until we find a place to stay." I smiled sincerely. "Sooo...if you guys happen to know of anything that's available, please let me know." I smiled, laughed, and returned to my seat to wait for the next person to stand up. The room was silent. Nobody moved or said anything. I guess it took a minute for my instructor to process what she had just witnessed. She finally mustered, "Well...welcome to LA."

In the months to follow, this teacher loved to bring this story up as a teaching tool/lesson to her students in her classes that followed thereafter. It came in very handy when her students would try to give her some lame excuse as to why they could not find someone to bring as a model to class. She would counter their pleas and shut them down, leaving them with no excuse at all, by saying, "Oh, really? You're from this area and you couldn't find one single person that would come to class to be your hair model? Well, then, explain to me how one of my students that lived out of her car when she first moved to LA had a model here with her every time the task was assigned? She made it happen. Now what's your excuse? Hmm?" I love that she got to use me as a positive example to one-up the slackers. I was finally feeling like a role model for once in my life.

‒‒ ‒‒ ‒‒ ‒‒ ‒‒ ‒‒ ‒‒

LA was great! I loved it there. I loved the challenge. I loved that everything and everyone around me was different. Every experience was new, surreal at best. I was miles away from home, and I loved being so far away from there mentally and physically. This was literally a fresh start. No hints of my past, no memories of old, and no one there to remind me that no matter where I went, my past would always haunt me. It was a kind of freedom and newness that I had never known and had always longed for. *Who knew?* LA was the place for me.

I had assumed that every person in this city would discount me as just some country girl, but they didn't, to my surprise. I was embraced and felt welcomed by everyone I met. In fact, I found more Southern hospitality here than I ever did in the closed-minded South I had just left. Here, I realized that the mentality at home was inside the bubble they lived in. No talks of what was going on outside of our little world. I was surrounded by culture here. Nashville was still very segregated; in comparison, LA was a melting pot, and I loved it.

I loved that you were appreciated in LA for those things about you that made you different. With such a big city, with so many people, different was what people wanted. At home, there had been things about me that I thought I should suppress so that people would accept me. I now started to express those parts of myself and my personality that I used to hide away. If I liked something, I voiced it. If I didn't, I said that too. It was actually encouraged, to just be you. I loved that people loved the genuine, authentic me. Like I said, I felt a freedom like never before. Especially in the clothes I chose to wear now, how I did my hair, and things of the like.

Another thing that I loved about the mind-set here was that people took pride in how they looked. They stepped out dressed to impress, every day. Both men and women alike looked like walking, talking runways on the daily. I loved it. I loved that women and men took the time before they hit the door to make sure their hair and face were on point. In the South, not all, but the majority of people step out looking however.

I loved the feel of the city; you best make a great first impression every day. In LA, you never know if the next moment will be the very one that will change your life. Opportunity abounded there. You could run into someone on the street and it could be a movie exec or a famous person, or who knows—everyone here was six degrees from separation. You could have an encounter here that could literally change everything. So I started taking more pride in myself—not just in the way I looked, but in all aspects of my life. As I started to feel more value in myself, I carried myself and thought as such. It was great! I felt great. For the first time in my life, I felt so confident, and the sky was the limit. I felt like anything was possible—who knew where my life could take off from here? It was a great feeling to be excited about the future. I finally felt proud of my life and not ashamed at all to tell people—or myself, for that matter—what I was up to these days. Especially when I would return home to Nashville for visits, I was no longer ashamed to be me. I wanted everyone to inquire about and look at what good LA had done for me.

Everything seemed to fall into place so easily for me here. Ethan and I would always jokingly say that I must have God on speed dial. It sounded like a great line at the time, but later on I would come to find that these words held more truth than I knew.

When I wasn't at school, I spent a lot of my free time at home listening to Joyce Meyer podcasts on my PC. Her teachings and what she had to say about God made sense to me and brought me a lot of comfort since I was so far away from home.

I tried to keep up a long-distance relationship with Ethan, but that didn't last long. As the world around me changed, so did I. My eyes were starting to open, so to speak. And like I said before, I was starting to see value in myself. There were some things that I was just not able to tolerate anymore once I saw my self-worth and understood more and more that I deserved to be treated well, not like a tossed-out piece of garbage that someone saved for scraps. I was finally starting to get some standards and set healthy boundaries with people.

Being in all this newness and wanting to move forward in that and let go of old, worn out, tired beliefs—keeping in contact with Ethan seemed to hold me back and keep me bound to my old life. With one foot in my past and one foot in the new, it was impossible to embrace this new revelation of being and move forward. I had to let go if I wanted to move on and see what was on the other side of happy.

It is never a good thing to hold on to a relationship for too long. We had been done for a long time. It should have ended completely before I even left. Sometimes we hold on to what we know, no matter how bad it is, just because it's what we are comfortable with. Walking away from what you know you should is never easy because you don't know what will happen as a result, but all I'm telling you is that when something is long past over, let go. There is another plan for you, but how are you supposed to go experience it if you won't step out?

As a result of trying to hold on to Ethan, I missed out on forming relationships and friendships with new people. I missed opportunities, missed parties, and missed lots of things I was invited to by several people on many occasions because I was too wrapped up in Ethan to care. (Either we would be fighting or he would be ignoring me, which would consume my thoughts and make me sad until he would take away my anxiety and finally call.) If I did get out, I would be sad because my mind was on him and what he was doing, so much that I couldn't fully enjoy any kind of life going on around me.

I wasn't in a good mood when I went out. I didn't want to interact with people; I just wanted to be left alone so I could have a pity party in my head and wonder if Ethan loved me or not and if he would ever text me back. That was no way to live. I sacrificed it all to pick up and move away. If I was going to come all the way to LA to do exactly what I had been doing in Nashville, I should have just stayed in Nashville. I had moved here to get away and start new. This was not new. I was in a new place, but I had dragged my past along with me.

I left a lot of things behind in Nashville when I got rid of everything in my house and bailed—this baggage was supposed to stay there too. I forgot to leave it there, and it was weighing me down. I was miserable. Miserable because I was homesick; miserable because I had let down my guard and had anything to do with Ethan before I left; and rekindling this mess was keeping me bound. I didn't go through all this and relocate just to end up exactly where I had been.

After months of this going back and forth, it finally happened: like I'd flipped a switch, my feelings for him changed overnight. I had finally had enough. I had always heard people talk about this sort of epiphany moment, but I didn't know it was for real, real. And I didn't know how to make it happen, or if it would ever happen for me in this drawn out, "if the horse is dead, you gotta dismount" relationship. I never thought I would see the day, but on this very day I did. In my head, it was over. I didn't feel anything—no passion, no want, no lust—just, "I'm exhausted. Would you please go away now? Leave. Bye-Bye."

In less than two weeks, Ethan had planned to visit for a week. He had also informed me that during his trip he was planning to propose. In the days leading up to this, I had been excited and looked forward to seeing him; then out of nowhere the feelings I had for him for so very long were gone. I even searched inside myself to find them, to muster up anything that could make me even fake it while he was in town—but no. This girl was done. My ship had sailed. I felt bad for him, but there was nothing I could do. It was just through.

I did my best to not let on that anything was different the week before his arrival. I didn't tell him to just stay home; I hoped that maybe when I saw him all those feelings would just come rushing back. But they didn't. I did my best while he was visiting to not let on that anything was wrong. I felt so guilty inside knowing that he was still hoping for a future with us, and I was no longer on board for that journey. Of course, after all that time and history together, I still loved him and I didn't want him to hurt, but I just didn't love him romantically anymore. The thrill was gone.

I did my best to stuff down the sadness I felt and just enjoy this time we had together, especially knowing that it might very well be our last. I remember that toward the end of the week, we walked on a trail next to the sands on the beach. Ethan stopped and sat on a bench facing the water. He had a smoke and returned some messages on his phone. I walked on a little ways ahead of him, and from a distance I turned back and just stood silently watching him as he looked down at his phone screen. He had no idea that I was standing at a distance just watching him, trying my best to take him all in.

In my inner knowing, I knew this would probably be the last time I would ever see him like this; the last time I would ever see him with us on these terms. The next time I saw him, we might not even know each other. We might barely recall the days when we knew each other like we used to. So I just stood and smiled and took in everything I could: his mannerisms; the way he sat, held his head, and crossed one leg over, placing his foot upon his knee; the way his eyes and his face squinted when he would direct his eyes away from his phone and look over the ocean. I didn't want to forget anything about this man whom I had loved for so long, this man who knew me better than anyone, and vice versa. I loved how it felt to hug this man around his large, thick hoodie. This man whom I at one time thought I would die without. This man that I had to say good-bye to and let go of, because I knew if I did truly love him, it was the best thing for both parties involved. I think that is really true love, when you can let go because you do love someone so much instead of letting go because you don't. And I loved him, and still do to this very day.

When we returned to our room later that afternoon, Ethan pulled out a ring and presented it to me. He didn't get down on one knee. He said nervously, "This ring is a promise to marry." In my mind, it was as though my head tilted to the side with a look of confusion. I thought, "Huh? So what is this? Are you asking me to marry you or what? I don't understand the question. And the presentation has thrown me off a little. Sorry. I really am trying to take this seriously, but are you? I'm not sure what's happening right now..." Then the all-time cutest, greatest thing happened. In his nervousness he went to remove the ring from its box, and he fumbled it across the room. It was as though he threw it at me. It was cute and sweet and awkward in every way it should be. In my mind, if we had married it would have been one of those amazing stories we would have gone on to tell friends at parties and our children. Like a "Kids, you'll never believe what your dad did! So typical of your father! Isn't he cute and all?" kind of thing.

I still wasn't really sure if he had in fact just proposed or not. I crawled around on the carpeted hotel floor, found the ring under the bed, and stood up. I placed the ring on my finger and looked up at him and just let out a "Yes." He hadn't really asked me a question, so I wasn't very sure of what the correct response should be. I just went with what I knew.

We went on about our day like nothing out of the ordinary had just happened. I think we went out for lunch and probably went exploring around LA. I remember that I didn't feel joyful and blown away like I had always imagined I would if he were ever to propose. It was strange. I'd finally gotten what I had always dreamed for and wanted, and I felt nothing. You would think after something like this I would have at least been on the phone or on Facebook spreading the news, but I wasn't. I remember at the time I even hid it from my mom and my best friend when he came out to visit. I wouldn't even let people know that we had talked.

This was all around not good—not normal, to say the least. I remember I didn't even wear the ring to school. I remember placing it back in its box after Ethan left California. I told no one at school that I was supposedly engaged. Yeah, I could safely say that those feelings I was wrestling with—whether I wanted to be with him or not—were official: I could safely say that I didn't want any part of this relationship anymore.

I didn't look forward to what was next. I couldn't keep up the facade. I had to step up to the plate, do what was right, and tell Ethan. I cringed at the very thought. I hated the thought of hurting him. I didn't feel like it was fair to him, for our feelings to be in separate places; but it also wasn't fair for me to drag this out and keep the truth from him. Neither side seemed like a win-win, let alone an enjoyable conversation to be had. But I had to put on my big girl panties and just get it over with. I was hurting us both more by letting it go on longer. Deep breath. Here goes. Just jump. Just do it already!

After Ethan had been back in Nashville for only a week, I finally mustered up enough courage to make the call to tell him my truth, that I didn't want to marry him and it was over. As expected, he was furious, and rightfully so. A few days later, I mailed the ring back to him. Standing across the counter from a postal lady at the post office, hesitating, through tears, I surrendered the package over to her. This was final. No going back after that package was out of my hands and on its way back to him in Nashville.

The feelings and emotions going on inside of me were perplexing at best. This was one of the toughest decisions I had ever made in my entire life. This was a game changer, a definite fork in the road. This decision was fate; it would affect my destiny. Both roads led to unknowns, as does any decision we make in this life, but I knew the outcome of one decision would be far better than the other.

What if this was the dumbest thing I could ever do? What if I look back years, minutes, and months later and cry out, "What did I do?" What if I never fall in love again? What if nobody but him would ever want me? What if I'm missing my one chance at marriage? What if he moves on and marries another, and I become a spinster who he laughs at and mocks?

But also there is that "What if?" Is this the right move? What if there is something, some life, some destiny, some person; a better, more enlightened version of myself waiting on the other side of the unknown? What if being with him was not in fact all part of God's plan for my life?

I decided to go with the latter. I let go. In that moment, still standing across from a disgruntled, annoyed postal worker who couldn't care less that this moment meant so very much to me (it wasn't pulling on her heart strings; I'll just say that), I looked up and let go of the ring. I turned away and walked out of the post office. What would come next and what my future held was literally and figuratively out of my hands. A door to my past was now closed.

━ ━ ━ ━ ━ ━ ━

In the days and months that followed, seeing how I hadn't given much effort when I first arrived in LA, a huge void was left in my life. A gaping hole now existed. It left empty space for me to think new thoughts. If Ethan was no longer a part of my life, then what would I think about instead? I had to adjust to a life with new activities and different motives, a new norm that did not revolve around him.

In times past, when we would break up in Nashville, I would fill this void with old friends, my mom, my dad, my uncle, my life, what I knew, my city. There was plenty to do and plenty of people around to keep me busy. But now I was here, with a big question mark over my head. I was so lonely, and I was bored. Of course, I was in LA, and it seems as though I'd find plenty to do and see to help the time pass; but since I had not made any real deep or lasting connections with the people at school (or anyone I had met, for that matter), I didn't have anyone to call, hang out with, or go do stuff with.

Sometimes when I did research cool places to go check out in LA by myself, going there alone made me feel and take notice of my aloneness more than if I had just stayed home alone in the first place. So I started staying at home instead, and just kind of gave up on venturing out, besides going to school. I found myself spending most of my Thursdays through Sundays, when I was off school, alone. It was consuming. I was definitely starting to second-guess myself and feel as though I had made a mistake. I even remember feeling like I couldn't wait to get the days over with, just finish school, so I could get back home to Nashville.

I had a prescription for Adderall when I went to school in Nashville, so I decided to refill my script with a local doctor in California. This medication seemed to dumb down how I felt, and kept me busy and distracted in my mind. It made the thoughts I had less obsessive. I found myself looking for tasks like buying furniture at IKEA just so I could take it home and put it together. It was a time filler.

I should have gone out and gotten a job—something part time, maybe—anything to take up space on those days that were idle for me. But the money that Robert wired me monthly covered all my expenses, so there was nothing pushing me to find a job. I always found some excuse not to do it.

The manager of a shoe store wanted to hire me, even as a key holder, and I ran. I never felt like I could fit in with those "real-world people." I felt like no job would last long because I would be "found out," so to speak, by the fellow employees. I also felt scared that the small wages I would earn would not be enough to motivate me to stick with the job and do my very best. I was also afraid of people's rejection, so I would reject them before they even had a chance to reject me.

However, contrary to this notion and way of thinking, I busted my butt at school and gave 100 percent at customer service, helping out staff and students when odd jobs needed to be done, like laundry, cleaning, whatever—you name it. I began to prepare myself for the real world and always showed up to school early, prepared for the day, and made sure my clothes were neat and my appearance was professional. Even though I didn't feel that I could give my all to a part-time job that wouldn't pertain to my long-term goals (or so I thought at the time), I did give my all to school and my future.

When I would be at home for hours on end alone, I spent all of that time watching Joyce Meyer episodes. I played them continually, back to back, all day, all night until I went to bed. As I found things to do around the house, I would leave Joyce playing as background noise, like you would do with music on a stereo. I was hooked. I guess it's not such a bad thing to get hooked on; there are worse things I could have spent my time with. Thankfully, in this arena of "alone," I was spending my time learning more and more and getting to know this God— the God I had always heard about; this God I had always visited; this God whose character and ways I'd never really understood or known much about.

As I listened to more and more of Joyce's teachings, I started to understand what a relationship with God was really all about, and I started to want more of Him in my life. I started to want to do things His way for a change and let go of how I had done things in the past. His ways began to make more sense to me than the world's ways that I had grown so systematically accustomed to. I was being introduced to a new way, a new life. Almost subconsciously I was stepping into a new life, a new way of life. But if you know anything about this amazing God we serve, you know as well as I that nothing, my dear, is done by accident or happenstance. Unbeknownst to me at the time, everything unfolding in front of me was part of His plan and what He had intended for me. And I thank God every day now that He did step in without me knowing. He had set me apart—aside, if you will.

I thought I was going to LA to start a new life on my own agenda. I had an idea in my head about how this new life was going to pan out. But I would later find out and come to understand that I was, in fact, there to start a new life; however, this new life had nothing to do with me. The move to LA was indeed about a new life, but a life with God, for God; a life that was about His will, not my own. I didn't know at the time that this was happening—a setup, some might call it. One that was met with a lot of resistance and a struggle for power. At times I begged God to leave me alone, insisting that this was not a good time for me. But now I'm so grateful that He set up these days.

I'm so grateful that God saw something in me that I never knew could or would exist. He saw something in me that I still cannot fathom. He saw something worth setting apart to use for His greater purpose and glory. And I now praise Him continually for stepping in when He did. Now I beg Him to never leave me or go away. And that is just one of the many great things about God: He is forever faithful in His promises. He promises never to leave us nor forsake us. He has never given up on or walked away from me. No matter how badly I mess up, He is still by my side and He still loves me. Thank You, God, for that!

━ ━ ━ ━ ━ ━ ━

At the time, however, being alone seemed to wear on me. I decided to stop listening to Joyce every day, replacing her with a playlist of my favorite songs. I thought, "This is crazy! Enough with this God stuff! It's gotten me off balance! For goodness' sake, take a break from this 'trying to live so pure and holy'! You've become a bore! I'm even bored with you! Come on, let that stuff go and think about you again and what makes *you* happy! Obviously this God stuff and trying to change your life isn't working for you! Nothing is getting better; in fact, you could even say it has made things *worse*! You spend all your time alone and you aren't out there experiencing *life*!"

I made a decision there and then to put God to the side, get back to living life, and "do me" for a bit. "Doing me" consisted of night clubs, drinking, drugs, late nights, partying, boys, casual sex, and drinking and driving. Whatever I thought would make me happy I did to the extreme. I did LA well. *And was it fun? You bet! Did I enjoy it? Yes! Did I feel like I had a life? Yep. Was I fulfilled? Did it ultimately leave me feeling good about myself?* No. *Did I feel like I was making lasting, quality, real relationships with those around me?* No. It was all surface with no depth.

I felt like all the friends I had could be gone in a New York minute. With one wrong move, their conditional "love" could be stripped away. So I gave them what I thought they wanted, and vice versa, and the cycle continued, off into nowhere. The life I went out and got was fleeting and hard to keep up with. I was being what I thought people and myself wanted me to be in order to keep up the kind of life I thought I needed to have to be happy and feel "whole." It was all a ruse. But it did look great on Facebook.

But something was different. Something didn't feel right about what I was doing. But how is this? Why? I had been doing these same activities for years in Nashville, just on a different level. The only things that were different now were the people's faces around me and the clubs that I went to. Why was I starting to feel like what I was doing now was wrong? I used to do this guilt free! What gives? Why now? If I was going to party, this was the city where I wanted to do it—I did not want to slow down and slack off now. I wanted to give it my all. (I was, trust me!) But now it was different; now I couldn't do it without a conscience.

What gives? How do I make these feelings of guilt and condemnation go away? Excuse me, God; this is bad timing for me! Now if You would please excuse me, I would like to snort this bag of coke without feeling like You are standing over my shoulder watching me! But try as hard as I could to stuff down these feelings that what I was doing was wrong, they wouldn't go away.

Although I couldn't understand it at the time, there was something going on deep down inside of me, at a soul level. A seed had been planted, and now God was making it grow.

If you had told me before I set out for Los Angeles that this would be the time in my life when God would feel it appropriate and the best timing to step into my life, I would have laughed in your face and called you crazy! *Of all the places to come calling for me, why in the world would God think that the city of vanity was the perfect place to do so?* Because He's God, that's why. And because, unlike so many of us would like to believe, this life—"your life"—does not, in fact, have anything to do with you. So step aside and put down your own agenda. Give it over to God. It doesn't belong to you, and it never belonged to you in the first place.

This scenario of God setting me apart from the life I knew so that I could hear His voice reminds me of when He told Abraham to step outside of his tent (his surroundings, his comforts, his normal) so that God could speak to him:

> He took him outside and said, "Look up at the sky and count the stars—if indeed you can count them." Then he said to him, "So shall your offspring be."
> —Genesis 15:5

CHAPTER 5

A HARD LEFT TURN

I PASSED THE STATE board exam and received a cosmetology license in the state of California. I had no plans to return to Nashville—I was so happy in LA! The opportunities there were endless! At the beginning of 2011, I moved to the coolest studio, located four blocks away from the ocean in Venice Beach. Los Angeles was starting to feel like home. I felt like I belonged there. The next objective was to find a salon where I could start my flourishing career.

———————

The day before Valentine's Day, I woke up in my studio to yet another beautiful day in Cali. I didn't look at my phone right away; instead I chose to be "easy like Sunday morning." I finally took a peek about an hour later to see if I had any missed calls or texts. To my surprise, there were several missed calls from people in Nashville, people I had not spoken to since I left. Only to cure my curiosity as to their sudden interest in me, I decided to return their calls. I hadn't a clue why they would be reaching out to me.

The first call I made was to an old girlfriend of mine. She told me that she and a few friends, including Ethan, had met up earlier that day for brunch. She assured me that Ethan had just left and was no longer among them during our call. She told me that Ethan had asked her to call me because the night before, someone had told him that I had committed suicide. He was freaking out trying to find a way to contact me. I laughed at the notion and very politely responded, "No, I didn't commit suicide."

I called the next number, which happened to be an ex-boy-friend of mine. (I dated him briefly before Ethan and I got back together, but that's neither here nor there.) Moving on, he said he had also crossed paths with Ethan earlier. Ethan asked him if he had my number, and if so, if he would try to reach out to me for him. I laughed again; this was kind of a far reach if Ethan just wanted an excuse to talk to me. "No, I'm alive," I said before ending the conversation and hanging up the phone. I called my girl Angie to share a laugh with her about all this. I suggested that maybe, just to mess with his head a little, she should go on my Facebook and post "RIP Gabriel." Thankfully, she didn't.

Amused by Ethan's story, which I assumed he made up to evoke a sense of urgency in the people he used as bait to get in touch with me, I smiled as I put down the phone. I was flattered that he would go to such extremes just to talk to me. I did always appreciate his flair for the dramatics. Somehow I had kept thoughts of him from running over and over in my mind for the past eight months—an impossible feat for a girl like me whose every thought and move she made the past ten years was consumed with him. And if I had thought of him, it wasn't in a way that would inspire happy thoughts and memories. But for some reason, on this day, this had all changed. I was delighted with the thought of him thinking of me. The possibility that we might give this thing called love another go brought me great joy and feelings of excitement.

As I waited for him to ring my phone or at least try to contact me by e-mail, I lay in my bed and pictured him walking up and down my hallway. He was a big, tall guy with a switch of the hips incomparable to any other. He had the cutest walk I'd ever seen. As I imagined him there, the look on his face, he seemed elated. There was a sense of joy and delight upon him. Was he, at this very moment, as excited as I was, thinking that we might come back together?

I checked my phone all day for some sort of "peep" from him, especially after all the commotion that morning. I just knew he couldn't do all that extreme searching for me to then abruptly give up. So I continued to expect a text or something from him before the day was out.

Later that evening, I lay on my belly in my bed facing my flat screen TV. As I lay there watching Eminem perform "Love the Way You Lie" on the Grammy awards show, I wondered if at that very moment Ethan was also watching it, thinking of me too. Then, *finally*, the phone rang. I thought to myself, "It's him! Hoorah!" It was actually a call from a mutual friend of ours. I was so relieved that the moment I'd been waiting for all day had finally arrived.

I took a deep breath and smiled, feeling excited as I answered the phone. *How cute! It's like elementary school where the boy is too shy to call the girl, so instead he gets one of his friends to call her.* I was almost blushing and so ready to play the "Do you like my friend? Check the box yes or no" game!

During the time it took me to grab the phone, look at the caller ID, and put the phone up to my ear, I imagined how the conversation would go down:

"Hello?"

"Yes, Gabriel, I'm sitting here with a mutual friend of ours. He's been telling me all day how much he loves you and misses you." Then a silent pause as he passes the phone over to Ethan.

I had butterflies in my belly as I looked forward to finally being able to hear Ethan's voice, that voice I knew so well. I took a deep breath and let out a sigh of relief. For a moment I felt so much better; even after being away for so long, I got that old feeling like I was home again. I snapped back into reality when the phone touched my ear and I heard the voice on the other end say, "Ethan's dead."

▬ ▬ ▬ ▬ ▬ ▬ ▬

As my best friend drove me to the airport, I thought, "God, I moved to LA to start anew, for something better, and to rid myself of past mistakes and a life of hurt. I start to get close to You and *this* is what happens? I thought going the 'God route' would make my life better! I thought if I started to live a life that pleased You, everything would be easy sailing from here on out and I would be happy! Now look what has happened! I thought my days of sorrow and troubles were behind me! This is not at all what I had in mind! This is not at all the future I had planned in my head!

"I thought I could control the good or bad circumstances in my life if I just made better choices! I considered a million possibilities for my future, but *death*? I never, ever considered death. Yeah, maybe I thought Ethan might move on and marry someone else. I thought I was about to ride off into the sunset of my happy ending! I don't know what to do with this! I am so angry right now! Why won't bad things stop happening in my life? I moved to LA to change my life and do better! What did I do to deserve this?"

I was now faced with the harsh reality that I am not, in fact, in control of my own destiny. No matter what we do or how we might try to control our circumstances, we do not have the final say on what will or will not happen in our lifetime. I thought I had been through enough struggles and hardships; I had paid my dues, so to speak. Why me? Why can't I see good days like other people do? I thought I had already learned the cruel truths of life, but on this day I was kicked in the face by what *cruel* really meant. Life will take us all through some unexpected and tough times, whether we think we are ready for them or not.

I cried out to God, "I don't want anything else to do with You! Leave me alone!" I continued to rage and war inside my head, but none of that would undo Ethan's death. It wasn't going to take away my hurt. I dreaded the days ahead.

━ ━ ━ ━ ━ ━ ━

One day before the funeral, I was riding in the truck with my dad. We were on an old two-lane road, headed out to the country where he was raised. I had asked my dad to take me out somewhere so we could shoot a couple of his guns. I needed to relieve some stress. I said, "Daddy, I was so mad at God when I found out Ethan was dead, but now, after only three days of being here in Nashville, I'm starting to see God's purpose in taking him and why this had to happen in my life."

"I'm so happy for you," Dad said to me. I looked at him, wondering why. He went on to say, "What you have come to understand within a couple of days—most people that takes a lifetime to get."

We rode a little ways on down the road just enjoying the drive, the countryside, and the time together. I said, "Daddy, I sure am dreading this funeral. I don't want to hear anything else anybody has to say."

"Don't worry," he replied. "I'll take care of that for you."

We reached our destination and stepped out onto the open land. Dad handed me a loaded, cocked and ready Colt 45 revolver. He took his long barrel rifle and proceeded to shoot off into the distance without waiting for me to go first. With his attention elsewhere, I quietly inspected what was in my hand. I rolled the gun over and onto its side, just checking it out. I turned the barrel up toward my chin and then back into a normal resting position in my hand. Dad fired a round and then looked back over at me. I continued to look down at the gun as I asked him a question.

"Daddy, what if I shot myself with this?"

"You won't do it," he said.

I looked up at him, then stepped away from the truck and walked over to where he was standing. We both walked side by side for a bit, then I found a great target to hit and paused to take aim. Before I pulled the trigger, I stopped and asked my dad if he had any ear plugs. "Ear plugs are for wusses," he retorted. Well, I didn't want my dad to think of me as such, so I manned up, took aim, ready, steady, fire, *boom*!

We fired off every piece of ammo we had on us. We shot at anything we felt was a great target—off into the woods, off into the great unknown. This is what I call therapy. I had one final shot left, and I pointed my gun out into a direction where we had not shot that day. I said, "Daddy, what do you think? Should I?" He shrugged his shoulders as if to say, "Your call." I prepared to shoot one last time for the day. I pulled back on the trigger and *click*. No bullets left. My dad turned to head back to the truck and said to me, "Now that's what I call divine intervention."

The next day at Ethan's funeral, I whispered over to my dad, "My ears are ringing from yesterday. I can't hear anything."

He leaned over toward me and replied, "You said you didn't want to hear anybody talk. I told ya I would take care of that."

CHAPTER 6

MOVED BACK TO Nashville brokenhearted. I had been unexpectedly slapped in the face by my mortality. I didn't want to miss out on any more time with my family and the people I knew who had meant so much to me. Unfortunately, the move back home only led to more depression. The life I had once known there no longer existed. The Gabriel I used to know no longer existed. I no longer had the circle of friends and the social scene I had before. I just didn't find any interest in the things, people, and places that used to be a part of my norm. My priorities and view on life had changed. I found myself not having anything in common with the people I used to hang with. I tried my best after several failed attempts to partake in social gatherings and whatnot, but I felt odd and alone.

I had only been gone for about two years; I was even surprised myself at how different I had become in such a small amount of time. So I stayed in the house. I once again found myself spending most of my time in the house alone. I tried to find comfort in my family but to no avail. This was even more disappointing to me, because in my mind I had thought I would be running home for the support. But this support had never really existed. This supportive pulling together of a family was only an idea in my head, an idea of what I would hope and yearn for in a family. It just wasn't there.

I also missed the excitement of LA. I found Nashville to be boring now. The people I was surrounded by seemed to lack depth. They had nothing interesting to offer or to say. I didn't understand at the time, that the "depth" I was searching for could not be found outside of me. This was a thirst that no human could quench.

━━ ━━ ━━ ━━ ━━ ━━ ━━

I found this letter that I wrote and addressed to Ethan during this time:

Saturday, March 19, 12:05 a.m.

You were right. I was and still I am sitting here alone. I thought I was doing something in my best interest. And for what? To spend my life in solitude and wait for something good to happen in my life. And now look at how things turned out. You're gone. Not just gone, but dead. Dead? Seriously? I want a recount. This can't be real. This can't be how the story ends. How dumb was I! How stupid could I have been? Wasted. I wasted us. I wasted a lifetime. True love comes in many forms. Ours came in a tumultuous package. If I had only known then what I know now, I would have ridden the wave until the very end. But who could have ever known? I could have given our story a million different endings, but not this one. Really? Dead? How can this be? We've been through awful things together and we've done awful things to each other, but I'd give anything to have you here again. It's amazing how death can answer so many questions for you. It's amazing how quickly you can learn to forgive when the past seems so miniscule compared to the big picture. I loved you like you were the only thing that existed on this earth. How

I wish I could go back and do it all over again. I'm sorry I didn't treat you better. I was ignorant and didn't understand things like I do now. I wish I could have looked past things that I thought were hurtful and just *loved* you. If any couple ever deserved a do-over, it's us. You and I took a lot of things out on each other because we were hurting inside. We both had pain that went down deep that neither of us knew what to do with. Our only way to release it was through each other. I'm sorry. Knowing what I know now, I would have told you to scream at me, and I would have held you so tight and not let you go until the pain subsided. I took your rages and actions personally, but it had nothing to do with me. I'm so sorry I didn't show my love for you more. I'm sorry for what I put you through. I'm so sorry. Even though ours is a sad story, I wouldn't trade you or our experiences together for the world. Even though we went through hell and back, you were and always will be my knight in shining armor. We weren't perfect, and even though we were nothing close to the fairytale, I'm so thankful that I do know what true love is. Even though my heart is broken and I'm filled with regret, in my lifetime I experienced a bond that could never be broken. Wait for me. Don't leave me here all alone. You're the only thing that matters to me. I want another chance at a lifetime with you. Next time I'll know what to do when it comes to loving you. Don't forget me, mi amor. My only goal now is to see you again. Thank you for loving me. I'm sorry I let you down.

--- --- --- --- --- --- ---

The time was also drawing near when my sugar daddy would be returning to the states for a week of R&R. Since Ethan's death, God had put it on my heart that it was time for me to lay this situation down and let Robert go. This was another reason why I decided to come home. I figured if I was to run out of money, or if I needed help or somewhere to live, my chances were better in Nashville than way over in California.

The night before Robert flew home, God spoke to me in a dream. It was the first time I'd ever had this happen. I've had wild dreams before but never like this. This one made me stand at attention and take notice. Although I didn't know at the time that God sometimes speaks to us this way, I knew like I knew that this was in fact a message from God.

In the dream, I kicked a digital clock and the screen read, "DON'T ANGER ME! DON'T TEMPT ME!" Then I saw myself at my friend's house in Miami. I was being offered a job at her building—a janitorial position, it seemed. The supervisor said to me, "I will give you shelter and provide you with the tools you will need."

At this point in my walk with God, I was still testing out the waters. I still hadn't fully come to terms with whether I thought He truly existed or not. I didn't know what would happen if I did as He instructed. I didn't really know if He would help me out or take care of me if I did get rid of Robert. All I knew was that I didn't want to test this God. Whoever He was, I had a feeling that He was not playing and that He meant business. I didn't want to take any chances and see what would happen as a result of me *not* doing as He instructed.

Later that evening, Robert called to let me know he had landed. It was the first of the month and bills were due. He had not yet wired me the money to cover all my expenses—all part of his control. I guess he was holding out and wanted to see me before he did anything for me, sort of like bait, to make sure I was going to do as he pleased first. Well, it wasn't going to work out so well for him this time. Despite whatever was to come next, bills paid or not, I knew I had to follow through and do as God expected. Through tears and a queasy stomach, I told

Robert that I wouldn't be seeing him while he was in town. I wouldn't be seeing him ever again, actually. And that was that. I hung up the phone, and I didn't hear from him again.

— — — — — — —

A couple of weeks earlier, I did what I thought was best in order to prepare myself for a life without Robert (or rather a life without his funds). I had just started working at a small salon in Nashville. I had only just begun to build a clientele, so the money I did bring in was slim to none. Looking back, I could have gotten a part-time job, but that still would not have covered all my monthly expenses.

I had no previous knowledge about how to support myself other than stripping. I needed some sort of safety net until I learned how to support myself in the "real world." Scared and nervous, I went to my dad, spilled my guts, and laid it all out. I told him the truth about how I had found the means to live so well without a steady job for over six years. I puked out the whole story as fast as I could to get it over with as soon as possible.

I finished and sat quietly waiting for his response to it all. I was flushed and blushing with embarrassment. I had just told my dad that I was a paid hooker. Then he asked me this question: "Does this man think that nobody loves you?"

I opened my mouth to respond but then stopped. I didn't know how to answer this question. "I'm shaking I'm so nervous. I can't believe I just told you all that, Dad." He simply replied, "A told secret holds no power."

I went on to ask my dad if he could help me at all as I adjusted to being on my own. I told him how badly I wanted out of this mess and that all I knew to do was just come to him, all guards down, and ask for help like I should have done many years ago—as far back as my club days.

He went on to say that it was fine, and that he was willing to cover my bills until I got on my feet. I went away feeling relieved. This heavy burden had finally been lifted off my shoulders. I felt free. I was more than ready for this to be over and out of my life.

— — — — — — —

Not very long after this, Gloria was diagnosed with ovarian cancer. I remembered a conversation with my uncle. "Well, I guess you got what you wanted!" he said.

I replied, "This isn't what I wanted! I would never wish this on anyone!" Truthfully, there were no words to describe how I felt. I was shocked at best. I just hated it for my dad, having lost his daughter to this disease, and now having to watch someone else he loved go through it.

— — — — — — —

It had been one month since I last spoke to Robert. My dad kept his word and paid my bills that month. It felt good to be free from Robert. I didn't feel bound anymore. It especially felt good to let my dad know the truth, and to know he had my back. I was beginning to understand the old saying, "The truth will set you free!"

The next month, when the bills were due, I called my dad. As soon as he picked up the phone, I sensed resistance on his end. He spoke reluctantly, struggling to find every word. He didn't seem to be listening to a word I said. Sarcastically he asked me how much I needed to cover my bills for the month. I knew he had a lot going on in his life, and I didn't want to make things worse. He sounded mad, so I brought the conversation to an end.

As we hung up the phone, I felt nothing but regret and guilt. I felt so bad calling him for money. My face flushed red hot with embarrassment. How dumb could I be? Why had I gone to him for such a thing? Why did I go lay it all out on the table and ask him for help? Obviously, I lived in a rich fantasy world in my head; one where I thought that this could go over smoothly! I felt awful going to him with my hand out...dumb girl.

I wasn't looking for a free ride. I thought he knew I meant I only needed help temporarily. Had I not done "some version" of what I should have done years before? And that "some version" was to go to my dad for help so I could get a leg up while I worked a normal job and rearranged some things in my life, and then finally pay my own way as soon as my life shifted into its new state of "normal."

I was so sick of doing bad things for money. I was sick of myself. Fast money; that lifestyle—it's a vicious cycle that sucks you in. Once you board that runaway train, you can't get off—not until it spits you out...I had just been "spit out."

I called my dad later that evening, hoping he would be in a better mood since he was off work. He answered the phone, "Hello?" After realizing it was me on the other end, he didn't have much to say. He dodged and danced around my every word. Finally, I said, "Dad, just say it!" After a brief pause he said, "I can't help you anymore. Gloria is my only concern now." The only sound I heard next was a dial tone.

▬ ▬ ▬ ▬ ▬ ▬ ▬

I had a full-time job, but as a stylist it can take several months—up to a year, even—to build a decent clientele. I was evicted from my apartment. I had never been evicted before. Now it would be on my credit history. I had to go to court to be served with the eviction notice. I found myself squeezed into a court-room, standing room only, among people I would have previously sworn I had nothing in common with. I felt like scum. A loser. Section 8, whatever that means. At the bottom of the barrel, I was now settled amidst the muck I had worked so hard to stay above. It was now my reality. And all because of a choice I had made—to say yes to God.

I walked out of court in tears. When I got inside my car, I cried even harder. I decided to take a chance and call my dad. It had been about a month and a half since we had last spoken. I was hoping that maybe, after some space, he would've had a change of heart. The phone rang and there was no answer. I thought nothing of it.

As I drove toward my mom's house, I received a text. It was my dad: "What's up?" I thought I was low before; now the entire world had just crumbled in on me. He had missed my call on purpose. He had placed a wall between us. To send something as impersonal as that text, it was clear to me that he was now unattainable. It felt like I had instead gotten a response from a guy I was dating who was trying to avoid me because he didn't know how to break up with me. My stomach twisted and felt sick. This realization irked me on several levels. I cried even harder; I was so sad—but what good would it do me? If this was what he wanted, I decided then to just leave him alone.

After several months of not speaking at all, I decided to show up at his house unannounced. His stepchildren didn't have to wait for an invitation to come over, so why should I? I don't know what got into me; maybe it was the fact that Gloria was sick. This wasn't just about my dad. I genuinely wanted to go see Gloria and see how she was doing after chemo. I wanted to see my dad too. I missed my family, so dang it, *I was going to go see them!* I felt I had nothing more to lose at this point anyway.

I pulled up in their driveway. My father stepped out of the door that led out to his drive and met me at the car. He looked at me with caution, not sure what I was there for (or, better yet, *there to do*). I couldn't tell if I was a wanted guest or not, but he went ahead and welcomed me into the house. The visit went well, just like any other time I had been there before—no awkward moments and no mention of what had happened in the past several months.

After saying my good-byes, my dad walked me back to my car. I got in, and before I could close the door to leave, my dad placed his hand on the door to keep it from shutting. He looked down at me and said, "You're a far better person than I'll ever be."

I gently smiled, acknowledging his words, and reached out to shut my car door. I then backed out of the driveway as my dad stood there watching me until I was out of sight.

CHAPTER 7

I DIDN'T KNOW WHAT to do with my life. I hated it back in Nashville. Things seemed stagnant for me here. So I received my refund from my taxes, quit my job, and decided to run back to California. I hoped things hadn't changed too much since I was there last so I could just slide back in and pick up where I left off. And sure enough, as soon as my feet hit that Cali soil, I picked my life back up exactly where I had left it.

I had only been back in LA for about three months before I had two great jobs doing hair at two excellent locations. One was a barbershop in West Hollywood, and the other was a "blowout bar" on Sunset Boulevard. It was fantastic! I couldn't have been happier working at these two jobs.

I rented a room from friends, a married couple with two small girls; the wife's mother lived in the guest house out by the pool. Actually, these just happened to be the same people who I rented my very first place from when I'd first moved to LA. They were awesome. It was like having a family even though I was away from my own. They let me take over their guest room until I found my permanent spot to call home. Things were going great! I felt good, I looked good, and I had hope for the future.

—— —— —— —— —— —— ——

One evening as I sat on the patio by the pool sipping a glass of wine, the phone rang out of the blue. Even though it was from an international number, it looked familiar. And then it hit me—I hadn't seen this number in quite some time. It was Robert calling from overseas.

Side note: The devil is such an opportunist. He always tries to slip a fast one in when we're at our most vulnerable, especially during those times in our lives when we either have a little or a lot. The Bible says in 1 Peter 5:8, "Stay alert! Watch out for your great enemy, the devil. He prowls around like a roaring lion, looking for someone to devour" (NLT).

Sly little devil, very sly; different day, but same old tricks. Now imagine a small devil on my shoulder telling me all the reasons why I *should* just go ahead and let Robert come back into my life.

The thoughts swirling around in my head sounded something like this: "When I made the move to LA, I made the trip with only a thousand dollars to my name (money I received from my tax refund). Being out here all the way on the opposite side of the country, all alone, it wouldn't be such a bad thing if I let Robert 'donate' to the cause…just a little, anyway. Besides, with the kind of cash flow that he can provide, I won't have to worry about making it without a thing. This might not be such a bad idea after all, especially while I'm out here all alone, trying to get back up on my feet. I still haven't found an apartment. That's gonna be expensive, what with the deposit and all, utilities…What about paying for food and gas? Not to mention all the other expenses, too many to mention, that could possibly pop up. Oh! And don't forget about when you asked your dad for some extra money before you left for LA. *He* told you that you needed to get to the point where you could survive on your own. So, seriously, if something happens to you or if you need anything, who are you going to call or go to?"

After spending a few minutes on the phone with Robert, just catching up a bit, and after I told him that I had been looking for a new place to live, he offered to wire $2,500 to my account to help out with expenses. How could I resist? And just like that, as if God were nowhere around to hear or see what I was up to, I was back in full swing again with Robert. I pushed aside any thoughts of possible consequences that might arise as a fore-taste of my disobedience. Here on the "west side" God seemed a little less real to me and definitely far off in the distance. I decided that denial would be the best road to take at this junc-ture. I felt like Eve when she was being tempted by Satan in the Garden of Eden.

> Now the serpent was more crafty than any of the wild animals the LORD God had made. He said to the woman, "Did God really say, 'You must not eat from any tree in the garden'?"
>
> —GENESIS 3:1

At this moment, instant gratification sounded much more fun than the alternative (i.e., having all the cash I needed instead of struggling and trying to make it on my own). Robert would be wiring the money to my account that night, and I could expect to see it there first thing in the morning. Once again I had plenty of money for anything and everything I needed. The vicious cycle had begun, yet again. Well, so much for closing that door behind me...and locking it...and smashing it into a million little pieces...and burning it to the ground.

CHAPTER 8

BY THE END of my third month back in LA, I received a call from my mom. A spot found during her recent mammogram was tested, and the results came back positive. My mom had breast cancer, and the doctor was scheduling her for surgery in three weeks to remove the mass. I said, "I'm coming home!" Mom said, "No, you are not! Don't you dare! Things are going great for you in LA! There's nothing here for you in Nashville!" I said, "Woman, you are crazy if you think I'm going to let you go through this alone! I'm coming home."

I returned to Nashville in August of that year. Mom had surgery to remove the mass, and she was diagnosed as cancer free. *Praise God!*

With the money sent from Robert, I was able to rent a house in midtown. Now all I had to do was find a job. I sent my résumé to a large corporation that consisted of seventeen salons. I knew it would be nearly impossible to find a salon that even came close to what I had left behind in Los Angeles. The salon where I had worked in Nashville just months before would have taken me back, I'm sure, but it was out of the way, and I felt like I needed something more.

As luck would have it, two weeks later I was hired at the salon I had my heart set on. I started working at my new job at the end of August. I was offered a spot at their newest salon near midtown only a few blocks away from my house. Perfect! Things seemed to be falling right into place.

However, when I wasn't working, I found myself in the same lonely, boring predicament as I had been in the last time I'd returned to Nashville from La-La Land. I sat on my patio surrounded by silence, looking at nothing but my house's brick walls. I was bored, and it made me sad. I had little to no social life at all.

I thought, "Well, this sucks. You can either sit here and sulk or get up and do something to change it!" So I did. I called old girlfriends, old guy friends, whoever, and gave it my best go at having a life. I finally started to enjoy life in Nashville again. It wasn't LA, but I had made the decision to come home, so it was up to me to make the best or worst of it.

CHAPTER 9

ABOUT FOUR MONTHS earlier, I had met a guy named Leo when I was getting my oil changed *right* before I left for LA. Throughout the next couple of months, he would text me here and there, and he would always ask me when we were going to finally hang out. I would always blow him off, though. I never felt "ready" to hang out with him. He made me feel shy. The thought of going around him made me nervous. I wasn't sure yet if I was up for the challenge.

When I first saw him, he blew me away. He was *beyond* gorgeous. And those eyes...that smile...I mean, *Whoa!* The only time I had ever been around him was the time it took to get my oil changed. He stood next to my car and talked to me while I waited. I could tell he was probably the "bad boy" type but at the same time the sweetest guy I had ever met. And when he laughed and smiled...man, he really sold it. I felt shy and giddy like a school girl on the inside (aka, a dork). I handed him my business card before I drove away. I didn't know what else to do! I hadn't found any real interest whatsoever in any other guys after Ethan passed away. This guy, though—I didn't want to miss out on a chance of maybe seeing him again.

I pulled out of the lot and stopped next door at the gas station. As I walked inside, I thought to myself, *he's the one.* I wondered if he was thinking the same thing about me. I also wondered if he "knew"; he had to, because I sure as heck did. I guess this is why I ran from him for so long. I didn't want to see him in person because I knew deep down that I was going to fall head over heels in love. Before running into him, I had grown quite comfortable keeping all interactions with men I encountered very surface, which kept me in control of who I decided to "let in." I was great at throwing my walls up before anyone even had a chance to say hello to me.

After Ethan's death, it was going to take *a lot* to convince me to date again. I told myself that if I was to ever meet someone I'd be willing to date, he would really have to knock my socks off. If there wasn't some kind of mind-blowing super spark, then I wasn't interested. I didn't want to just go on date after date and see what would happen. If I would ever take another guy seriously and let him into my heart and life, I was going to have to know from the jump that this was the *one.* I had promised myself that I would never love someone again like I loved Ethan, because losing him hurt too much. So I was also OK if love never happened for me again. That was probably the smartest and safest plan anyway.

After several months had passed, one day in August I finally gave in and responded to one of his texts. We made plans to get together one night that week. Of course, as to not surrender all the control, I had to have the evening's plans on my terms. I invited him out along with me and some friends. I guess I subconsciously thought that if we were out in a group then it wouldn't really be like we were on a date. I let my walls down a little. I wasn't ready yet to let go of *all* my boundaries. Hey…a step is a step.

▬ ▬ ▬ ▬ ▬ ▬ ▬

Someone I knew from the salon just happened to be doing a show that night. It felt like home away from home, with me missing LA and all (especially West Hollywood). So I invited Leo to meet us at the club where my coworker and several other ladies would be performing that night. The fact that he agreed to such without even a flinch of hesitation; this boy was winning me over already.

We decided to meet up in the parking lot before going inside. As he walked behind our car, I stepped out of the passenger side and continued to watch as he walked toward us. He wasn't at all like I had expected. This time, seeing him, he seemed different to me. Not in a bad way at all; I guess only seeing him in that brief moment while getting my oil changed, I hadn't gotten to take him in as he really was. I guess when you get to know someone over the phone, you create an image in your mind of what they would be like—their mannerisms, what they looked like when they smiled, the way they walked, talked, or even laughed. Yes, I know, we do live in a technology age—he had sent a few selfies to my phone, and I had seen many pictures of him on his Facebook—but seeing him in person was much different. It was better than I had imagined. He had a swag about himself, a charisma. Seeing him this time in person, I felt drawn to him, as if I knew that after this moment, my life would never be the same again. Everything about him was beautiful, not to mention exotic, especially compared to the other boys around these parts. His dark hair was cut short, almost shaved on the sides, and from front to back he had a wide Mohawk.

He finally made it over to where I was standing. We both smiled, and then with my arms wide, I went in for a hug and to say hello. I stepped back to look him over again. I started at his feet and scanned all the way up until we made eye contact. I asked him, "Are you real? You really do exist."

He flashed that gorgeous, boyish grin and let out a laugh. "Yeah, I'm real."

After this night, that was all she wrote. We had both gotten ourselves into something we couldn't back out of now (we wouldn't have backed out if we could have, anyway). Neither of us was prepared for this, but we were in for the ride of a lifetime. We didn't expect this thing called love to suddenly grab a hold of us, seemingly out of nowhere, and speed away like a runaway locomotive ("Loco" being the operative word here). When love hits you, you barely realize the gravity of what is taking place. And before you know it, it has taken over and it controls you—you don't control it.

We were both caught off guard; we never expected a life-altering, game-changing thing like this to occur. But it had, and it did. So there was nothing left for us to do but to just go all in instead of resist it, and to enjoy every bit of it, every second, and every ounce of each other. Wow. The unthinkable had happened. I had fallen in love, I could easily and truthfully say, overnight. That love at first sight kind of thing. And yet we were both still scared to admit to ourselves and to each other that this was really happening.

After we were together for a month, he told me, "I didn't want a girlfriend at that time in my life, the first night we hung out, but then..."—he shrugged his shoulders and pointed over at me, still looking confused by it all—"I met you. I've never had feelings like this before for any girl I've ever dated. I mean, I've been in love, but not like this."

━ ━ ━ ━ ━ ━ ━

I recalled all those promises I had made to myself before I met him about not falling in love again, the fear of being hurt by love, blah blah blah; it all flew right out the window. It never entered my mind that I had said what now seemed to be such "foolishness." He made me forget every reason why I shouldn't fall in love, and he made me *run* toward every reason why I should. I was crazy about him. We were crazy about each other. To call me a "smitten kitten" would be putting it mildly.

By mid-September, he looked at me and said, "I guess when we're both seventy-four, we'll look at each other and say, 'How did this happen?'" We were on such a whirlwind that it wouldn't hit us until we were old and gray and too far gone to realize so much time had passed. All we would know for sure is that we had somehow made it there together, inseparable since the day we met—and that's all that would really matter anyway.

━ ━ ━ ━ ━ ━ ━

This kind of love, no matter how euphoric, is dangerous. The kind that makes you lose all common sense. The kind of love where you don't feel like you were experiencing life until you met this one person. Nothing matters anymore but this love. You can't breathe when you're away from each other. You feel anxious until you receive their call at the end of the day. Your day doesn't begin well if you don't receive a text from them before you wake up. Days are dull when you don't see them. You live every minute just looking forward to the next time you will be able to see them again. This kind of love is a drug. All other drugs pale in comparison.

We tried our best to resist what was happening, but to no avail. We would fight over the dumbest things, find excuses to break up, and distance ourselves from another, but the distance only made us want each other that much more. When we would fight and break up, sometimes for weeks at a time, I would go into a state of grief. I longed for him. My life had no meaning unless he was in it. To have known love before, I never thought in a million years I'd ever love again. Not like this. But I did. And this love I was feeling was ten times more than the previous love I had lost. And that loss almost killed me.

I remember my love before, at times still feeling sad for that loss. But all the hurt I suffered from that loss was now a distant memory. This love had taken over. It consumed me. I had never loved someone this much before. I loved him more than any one person I had ever loved before in my life. I loved him more than I loved my family. He was the person who mattered most to me. He came before everything: my job, my life, my dreams, money, sleep, myself, my sanity, and God. Some might call it lust or obsession—call it what you will, but I was in love. Never before had I known how true love felt; nor had I known, until now, the extremes you will go to in order to defend it, protect it, keep it, and savor it. I was head over heels in love.

━━ ━━ ━━ ━━ ━━ ━━ ━━

It was October. My thirty-third birthday was only one week away. One morning, I sat out on my back patio having coffee and a cigarette before going back inside and getting ready for work. I had been out there no more than fifteen minutes when suddenly, Leo came stumbling out the back door. For a moment, he looked around like he had no idea where he was. He then looked over at me and started to walk toward me. He appeared to catch his bearings somewhat before taking a seat next to mine. He said, "Baby, something just held me down in the bed. I tried to raise up and call out for you but I couldn't. It was like I was paralyzed. Then, all of a sudden, it was like it just let go and I could move again."

A couple nights earlier, I'd had something poke me and wake me up in the middle of the night. I also heard it growl when I was trying to go back to sleep. Afterward, I assumed the place was haunted, but I never thought to mention it.

I stormed back in the house and grabbed my sage stick. I lit it and started wafting the smoke around the room. "Not cool!" I yelled. "Don't do that again!" I asked Leo, "Did you hear it make any sound?" He answered, "I didn't want to tell you this, but I could hear it doing this." He then pushed his breath out slowly to show me what it sounded like. "It was like it was breathing into me," he said.

CHAPTER 10

I FELT SICK IF I wasn't with Leo. I literally felt zapped of my strength both physically and emotionally when he wasn't around. When I was at work, my mind stayed on him. I worried continuously about the future and how I would survive if he ever left me. I spent my days looking forward to the next time I would be able to see him so I could get my next "fix."

Over the days and weeks, things started to slowly change between us. The feeling of love I once knew was still there, but now it had turned more and more into an obsession. I would fill up on Leo when he was with me and dread the moments before he would have to go. I knew all I had to look forward to when we parted was agony until I would be in his presence again.

I always kept my phone near me, waiting for him to text. After receiving a text from him, the minutes would drag by like hours until he gave me what I needed and I heard from him again. He became my lifeline. Life wasn't worth living without him in it. I'm still surprised to this day that amidst all this, I still did really well at work. My brain stayed on him, but somehow I was still able to keep some kind of balance and excel in my career.

Nothing was more important than my relationship with Leo. It held first place over all. I had lost interest in everything, even myself. How he treated me dictated how I felt about myself. He had a large family and two sisters that lived at home. They demanded a lot of time from him as well, so he would put me to the side and make me wait my turn. Instead of having my own life, I would sit at home and think of him and wait for the moment he would show me some attention.

I lost myself in this. I lost my identity. I knew this was different, although I couldn't explain it to myself. *Have I acted like this about a guy before? Was I ever this desperate when it came to Ethan? What is going on with me?* It was like I was in a daze. I couldn't see two feet in front of me, so I stayed trapped in this bubble. It felt like passive-aggressive control. *Where is my self-esteem now?* I lost my self-worth. I thought about how lucky I was to have him and even felt bad that such a beautiful guy like him would downgrade and date someone like me.

My mind was foggy. I knew this addiction to Leo wasn't healthy, but I didn't know how to get out. I didn't have any real friends around me so I could mirror myself, and no family to talk to, so I just stayed isolated and in this haze.

Mama, Don't Let Your Babies Grow Up to be Cowboys

I received a text from Leo while I was at work, and it said, "Babe, can I ask you a question?" I was excited that he texted me at all, and my heart jumped up in my chest as I wondered what this question could be. *Will you marry me?* was what I hoped for. I texted back, "Of course. What's up?" He responded, "Would you cosign on a bike for me?"

My heart sank. Disappointed, I waited a second to think about it. I loved him so much, and I would do whatever made him happy, especially if that "whatever" might convince him to stick around a little longer. It wasn't exactly the most romantic thing he could ask, but I reluctantly replied with a yes. I warned him that my credit wasn't the best so it might not work, but we could give it a try. I never thought it would pan out, but it did. My boyfriend was now the proud owner of a Harley Davidson.

What have I done? I thought. *What happens if he gets hurt? Then it'll be my fault.* And what's worse, the boyfriend that I begged to find more time for me now had something in his possession that would suck up even more of his time—the time that I so desperately craved. Smart, Gabriel. Real smart.

— — — — — — —

In the background of all of this, there was still my sugar daddy overseas. He still took care of all my bills. I felt guilty from the moment I fell for Leo, knowing in the back of my mind that this was still going on. I never told him, so the guilt started to wear on me.

Robert would be coming home to visit in March. That same week, Leo would be away on vacation with his family at Disney World. Even though Leo would be gone and I could have possibly gone behind his back, I just loved him too much to see another man and then lie to Leo's face when he got back home.

About a week before Robert got to Nashville, I broke it off with him and told him I didn't want to see him anymore. I wasn't making enough money to make it on my own yet, but I didn't want to chance it. To risk losing Leo, if he were to find out—it just wasn't worth it to me.

The stress of keeping this all a secret ate me alive. I grew weaker every day wondering if I made the right choice. I felt like I had to continually work at it and try to convince Leo to stay with me. I had to work for his love. I never knew one day to the next if that would be the last day I would ever hear from him. I felt like if I didn't text or call him then I might not hear from him again. This was all so confusing—why was I begging someone to treat me right? Why did I feel like to him, I wasn't worth keeping? I was giving up my "security" for something that didn't make me feel secure at all. I didn't feel good about the decision to drop Robert, but I didn't know what else to do. I felt, if anything, love over money was always the right choice. So I took the leap into the great unknown.

I got a roommate, a guy friend who actually used to be Leo's best friend. I squeezed my stuff into the smallest room in the house, giving him whatever he wanted just as long as he would move in. I asked Leo if he was OK with this before I made the decision, and he told me it was OK. But it wasn't. He didn't like that I lived with a guy, so he became more distant.

As my surroundings in my home closed in on me, I also started to suffocate with the way Leo continued to ignore me and not give me the time of day. He also had the bike now. We were now, more than ever, living in separate worlds. He was excluding me from his more and more as I begged him to spend more time with me. I was miserable and spent most nights at home by myself. Every night I would drink until I was drunk, and then I would take sleeping pills, equivalent to horse tranquilizers, before going to bed.

CHAPTER 11

I N LATE APRIL, I received a text from my uncle saying that my dad had been rushed to the hospital. I was out at dinner with Leo when I got the news. I put my phone on the table and slid down in my chair. I knew what this text meant. Deep down I knew it was all downhill from here.

— — — — — — —

My dad was in and out of this particular hospital for about three months. I stayed with him most nights. Leo would go out while I sat there, concerned for my dad, and at the same time wondering what Leo was up to. The difference in our ages started to show more than ever and began to take its toll; he was twenty-two and I was thirty-two at the time. We were living in two completely different worlds. I wasn't in a place in my life where I could be easy breezy and do as I pleased just on the basis that it was fun or made me happy. I needed support that Leo couldn't give me. He was just a kid; how could he have known what I needed? He even mentioned to his cousin that this was the first real "grown-up" relationship he'd ever been in.

My mother sure couldn't give me the support I needed either. She was too busy trying to make it about her and how Dad's illness affected not only me but her as well. Gloria wouldn't stay with my dad because she would get too jealous of the nurses. She and her daughter would come breezing through whenever they had a second to stop by.

I didn't have food, or the money to buy it. Gloria wouldn't get me any money from my dad, and I was too afraid to ask. Most days I'd go without bathing, due to lack of time and effort. I didn't have a lot of time to go between the hospital and work. I remember thinking how good Gloria and her daughter smelled and how they looked so pretty in comparison to me and Pops.

What made it worse, even though I was there to help, my dad made me feel as though he didn't want me there. He would barely speak to me, and when he did speak it was usually an underhanded remark expressing his disdain for me. "You know, my father had my sister removed from his hospital room, even on his death bed." I had a feeling this was a shot at me, but not knowing what I had done to make him want to kick me out and not wanting to leave him there by himself, I just did my best to stay out of his way and keep my mouth shut.

One morning just before 7:00 a.m., I was woken abruptly by my dad shuffling around the room. He walked over, stood at the end of my bed, and starting searching through his overnight bag sitting on the windowsill. As I raised up, trying to catch my bearings, I asked him, "Whatcha need, Daddy? I got it. I don't want you to fall—go get back in your bed."

As he continued to look through the bag, he said, "You're not ready. You're not ready. If you were a boy you would know what to do. Boys are problem solvers." My father always held the fact that I wasn't a boy against me. My mother once told me that when I was little, around four years old, I fell to the ground in front of him and started to cry because I scraped my knee. She said he didn't get out of his seat, he just looked at me and said, "Wouldn't have cried if it was a boy."

I would call Leo and scream and cry, telling him I needed him, but he just didn't know what to do for me or how to be there for me. He would call me on his lunch breaks, and I would feel like I needed to talk. But I wouldn't get much more than a "How's your day?" before he would get off the phone to eat his lunch. It would be hours before I would hear from him again. I had no one to talk to, so I just continued to keep everything bottled up.

━ ━ ━ ━ ━ ━ ━

One day in May, I kept hearing the word *precipice* over and over in my head while I worked. Precipice…precipice…precipice. It was persistent, like someone was relentlessly trying to catch my attention, *forcing* me to listen up and understand what this word meant—like a little kid holding one finger out to touch my arm but never making contact, saying, "I'm not touching you! I'm not touching you!"

I spent hours trying to brush it off and ignore it away, but to no avail; it just wouldn't let up. (Mind you, just so we're clear before moving on, I wasn't hearing voices in my head like a nutcase! When I heard the word, it was not from an audible voice. It still sounded like my thoughts and my voice; but this was different. It's like I "knew" it was coming from somewhere else. This is where discernment comes into play, and hearing the Holy Spirit—that still, small voice. This was my first real introduction to what it was like to hear Him.)

Finally, by the end of the day, I let go of the fear of sounding like a complete kook and asked my client, "What does the word *precipice* mean?" He was a surgeon, so based on all the time he spent in school, I assumed that he would have acquired a broad enough vocabulary to answer this question. He answered,

"Yeah, a precipice. It's like…well…imagine you're standing on the edge of a tall cliff, looking over a broad area. You see two crossroads down below in the distance. From this viewpoint, you can get an idea but not the full picture of where these two options will lead you."

After hearing this description about the word that I, before today, had no former knowledge of, the one that was going off in my head like my brain had Tourette's—no offense; I have, as of late, acquired my own little tic. But I'll throw that in when we get to it—anyway, like I was saying, after hearing this I was like, *Wow…Hello, God!*

▬ ▬ ▬ ▬ ▬ ▬ ▬

During this time, God put it on my heart that the time would be coming very soon for me to part ways with Leo and lay this situation down. My defiant attitude toward this instruction was like a child not wanting to put away her toys. "But God, I'm not through playing with this! It's fun, it makes me happy, it's an escape from my reality, it's pretty, it makes me laugh, and it makes me feel wanted and loved—well, sometimes. And I *love* it, God; I don't think I can live without it! Take whatever else You want, but *please* don't take this away from me!" Yet no matter how I squirmed and tried to bargain my way out of it, I knew I was hearing Him right. No matter how badly I didn't want to go through with this, I knew it was time. As much as I didn't want to let go, I knew God meant business because He had other plans for my life. Breaking up with Leo was going to suck, but I also knew that it was going to suck a lot worse if I didn't.

I had no clue what God had planned for me instead. He never gave me a blueprint to my destiny with a map that showed me how to get there. At this time in my life, I didn't share with those closest to me my experiences with hearing from God. I never "checked" with anyone like a pastor to confirm the validity of what was happening. I just knew like I knew like I knew that I was hearing God speak, so much so that I did my best to put my own agenda down and walk it out and follow His lead. At times I thought doing so just might kill me. Little did I know at the time, that was exactly the point.

Truthfully, it took me a minute to let go. Not too long after God had spoken these words to me, I was still dabbling here and dabbling there trying to hold on to what he told me to let go of. And trust me, I tried to hold on tight and "fix" the relationship with Leo. I hoped that God might find it pleasing and acceptable so Leo could stay and come along with me for the next part of the journey. At this point, I was figuratively holding what was left of us by a string. No matter what I did, we continued to unravel and slip out of my hands until I had no option but to just let go.

I have heard it said that some people are only meant to be in your life for a season; no matter how much you love them or think you can't carry on without them, in truth, some people you just can't take with you. It doesn't make them bad people; it just means that their part in your story is over. First John 2:19 says, "They went out from us, but they did not really belong to us. For if they had belonged to us, they would have remained with us; but their going showed that none of them belonged to us."

While struggling with what I wanted and with what God wanted, much like Jacob did in the Bible, I came across a scripture that I had never read before. It was Isaiah 43:19 (NLT): "For I am about to do something new. See, I have already begun! Do you not see it? I will make a pathway through the wilderness. I will create rivers in the dry wasteland."

It was as if the words leaped off the page and popped me right in the face, screaming, "*Wake up, you fool! A change is happening, can't you tell?*" There is a reason that God's Word is called the

"Living" Word; it is very much alive. If you think you can't hear from God, just pick up a Bible. Everything you need to know and every answer to any question is right there in that book!

━ ━ ━ ━ ━ ━ ━

By the end of May, I had broken things off with Leo. The months that followed were excruciating. He still consumed my every thought. Work was also tough. I spent my days in a very tense, passive-aggressive environment. It was plain to see that my fellow employees didn't want me there. I was the daily topic amongst the rumor mill in the break room. Everyone smiled in my face, but as soon as my back was turned, eyes would roll and all you could hear were whispers and jeers.

I stayed busy, though. My clientele continued to grow, and I stayed booked. I did the best I could at being a great employee. I kept the conversation with employees and employers to a minimum. The people I connected with were my clientele. They were all that really mattered to me anyway. They loved me and thought a lot of me. If it hadn't been for them, I would have given up on the job a long time ago.

It was hard keeping up the act that I was "OK." As a stylist, you always have to be "on." You can't have a bad day in front of your clients. Being a stylist is very draining on your physical and emotional self. My clients found me cheerful and uplifting to be around; no one knew that I was dying on the inside. No one knew that every night I went home and spent my nights alone, crying.

One night after work, my roommate returned home and found me kneeling on top of my bed, sobbing, with my body leaned to the side, pressing up against the wall. I ached all over. The stress of my job and life took such a toll on my body that I found it hard to even hold my head up. All the stress gathered at the base of my neck, and I would unknowingly shrug my shoulders from the tension. It was as though my body was trying to keep how I felt squeezed inside of me so I wouldn't burst.

I felt like I was running out of the strength I needed to keep pushing through. And at what cost? I worked so hard to be good at everything—my job, life, a relationship with Leo, trying to be what people wanted so they would like me, trying to be pretty enough so that maybe people would like that about me—but nothing worked.

I was killing myself, depleting, giving and giving out more and more with no return on my investment. I had tried my best at everything. I was at a loss as to what to do to make my life "work." If I gave my best and it wasn't good enough, then what else was there to give? If giving my all didn't make me acceptable in any area of my life, then what else could I do? I had nothing left to give. What was I supposed to do to have a "good" life? I tried "good," and I tried "bad," and still nothing had worked.

I was so overwhelmed with sadness at this point that I was completely miserable. I tried to live my life in a way that the world considered to be "good," but nothing had changed. What's the point of trying to do better if it gets you nowhere? In fact, I felt just as unhappy—if not more—as I did before I decided to "change" my life for the better. I was starting to think that I was just foolish to believe that I could ever have better. Who was I to assume that I deserved to have such a great life?

CHAPTER 12

For we wrestle not against flesh and blood, but
against principalities, against powers, against
the rulers of the darkness of this world, against
spiritual wickedness in high places.

—EPHESIANS 6:12, KJV, EMPHASIS ADDED

IT JUST SO happened that Gloria's birthday fell on one of my days off. I had two days off per week. I spent those days in one of two hospitals, in the nursing home in Murfreesboro, or at Dad's house; wherever Dad and Gloria might be located at that time. By chance, Gloria and I were able to spend this day together. Just she and I, solo; I was honored and grateful, especially since this might have been her last birthday. Some might have considered it ordinary or uneventful to have lunch with her, at a no-frills barbecue joint in Murfreesboro, but to me it meant a great deal.

I missed Leo with every breath I took. My thoughts were never far from him. But in the back of my mind I knew that if he and I had still been together, I would have missed out on times like these with my family.

━ ━ ━ ━ ━ ━ ━

For days I dreaded the arrival of Leo's birthday. I braced myself for how bad I would feel and how bad that day would be for me. I longed for him. There was no letting up in sight from my feelings and my love for him. I resisted the urge to reach out to him, but against my better judgment, I texted him at the very last part of the day. It was 11:30 at night; I just couldn't take it anymore. At midnight this day would be over and I would have missed my chance forever to tell him happy birthday. Besides, if I didn't, he might think I didn't love him anymore, right?

"Happy Birthday" was all I wrote and sent to him in a text. I waited and waited and heard nothing back. "I'm an idiot!" I told myself. I sat on my back patio, alone in the night, criticizing myself for making such a stupid mistake. Thoughts like "You're so weak! He's not thinking about you! He's forgotten you even exist! Dumb!" jumbled my mind. Then my phone chimed. It was him. I felt relief and at the same time fear of what his response might be. What if it wasn't something good? How would it make me feel then?

His text read, "I wondered if you would." We spend the next hour chatting back and forth via text. Small talk, nothing deep or wordy at all. I always felt like I had to drag words out of him. After every text I sent, it was as though it took a lifetime for him to respond. After every waiting moment, sometimes I would even find myself wondering if he might never text back at all. He was my drug. I was always waiting for my next hit. If he didn't give it to me, I went through withdrawals for days until he would give me another dose. I never felt good unless I felt wanted by him. I was screaming on the inside for him to want me back, but I was always left wanting more.

"I'm alone on my birthday," he said. "Pretty lame, huh?" After a moment went by, he sent another text. "I'm sitting here listening to '21 Questions' by 50 Cent and I can't help but to think of you."

In reference to all of those "21 Questions," I told him that he knew what my answers would be. I had answered each and every one of those questions throughout our entire relationship, if not by speaking words then definitely by my actions. I told him that he knew, without a doubt, how I felt for him.

An hour went by, and I kept wanting more from him. I still wanted to pick up the phone to plead with him and tell him how badly I needed him. *Doesn't he want me too?* I wanted to tell him that I needed him to stay alive, to breathe. But with no words left to say, we told each other that it was great to hear from the other and said good night. Afterward, I just sat there in the night air, in the darkness; left wanting, depleted, and yearning for him.

The following day, I kept checking my phone but never heard from him. Surely he was excited like I was to talk again. Surely his mind stayed on me like mine stayed on him. He wanted to be together, didn't he? I checked my phone all that week, and nothing. I was so let down and heartbroken. How could I be so in love and missing this guy when he showed very little concern for me?

Deeply mourning the loss of him in my life, I had no choice but to just let the days pass. Was it because I'd broken up with him? Was that the reason he wouldn't reach out to me, to try to get me back—because of his pride? Was it my job to reach out to him? I felt like I had done all the reaching when we were together, and even still, it seemed pointless. It certainly didn't do me any good to chase him down while we were together. It felt like even if I took super glue and stuck him to me, I couldn't keep him with me. Was it his pride that was keeping him silent and staying away from me? Or did I need to face the fact that he never really wanted me in the first place?

It was all very confusing. His words never matched his actions. If someone says they love you but doesn't act like it, is that really love? My self-worth depleted with each day that passed. *If he didn't want me, then it must be true that I wasn't worth much.* I felt great about me, or so I thought, before he came into my life. Why was I so overcome by feelings of being worthless now? It all didn't make much sense to me. How could one person tear down everything inside of you that said you had worth and value? This one person's rejection made me forget anything that was good about me. It was like I was trapped inside a bubble that I couldn't escape or see clearly through. Why? What happened to make things this way? Why this person? I hoped that one day his memory would just fade away.

— — — — — — —

I had two weeks left on my lease. I planned to move out at the end of July and move down to my daddy's house in Murfreesboro. My dad had a shop behind his house with an apartment on the side just in case anyone needed a place to stay. Money was tight, and I still didn't trust myself to be able to live on my own and pay my own bills without Robert's help. I also thought it could be a "two birds with one stone" kind of situation, because being there meant I could help with the care of Daddy and Gloria. I thought it wouldn't be a bad idea if I was there to take up some of the slack. Even though they had nurses and family at the house 'round the clock, the need for one more hand always presented itself. I figured I could make the hour-long drive back and forth from Nashville for at least a few months; it seemed a small sacrifice to get the chance to help my parents out and to save money on bills and rent. The pros seemed to outweigh the cons. Besides, a change of scenery might do me some good and help me to get over Leo.

— — — — — — —

This oppressive ache I felt for Leo at times seemed almost too much for me to bear. My boss even insisted that I take a week off work to clear my head. I was starting to break. The pressures from my personal life and my work were starting to take a toll on my capability to deal day to day.

During a text conversation with Leo, I told him that I had taken a week off of work. He responded, "I bet you're having fun, huh?" *Fun?* I thought. *What's that?* Not to sound like a martyr, but it had been such a long time since I'd had any fun at all. Did he really think anything about my life was fun right now? Did he think I even had time for fun or that I was capable of finding anything fun to do considering that every moment of my life was filled with thoughts of him? Had he forgotten all I was dealing with? Let's see ... sick parents, not to mention missing him, paying bills, and a job that sucked to be at. Yes, Leo, I'm having so much fun. His blatant lack of concern for me made me sink even lower. He obviously knew nothing about me and never had, even when we were together. I guess it really was all about him and what made him happy. The reality was starting to sink in: he had never really cared about me, and he never thought about how his actions might affect me—it was all about him. As long as he was happy, everything was all good ... for him. I could only hope to be that oblivious.

I reached out to him on several occasions, giving him the opportunity to see me. I gave him an open door and left it sitting there wide open, so to speak. Sadly for me, he never reciprocated. Finally, after several failed attempts, I no longer cared how desperate I might seem or whatever negative light it might shine on me; my need to see him trumped any self-respect or dignity I had left. I should have just walked around with a sign around my neck that read, "Please, somebody love me."

I sent him a text inviting him to join me at my nail shop while I got my nails done. We had been there a time or two before. He even got his first mani-pedi with me using a gift certificate I bought him at Christmas. I didn't know how else to coerce him, so I grabbed at anything. I followed it with a text that said, "If you turn down this chance to see me, then you are a crazy man!" I guess I took a stab at his competitive spirit or his pride; he was always up for a challenge. Whatever—I didn't care just as long as he showed up. Any fool could see that if the boy wanted to see me, he would have been there before I even had a chance to press the send button. But no, this wasn't the case.

He bit the line, finally. When he showed up, I played it cool. Still sitting waiting on my nail tech, I watched him walk past the window and in the door. He walked up to me and stopped. He looked down, and with his arms wide he waited for me to stand. "Well?" He waited for me to reciprocate. I stood up, gave him a hug, then sat back down and went back to what I had been doing, choosing a nail color. I wanted him to think that his arrival was no big deal to me. He sat in a chair next to me, as close as he could get, facing me. He continued to stare at me like he was mesmerized, in wonder. I could feel his stare as I watched him out of my peripheral. When I finally looked over at him, we locked eyes, and he said, "It's like I'm seeing you again for the very first time."

After my nails were done, we decided to go over to a restaurant we used to frequent. It was actually one of the places we went to on our first date. It was a bar and grill. We sat at one of the picnic tables on the patio. He sat across from me, staring intensely into my eyes every chance that he could get. As I nibbled at my food, I would look up at him while he talked, then quickly look away. He told me that if I would give him a chance, I could trust him, and that he wouldn't hurt me this time. He promised. All I could do was shake my head at his promises. I knew deep down it wasn't right, but I no longer had the strength to stand up for myself. I had no sense of identity left.

After we ate, we moved to a tall community table inside. The table was almost full, so we sat beside each other on one side so we could both see the TVs. After a minute, we both turned our faces toward each other and slowly leaned in. Our lips met for the first time in months. The kiss was slow and gentle. His lips felt incredible. I felt the electricity move from my lips downward throughout my body until finally my entire body was enveloped with this passion I felt for him.

We stopped for a moment, and I looked into his eyes and asked, with our faces still close enough to touch, "What is that? Do you feel it too? It's powerful when we touch. What is that?" We paused for a moment, taking each other in. The pull between us was so magnetic that neither of us could deny it. We were both perplexed by what it was that kept us from being able to let each other go, both of us recognizing how hard it was for us to be together and make it work in the "real world" but at the same time powerless to make the feelings we had for each other go away, try as we might, over and over again. Out of sight, out of mind, right? No, that didn't even work. The way we felt for each other never diminished while we were apart—in fact, it only seemed to increase. You would think this kind of love would be a good thing, but it was more like torture. I kept looking into his eyes hoping I might find the answer there, and then suddenly it came to me: "This must be what love feels like."

The next two weeks were spent in bliss. I floated on Cloud 9. Suddenly life didn't seem so bad. Everything was still the same, but now he was in my life again. The tough stuff seemed doable as long as he was in the picture and all was in harmony. We vowed to work hard and do better this time around. We were convinced that we could make it work, based only on the fact that we loved each other so much. We also agreed that we could make it work, even if I moved to Murfreesboro for a short while. Actually, Leo told me how excited he was about this. He said it would give him an opportunity to work that much harder to prove that he could be good to me. He was dead set on proving to me that he could be the man I needed him to be.

The following weekend, he showed up to my house with flowers and groceries. He planned to cook dinner for us. We both got into the kitchen, and I turned on some music while he cooked. I danced around on the opposite side of the room in an attempt to lighten his mood. He was overwhelmed with the pressure of cooking me an extraordinary meal. It was kind of funny to watch; I've never seen someone expect so much from themselves, especially over stir-fry. Poor guy—he almost made his head burst.

I couldn't help but giggle and playfully joke with him as I watched him take this cooking thing so seriously. He was awfully cute about it. I loved that he wanted it to be perfect for me; but if he only knew that I didn't need more than him just being there. I was terribly in love and could have floated away if I didn't ground myself to the floor. Everything was perfect. We were having so much fun together . . . I just knew everything was going to be OK.

Then his phone rang. It was his stepmom. She and his sisters were out of town visiting her mother, and she was calling to see how everything was going back at the house. He still lived at home in a small apartment, of sorts, right off of the garage. I only wished I had a cool family to stay with and a place to live where I wouldn't have to worry about rent. His family actually liked—well, loved each other. It was always really cool to watch and to experience what it was like to be part of a family like that. I loved it. I loved it for them; how fortunate!

Then I heard him say, "I'm not there." When she inquired of his whereabouts, he stumbled with his words and quickly blurted out, "I'm somewhere else." I stopped dancing and turned to face his direction. *He used to always tell them he was with me if they asked. Why isn't he now?* Just then, his stepmom handed the phone over to his teenage sister so she could say hi. (This was the sister I had always competed with for his time. She might as well have been "the other woman"—it sure felt like it.) He looked up at me and quickly hung up the phone, tossing it onto the counter. *No he didn't!* He turned his attention back to the food cooking in front of him. He tried his best to recover from this fumble as if nothing had happened. I grabbed the skillet he was cooking in and moved it off of the heat. "Don't worry about cooking for me." Then I turned to walk out of the kitchen.

I was livid. How could I not be? It *hurt.* After everything he had promised to me in those past two weeks, he was *still* keeping me separate from his life. Clearly, he didn't want his family to know he was with me. I felt ridiculous for *ever* assuming that he would include me someday. He was never going to make me feel like I was important enough.

I stood in the doorway between the kitchen and the dining room and said, "You couldn't even tell them where you were?" He brushed his hair back and looked down at the floor, searching for an answer. Then he said, "Yeah."

I was shocked at first that he answered by agreeing with me. Then he delivered the sucker punch to my stomach: "I guess that did seem kind of obvious when I put the phone down before my sister could pick up." *Ouch.* I was humiliated, embarrassed by my previous optimism, but most of all I was disappointed. My floating heart had dropped. I walked out the side door that led to the patio and sat on the steps near the end of the driveway. Frustrated, I had no idea what to do next. I loved this guy so much, but *wow*! He didn't treat me well. But why? I couldn't make sense of it all.

In my mind I started to list all the people who did love me and all the people who had loved me before. He had never met most of these people or seen them interact with me; he had never met the people who thought I had worth and value— maybe this was why he thought I didn't. I just couldn't under-stand why he was the one person I couldn't seem to convince that he should think good of me.

Leo stepped outside and walked up behind me. I turned to look up at him as I stood and said, "Do you think I've never had anyone love me before?" I guess I should have explained myself instead of saying just that one sentence, because what happened next I never saw coming. Leo's face turned to anger. He looked at me, scowling, and said, "Well then go get that guy!" When he said this, the first person that crossed my mind was Ethan. I looked at him sadly and with what I had assumed was a sincere notion, and said, "I can't...he's six feet deep."

I never meant to make Leo feel as though I wanted Ethan over him. I guess in some strange way I said this because I wanted Leo to understand the deeper parts of me, the parts that got bruised when he acted so carelessly with my feelings. But that wasn't at all how he took it. Riled with anger now, his body stood firm as he took a step back, cocked and ready as though he was preparing to fight. I had never seen Leo this mad since I'd known him. How had our relationship come to this?

Everything was spiraling and unraveling out of control. This night was turning into something neither of us had intended.

I kept looking into his eyes, wondering how to bring us back from this place, but I didn't know how. He was too far gone; all I saw in his eyes was rage and war. He started to heave large breaths as the temperature inside him rose. I reached out for him and said, "No, Leo, don't. I didn't mean it like you heard it. Please!" He jerked away from my touch and said "No!" as he turned to go back inside.

As he went, I stood there and watched, crying in desperation. I wanted to turn it all around, but something in me knew it was now out of our control. I followed behind him and turned to find his whereabouts. I walked toward the front living area—no Leo. I called out for him—no Leo. I called out for his dog—no dog either. I looked out the storm door—there was no sign of Leo, but his truck was still parked in the front of the house. I guessed he'd gone for a walk. I thought some space and a breather might do us some good, so I went back to my bathroom to splash some cold water on my face.

I put on some music, applied my makeup, and tidied up a bit. I poured a glass of wine and just tried to let it all go. Let bygones be bygones. I loved him. Deep down I believed he loved me. Couples have problems, right? We could work this out. He would return to the house feeling better, and we could get through this. It was just a hiccup. We'd said we had work to do; this was just part of it. When we got back together we had both agreed that we were willing to put in the work. My love for him outweighed the bad. I thought his for me did too.

Just then I realized that Leo had been gone for a really long time; it had been more than an hour. I looked outside again to see if his truck was gone. Nope, still there. Concerned about his whereabouts, I grabbed my phone to call him. It rang twice, and he picked up. I heard *loud* music in the background. *"Leo! Where are you?"* I thought to myself, *Oh my gosh, is this guy out somewhere? Is he out having a good time?*

He quickly hung up. I started to pace the floors. I just *could not believe this! You mean to tell me that I'm at home by myself thinking about us and how we are going to work it out, and he is out having a good time? Wow!* I just could not believe it. This just took things to a *whole* new level. And here I was, looking like a fool, thinking how romantic it would be when we worked it all out! I was trying to give him the benefit of the doubt, and he completely flipped the switch on me! I knew deep down that this was the kind of guy he was. And *here* was my proof!

A few minutes passed, and I found Leo sitting on the steps of my front porch. He was drunk—not just kind of drunk, but *drunk.* His eyes were glazed over when he turned back to look at me, his body swaying back and forth a bit. I locked the storm door and shouted at him, "You suck, Leo!" I turned and walked back toward my bedroom.

Suddenly I heard a huge *bang!* come from behind me. It rang out like thunder. Shocked, I jumped from the noise and turned to look. To my disbelief, I saw Leo kicking in the door. The plexiglass from the door stayed in one piece but flew into my living room area. Leo reached in to turn the key on the other side of the door and made his way inside. I had never seen this side of him, so I didn't know if he intended to hurt me or what his motives were. So I went with my instincts and fought back, just like I would have with any intruder.

Before this moment we had never laid a hand on each other in anger. I grabbed onto the neck of his shirt and started punching him over and over again. I wasn't sure where the punches were landing or if they were doing any good. I did all I could just to slow him down. He pushed me and I fell back, still holding his shirt. Little did I know that I also held on to the crucifix he wore around his neck. (He had told me stories about times in his life when this crucifix had saved him from getting into trouble.) I didn't let go, and the force from me falling away snapped his necklace in two. The couch behind me broke my fall.

I looked up at him in shock; I think we were both in shock. He turned around and stormed out of the room toward my bedroom. Before entering, he kicked his foot straight through the old house's wooden door. I got up and ran toward the noise only to find him tearing up anything and everything he could get his hands on: lamps, blinds, the windows, a room fan—everything. It was like watching a tornado rampage through my home as I stood there, helpless to make it stop.

He then picked up the bottle of liquor that we had bought for that night, which was sitting on my night stand. He turned the bottle up and started to chug it. I ran toward him and grabbed for the bottle. "Leo! No!" He yanked it away before I could grasp it, causing it to spew everywhere behind him and leaving the wood door to my closet covered in white spatter (the combination of the alcohol and the wax used on the door caused the discoloration). My house was a mess—not my house, actually, but the people I rented from; their house was a wreck. The house I would be moving out of in a week. The house that I had rented for a year, planning to get my full $1,000 deposit back. Before this incident, no damage had been done to it while I lived there.

He walked over to my big flat-screen TV, grunting and yelling out of frustration, and punched at it. This TV had sentimental value to me. I bought it while I was in LA. I always took pride in the fact that it made it all the way from there and survived several moves without a scratch on it. After I had taken such good care of it, and it had been such a good soldier and survived all I had put it through, our strong will to survive would now have been in vain—a long journey, torn down by the hands of someone else, suffering defeat in one fatal blow. Now I was just going to stand by and watch this happen?

I tried to grab for his hands to make him stop. "Leo! No!" He seemed out of control, an unstoppable force, like a runaway train. Then I stopped and looked into his eyes. He wasn't there. I did my best to get his attention, hoping he would just snap out of it. All of a sudden, I wasn't mad anymore. I just wanted it all to stop. I wanted Leo to know that it was going to be OK. I wanted to hug him, to somehow shift what was happening and let him know that he was in a safe place. And to tell him that I loved him. I put my arms around him, and he resisted my embrace. He was too far gone. This night was too far gone. How could we have possibly gone from happy and in love into this so quickly?

"God, We Have to Stop Running Into Each Other Like This"

My iPhone was linked to two small speakers that sat next to the bathroom sink. I played every "I hate men" breakup song I could think of. I turned the volume up as loud as possible. I hoped that in the midst of his rampage the lyrics of just one song would make him stop and realize what he was doing to me. The chances of this happening were about as likely as him realizing that we were still in the same house together. The mixture of alcohol and rage coursing through his veins made him unaware of the casualty sulking on the bathroom floor. No matter how badly I wanted him to, he wouldn't be bringing any relief to my pity party of one anytime soon. It's a lonely feeling when someone is so very unaware and unconcerned of your whereabouts and your feelings—especially when you are so very aware and concerned with theirs.

On the other side of my house, I heard every move Leo made, and I listened to every word he uttered. He was talking to someone on the phone as he paced back and forth through my house like a wild animal. "I guess I just can't be good to *any* girl, man." I couldn't tell who he was on the phone with. Later on I would find out it was his cousin, Damien. Leo talked with a sense of urgency and paced the floors in a confused state of panic, like a little boy who wanted his mother. Then at other times he sounded amused at himself: "Man, there's half eaten candy bars all over the floor! I must have been really messed up." He laughed as though he had *just* been informed about what kind of jerk he really was.

As he continued to pace back and forth throughout the house, he passed by the hallway near the bathroom where I was sitting on the floor—if I were a snake I could have bitten him—but he never noticed me sitting there. Damien even asked Leo where I was—I heard him reply, "I don't know where she's at."

With a half empty bottle of wine in my hand, I sat Indian style on the bathroom floor. My knees faced the small wooden vanity, and my back was propped up against the door. It was the ideal setting for a damsel in distress—a pity party that only a returning offender could love!

Leo's blood was all over the floor. On his tangent he had also made his way into the kitchen at one point, punching his fist through the glass cabinet doors. He left a trail of blood throughout the entire house. I didn't really care that it was all over me and my clothes. Honestly, I didn't really care about much at the moment. I just wanted to know when this would be over. I probably should have been thinking of ways to make him pay, but instead I just continued to sit there. For the first time in my life, I wasn't going over and over in my head who was right or who was wrong, or even trying to figure out what led to all this, how we'd gotten here in the first place. It was too late for all that. I put the bottle of wine up to my lips, turned it up, and took a big swig. The only thing left to do was get on with my life—that is, as soon as this maniac got out of my house.

I was exhausted and sad. I'd been crying and fighting all night. I took a deep breath and let out a loud sigh. Under my breath I said, "God, where are You?" Without a moment's hesitation, I heard Him reply, "I'm right here!" as though He had been sitting there on the bathroom floor right beside me the entire time. "Where else did you think I would be, silly?"

An image of what Jesus would look like sitting there next to me entered my mind. His legs were crossed Indian style like mine. He wore a striped shawl of many colors, almost like a large sweater with half sleeves, and cut-off faded denim "jorts" that frayed at the knee. He had long, brown hair, of course, that stopped just past His shoulders, a beard, and the most beautiful tan skin. He appeared to be no more than thirty-six years of age—a young thirty-six. There was a peace about Him, a calm, a knowing; in this, I could sense that He was very wise.

He reached over as I passed the bottle of wine to Him. He took a swig and then rested the bottom of the bottle on His calf. "So, how's it going with that boy I told you to leave alone?" I closed my eyes and winced, like you would right before receiving a punch in the face. In all honesty, it probably would have felt a lot better if He *had* just punched me instead. My heart sank as I realized that He had actually been there the entire night. I felt bad now for asking Him where He was. I tried to blame Him for something bad that happened because He wasn't there, when the truth was that He had tried to keep this from happening months ago. None of this would have happened if I had heeded His instructions *and* stuck to them when He told me to let this relationship go. I had no one to blame but myself. The consequences that would result from my poor decisions rested heavily on my shoulders. Thankfully, He was there to help me carry the load.

God's Word says, "Be strong and courageous. Do not be afraid or terrified because of them, for the LORD your God goes with you; he will never leave you nor forsake you" (Deut. 31:6). Unlike most humans, God doesn't give up on us or stop loving us when we *do* mess up, no matter how many times. I was so happy to know He was there, even though I was ashamed of my mistakes. His presence reassured me that I was not in harm's way, so I felt safe to sit there and ride out the storm until it passed.

At that moment, I heard Leo instruct Damien to call him back when he "finds out." *Finds out what?* I hadn't a clue. Leo was so anxious and nervous, like a caged animal looking for a way out; he seemed to be looking into the atmosphere that surrounded him for an answer, a resolution. The door was wide open; why wouldn't he just go? As he passed by the hallway once more, I caught a glimpse of him looking up toward the ceiling and opening his mouth to cry out. I had never heard or even seen Leo cry before. I was shocked that he might take a chance in letting me see him appear so vulnerable. I don't care how drunk he was—he had always taken a lot of pride in the fact that he had not "allowed" himself to cry for years. He wailed out loud three times. The way he cried, I could hear and almost feel the pain and anguish he truly felt inside.

I heard him in the kitchen, quiet for a moment, sniffling a bit, trying to gather himself as his tears subsided. Then I heard his phone ring. It was Damien calling him back. "Hey, anybody that's up at one o'clock in the morning cooking out is good with me!" Leo said. After I heard him say that, I realized that he'd resolved to search for someone with some weed.

I must say, I was a little jealous; he was about to leave my house, and soon he would forget all about this. I, on the other hand, would not be so lucky. I would be left alone to survey the damage—no escape for me. I was also riddled with guilt when I thought about how I was going to explain this mess to my land-lord. How was I ever going to pay for all the damage? Without a warning, this evening had turned into a war zone. I'd started the day off hopeful—we both did—and now we were ending it in defeat. No matter how much I loved Leo, I knew this was it. There was no going back from here. So much for that "happy ending" we were both so excited about.

In the shadow of the previous night's events, I remember regretting one decision the most. When I listened to music on my iPod, I should have listened to praise and hallelujah songs that glorified God. When I was sitting there in the bathroom, God put the story of Jericho on my heart. This is an example of why it is *so* important to read the Bible and know God's Word for yourself.

> This is the new covenant I will make with my people on that day, says the LORD: I will put my laws in their hearts, and I will write them on their minds.
> —HEBREWS 10:16, NLT

I should have honored God in this moment; I should have stood up for the kingdom, but I didn't when I had the chance. I hoped He wasn't disappointed in me, enough to make Him give up on me. I vowed then and there that the next chance I got, I would stand up for Him! I just hoped He would give me another chance to do it. I remembered that Leo and I had crossed paths right before I went and sat down in the bathroom, and he said to me, "There's food in the kitchen. I hope you choke on it with your righteous self!" I regretted that I didn't respond by playing gospel music loud throughout the house for Leo to hear, in effect saying back to him, "Yes, I am righteous! I was made righteous through the blood of Christ!" I regretted that I didn't let Leo know whose house this was and whom I belonged to.

> But Joshua had commanded the army, "Do not give a war cry, do not raise your voices, do not say a word until the day I tell you to shout. Then shout!"
> —JOSHUA 6:10

At the Battle of Jericho, the soldiers came face-to-face with their opponents, and instead of taking matters into their own hands, God instructed them to let out a *shout!* This caused their enemies to become so confused that they turned on themselves and killed each other instead. This loud burst of *shouts!* also made the walls of Jericho come tumbling down. What would you do if you knew you couldn't fail? Furthermore, what would you do if you knew you had no enemies or opposition? Romans 8:31 says, "What, then, shall we say in response to these things? If God is for us, who can be against us?" The battle has already been won. Little did I know at the time that the lesson learned from the Battle of Jericho would be a two-parter.

I was having problems with fellow employees at my job. In six months' time I had built a clientele faster than anyone before in such a short amount of time. All I was trying to do was make money. I was making waves and ticking people off at the same time. I didn't act haughty, nor did I flaunt it in anyone's face. I was just doing what I thought was best, but I guess this put a mirror up to others that highlighted their flaws and shortcomings.

All I wanted to do was work. Stylists would catch me in the break room and question how I had done so much in such a short time. My only reply would be, "God." No one took that seriously except me and God. The more mature stylists who had been at this profession for over twenty years were hip to my game. One of the older stylists said to me, "My former employer once told me that the best stylist is one that's in debt."

The environment at work was tense. I could tell that no one was a friend. Backstabbers were running amuck. I did my best to just keep my head down and nose clean, and to give all my attention and efforts to my clients. I didn't hobnob with other employees; I could tell they didn't care too much for me. But they wouldn't just let sleeping dogs lie. The fight was on. It was one sided. I wouldn't give them what they wanted, and what they wanted was a reaction. They wanted to push me to act out so they could claim I was a problem to corporate and have me pushed out of the door. But I wasn't going to cater to their childish games. I remember at one point telling my female manager that she wasn't going to *make* me into what she wanted me to be. With no relief for the pressure building up in the valve, it finally all came to a head in one single day. Tick…tick…*boom!*

One morning I stepped around my station to find one of my clients in another stylist's chair. Both of us looked at each other puzzled and in shock to see the other. She was special to me and vice versa. She owned a nonprofit in Washington, DC, and when she would visit her hometown of Nashville, she would make it a point to stop by and have me do her hair every time she was in town. "What in the world is she doing in someone else's chair?" I thought to myself.

When I ask her what happened, she said, "They told me you weren't here!" I replied in disbelief, "You have got to be kidding me!" I glanced toward the front desk and at my manager to see if anyone noticed that we had caught their plunder. My client asked, "Is this guy any good?" I wanted to snag her out of his chair and finish what he had already started. Without any inkling to a resolution, I replied, "Well, he's not me."

The following Monday, on my day off, I got a call from a man at corporate asking me to stop by his office. I sat down in a chair in front of his desk. I was nothing but smiles; I didn't feel scared about being pulled into court. I didn't fear the conversation, because I had nothing to hide.

I told him the truth, and all of it—even about the time I pulled the sheet rock off the wall of his brand new salon when I ripped down the dry erase board. I told him everything, even the parts I probably should have kept to myself. Like the time I was no more than ten minutes late to work after leaving the hospital with my father. I had made the salon aware of the situation and told them I might be a moment or two late. When I arrived, my manager screamed at me in front of other employees, saying, "Your clients come first, Gabriel!" I totally agreed with her; other days I made it on time. But due to this day's circumstances, I figured a few minutes wouldn't hurt. My manager's reaction made me think that my client might have been mad about having to wait, so I stepped around to the waiting area to ask her if she was OK. She looked at me, puzzled, and said, "Yeah! I just got here." After finding out that everything was in fact OK, I was livid that my boss would jump on me at a time like this. Didn't she know where I had just come from? Didn't she know my dad was sick?

I told the man from corporate that while looking at the back of my manager's head as she walked away after screaming at me, I visualized myself grabbing her by her hair and slamming her face into the wall. I held back nothing. I didn't know what the repercussions would be; I had no expectations.

After I finished telling him my side, I sat silently and waited for his reaction. "Get out of my office!" could have been his response, but instead he chose team Gabriel, saying he wouldn't stand for stylists sabotaging other stylists. He told me I'd done the right thing, exactly what I should have done. He had called me to his office to fire me that day, but instead he was going to meet with my two managers and me at Starbucks the next day and tell the managers they would have to get used to me working there. He would not put up with their behavior.

This is where the second part of the Battle of Jericho came into play. I was literally going into a battle with no enemies. God told me to stand boldly at the battle line, and I did. He promised that no weapon formed against me would be able to prosper, and it didn't.

CHAPTER 13

ONLY A FEW short days after the incident with Leo, I moved out of that house and moved all my things to Murfreesboro. However, I didn't feel a very warm welcome from my dad when I mentioned moving into the shop. So I called my mom and asked if it would be all right if I came and stayed with her. I couldn't get an apartment because of what had happened at the last place. Rightfully so, the realtor I rented the house from told future landlords that he would never rent to me again. The damages Leo did to the house also put me $3,000 further into the hole. I was livid. I couldn't afford to get my own place. I had a place to stay at my mom's, but all she wanted to do was fight. What made this situation even more depressing was that I had given Robert up so Leo wouldn't leave me. If I hadn't let Robert go, then I wouldn't be worried about money—I'd be sitting pretty, with my own place to live. But now, there I sat; busted, disgusted, and alone.

In the days that would follow, I didn't find much to be happy about. No sign of better days to come. I was mad about life. I was just mad in general. I stayed angry and bitter inside my head all day. Mad that my dad was sick. Mad that things were so awful with Leo. Mad that they hated me at work. Mad.

As I drove to work one morning, I told God, "I need a break. I don't want to hear from You today. If You try to talk to me, I won't listen." I felt confident in the line I had just drawn in the sand. Feeling vindicated that He would follow my new rule, I strolled into work. Throughout the day, I did my best to throw God to the side and ignore Him if He started talking to me.

After hours of this back and forth, casting Him down as best I could, and disregarding Him when He spoke, I heard Him say something that made me stop all this behavior completely. As I blew out one of my female clients' hair, when God had my full attention (there was no other distraction around me; all I could hear was the hum from the hair dryer), I heard Him say sternly to me, just like a dad would speak to a disobedient daughter, "How did you get all this clientele in such a short time, anyway? Do you think that just happened? Do you think that was done on mistake? Did you do that yourself?" In my thoughts, I answered, "No, God. You did." He went on to say, "As quickly as I gave it to you, that's as quick as I will take it away." Knowing I had just been put in my place, and rightfully so, my spirit sank as I realized how awful I had treated God that day. I continued on with the blowout and answered in my spirit, "I humble myself under the mighty hand of the Lord."

━━ ━━ ━━ ━━ ━━ ━━ ━━

One night I sat on my mother's back patio drinking a beer. Surrounded in the empty, oppressive silence of the night, I looked up into the night sky and said, "God there are so many questions I have for You. So many parts of my life are in a mess. But if there was one question I could have You answer, it would be this: What are You going to do about my broken heart?" Without a pause I heard the Lord say, "I'm going to break it open so wide that it will have nothing left to do but to come back together whole."

THE TRUTH WILL SET YOU FREE

I was off on Mondays, so one Sunday I went to spend the night with Gloria. At the time, my daddy was in the nursing home, Jackson lived out of state, and Rebecca was at home with two kids and a husband. I decided it was the least I could do to try to help out. Gloria and I sat at the island in the middle of the kitchen. I pulled a bar stool around across from where she sat so I could look at her while we talked. Sometimes that's where she would sit to smoke. She would turn on the air vent on the griddle to draw the smoke out of the house. It was a nice, quiet night. No news is good news; I don't even think we had the TV on. We were almost like strangers that knew each other well yet knew nothing at all about each other.

I forget how the conversation started, but Gloria mentioned the fact that my dad used to send me home with six hundred dollars when I was a kid. I looked at her in disbelief. "What? "Six hundred dollars?" She gestured with her hand, a lit cigarette in between her first two fingers, and said, "Yeah. I don't know what a little eleven-year-old would do with that kind of money. I guess you went home and spread it all over your floor and played with it." She shrugged her shoulders.

I replied, "Gloria, I didn't even know he sent me home with that much money. I always thought he sent me home with about one hundred dollars. That money meant something completely different to me." At this point tears streamed down my face. I looked her in the eyes and said, "That money sealed my fate. Every time I would beg my dad to not take me back to my mom's, it seemed to fall on deaf ears. He would hand me the cash as if to say, 'Run along, now.' I remember that I'd look down at it in my little hand and my shoulders and spirit would drop because then I knew how my next few days ahead would be. Nobody would listen to me, so I had to go back to my mother's—to my prison, to the house of horrors. No one was going to save me from it either. As I continued to look down at the cash in my hand, that cash was an agreement to a vow of silence, and I would have to suffer and survive this lonely hell, alone."

The tears gushed now and so did my words. It was like the dam had been broken and I couldn't hold back even if I wanted to. It was time. It was time for the silence to be broken and for her to know my truth. Until this very moment I had always let people assume what they wanted to about me—call me wild, a trouble child, whatever; it didn't matter. This was how I protected my mother. As long as everyone else thought I was acting out just because I was "bad," no one would find out what I was dealing with at home behind closed doors. I carried the blame so no one would point the finger at my mom. I didn't want people to know that she was capable of doing such things, especially to her own child. I kept her (our) secret close to me.

Since no one protected me from this monster, and I really didn't care much about the monster's feelings because it didn't care about mine, I stopped caring about repercussions and the cause and effect of my actions. They didn't give a care about me, so why should I care what happens to them *or* me? They obviously saw me as worthless, having no value, so I carried on as such. *Who cares? Burn it all to the ground! Leave no survivors in my wake!* What had been created was a monster. A monster birthed another monster. You reap what you sow.

> Don't be misled—you cannot mock the justice of God. You will always harvest what you plant.
> —GALATIANS 6:7, NLT

Gloria looked at me with tears in her eyes. "Why didn't you ever tell me? We just always assumed something was wrong with you." I looked at her and shook my head because I didn't have an answer. "I didn't know what to do," I said. She went on to say, "If I had known, I would have protected you. I would have kept you with me and kept you safe." We both sat there in tears, stunned by this new revelation. Oh, the years we had wasted and the pain we could have been spared if we had only talked to one another! Instead, we all just assumed what we wanted to be the truth. Then Gloria said, "Your mama could have gone to jail for what she did to you." All of a sudden, as we sat there across from each other, the person in front of us whom we thought we'd known for so long gradually started to change right before our eyes. Two women that had been at war for so long began to see each other through new eyes. And then, unexpectedly, I wasn't the same, and neither was she. The imaginary war we had fought for so long was now over. In the blink of an eye, two nemeses became down for each other like four flat tires. In the weeks to come, I would say to her, "We had it all, didn't we? You, me, Dad, Jackson, Rebecca; when we came together as a family, we had it all and we didn't even know it."

As we sat there and continued to talk about our newfound realities, suddenly it crossed Gloria's mind that she and my dad might not be around too much longer. She admitted, "I always worried if something were to happen to me and your father that you would be left all alone." I tried to reassure her by saying, "Gloria, I'll be OK. I won't be alone, I promise."

She tapped her cigarette on the corner of the ashtray, propping her elbow up behind her on the back of her barstool chair, and then rested her head in her hand. She cut her eyes up and over at me, looking at me as though she knew better. She was aware of a truth that I, at that time, preferred to cover up in my denial.

During a time when my father stayed a couple months in the nursing home, I had to take Gloria to the emergency room at midnight. She complained of stomach pains and nausea. After an MRI, we were told that her intestines had backed up. The doctor said she should be taken to another hospital for emergency surgery. He pulled me away to speak with me in private. "This woman doesn't know how sick she is, does she?"

This cold, hard truth sent chills down my spine. Her children hadn't told their mother that not only did she have ovarian cancer, but she had been recently diagnosed with intestinal cancer as well. When they had updated me recently on this new diagnosis, I never thought in a million years that they would hide this newfound knowledge from Gloria and my dad. I hadn't discussed it with them either. I thought surely they were aware. It was like the pink elephant in the room, I thought, an unspoken truth. I felt no need to rub their noses in it, so to speak, by bringing it up. It was almost like following the frame of mind that whatever you resist, persists. It never occurred to me that I should have spoken up and said something. How was I to know? Her kids were the ones to whom the doctor relayed this information. Who could have imagined that they wouldn't convey this news to everyone, especially their mother?

Being kept in the dark about this newfound truth, Gloria kept eating normally. And we all kept feeding her normally. This diagnosis should have procured certain life changes, like keeping her on a strict diet. Without making such changes, this is how she had reached her current state. Her bowels were completely blocked, unable to digest food.

Gloria was rolled out on a gurney as the medics prepared to load her into an ambulance. Before she was taken away, I leaned in toward her, looked her in the eyes, and asked her, "How far do you want to take this? They're talking about the possibility of taking body parts at this point. If you wake up after surgery with a colostomy bag, are you going to be mad at me because I gave the doctor permission?" She sincerely answered, "I'm not ready to die yet." I stood up and said, "Well, OK. I'll meet you over at the hospital." The paramedics rolled her away from me, toward the double doors that led to the ambulance parked outside. I got in my car and drove thirty miles to the hospital. Upon arrival, I found the room she would be admitted to. Gloria's parents and her daughter, Rebecca, were also there, awaiting her arrival.

About an hour later, Gloria was fully settled into her room. We sat with her as we waited for her to be taken away for surgery. I sat in a chair across the room, facing Gloria's bed. Rebecca sat in a chair adjacent to me on my left.

As Gloria talked away with her parents, who were sitting on the couch to my right, I took advantage of this moment and pulled up the notes app on my iPhone. I wrote the words, "Did you guys not tell your mom how sick she was?" I then passed my phone over to Rebecca. After reading it, she wrote, "I think so," and handed it back to me. I replied, "Did you not tell my dad?" She read it, shook her head, and shrugged her shoulders as if to say, "I dunno." At the same time she said, "Yeah, I think so." She left the phone in my hand and turned to look over at her mother as if to avoid any further questioning.

Tired and in need of rest, I decided to leave knowing that Gloria wouldn't be alone with her parents and Rebecca there. On my way back to Murfreesboro, I stopped by the nursing home to see my dad and to give him the latest update. "I had no idea they hadn't told you, Dad," I said. I felt sick having to relay this new truth to him. "I thought for sure, if anybody, they would have told you, especially with your medical background." He just sat there looking out into nowhere, shaking his head in disbelief. He looked as sick about all this as I was. "They shouldn't be in charge of her care anymore, Dad. This just proves that they can't be left responsible when it comes to their mother's best interest. She should have been put on a strict diet right after her last diagnosis," I said. My father agreed.

I sat in the recliner to the right of his bed and pulled back on the lever, lifting my feet so I could stretch out. We lay there together, side by side, in the silent room. I felt overwhelmed by recent events and the circumstances. I had done my very best to hold back my tears for months. I had assumed this was best for Gloria and Daddy, to show them strength while they went through such a tough time. But in this moment I couldn't hold the tears back anymore. Tears rolled down my checks as I gasped for air. "I'm sorry, Daddy. I don't mean to cry in front of you... I can't help it. I apologize... This just isn't fair." With soft words, he simply responded, "I'm just glad to see you finally show *any* emotion." I hadn't realized up until now just how much I *had* held it all in, hoping to appear strong for my parents' sake. After hearing my father's words, it became clear to me that it was *OK* if I wasn't strong *all* the time. I said, "Daddy, it's like we're all on a roller coaster and we can't get off." He agreed with me and said, "I know."

We continued to sit in the silence, both of us looking up toward the ceiling as we contemplated this thing called life. The sun had now fully risen. Light showed through the sheer curtains covering the window next to Daddy's bed, making the room appear to be a hazy yellowish orange. The warmth of these colors enveloped everything around us. A peace and calm seemed to settle over us, wrapping us in its loving embrace.

Before returning to my dad's house to try to get some sleep, I decided to run by my chiropractor's office. My neck was killing me from the stress; I figured a quick visit wouldn't be such a bad idea and might help me relax a bit. I was her first patient of the day, seeing how she had barely opened up for business before I arrived. The time now was ten o'clock. Most people were just starting the day; I, on the other hand, was on the opposite scope, coming to the close of mine.

I lay facedown on her table and began unloading to her the events that had occurred in just the past twenty-four hours, accounting for any tensions and the amount of stress she might be sensing in my body. When she finished my adjustment, I was unaware that anything I had said was of any importance to her at all. I lifted myself up, sat on her table, and proceeded to fix my disheveled hair, pulling it back into a ponytail.

My chiropractor said, "Gabriel, I started my day by getting into a fight with my husband." Hearing her speak, I placed my hands in my lap and gave her my full attention. "I thought I was having a bad day," she said. "I even came into work crying. But then you come in here and you have *real, valid* problems going on in your life. As you told me everything that was going on, all I could think to myself was, 'My problems aren't problems! What in the world am I crying about?' As you continued to share with me, Gabriel, your family's recent struggles and heartbreak, at the same time all you talked about throughout the entire conversation was how wonderful God has been to you. Can I just tell you, I'm so glad you stopped by this morning. You have completely turned my day around for the better. I am in awe of your faith and your love for God. After you leave here today, the first thing I'm going to do is call my husband and apologize. What we were fighting about seems so silly to me now."

CHAPTER 14

GLORIA KEPT GETTING worse. Her surgery to remove part of her intestines resulted in her needing a colostomy bag. The wound from the scar had developed gangrene. I sat on the couch in the den and watched as my father made the call to have hospice send someone to the house. I was always impressed when I heard him talk to other medical professionals. He was a smart man; a lot of people considered him to be a genius.

My aunt, who was a nurse, had been asked to stop by for a second, for a third opinion. She, my uncle, and I all sat around my father and awaited the decision about whether hospice would send out a nurse or not. It was quiet where we sat. All we could hear was the noise and chatter coming from the back bedroom. Gloria lay on her bed surrounded by her daughter, her four grandchildren, and her two nurses. Throughout the evening, I kept going back to check on Gloria and then to the front room to give a report to my dad. One of our reasons for concern was that on several occasions I heard Jackson and Rebecca tell the nurses how to administer care to their mother.

As we waited patiently for hospice's response, we heard someone on the receiving end: "Mr. Pearson, we're sorry but we can't give you that information."

"Why is that? I'm her husband," Dad insisted.

"You don't have power of attorney," she replied.

My father hung his head in sorrow. My uncle, aunt, and I all looked at each other in disbelief. Then I looked over at my father, helpless. As a sordid confirmation, all of our attention was then directed out the window into the front yard. There stood Jackson yapping away on the phone authoritatively. There stood the defiant "power of attorney."

We asked everyone to meet us in the living room for a chat. Assuming she knew what this was about, Rebecca stomped into the room defiantly, leading the rest behind her. By this time I had moved to a seat behind my father's recliner and sat on my uncle's knee. I wanted to fight, I wanted to speak out, but my Uncle Gary held me there with him, securing both arms to my sides. My aunt sat before us also, on the left side of my father.

Those who had been called to court walked in a single-file line and sat on the couch in front of us. It was a house divided. My father told them how he had heard the news of their taking "power of attorney" from him, and how this hurt him. Rebecca jumped to her feet, lunged toward my father, and pointed her finger in his face. "That's *our* mama!" she yelled. "Poor James! I'm so sick of your 'poor me' act!"

I went to stand, and my uncle pulled me back to his lap. I wanted to take up for my dad. How could these people be treating him this way? I balled my right hand up into a fist and punched my uncle's leg over and over again, never turning my eyes from Rebecca's face. I vehemently sat there and watched her scold my father as though he were a child.

My dad hung his head down and looked at the floor. Then he said to her, "I've taken care of your mother and paid for all her care. Do you want to take that responsibility also?"

Rebecca headed toward the door to leave. Before closing the door behind her, she pointed at my father again and said, "I love you, but I'm mad at you right now!" Then she turned away and slammed the door shut behind her.

━ ━ ━ ━ ━ ━ ━

I took the following Tuesday off and spent the day hanging out at my father's house. It was a beautiful day. The weather was lovely, so my father wanted to get outdoors for a bit. He requested to walk down to his shop, so I placed his walker in front of him before we prepared to walk out the door. We stepped out and headed down the driveway. "You're moving fast today, Daddy!" I exclaimed supportively. "You need to paint some flames on the side of your walker!" He said to me, "It's because I'm going downhill!" and then chuckled.

We got down to the covered carport area next to his shop, and me, Dad, and one of his brothers sat in three old chairs from Daddy's drug store. We had the best time together, just sitting and enjoying the day. My dad said to me, "I want to shoot my BB gun. Baby, you know where it is, in the cabinet in there. Go get it. And you know what pellets go with it—grab those too." I felt honored by his request and the fact that he trusted I knew what pellets to grab. I felt like a little kid walking proudly with his chest puffed out after his father had patted him on the head and said, "Good job! Way to go, you!"

I returned to my father, handed him the gun, and returned to my seat next to him. Dad playfully took the pistol and pointed it at something behind me. I watched him as he pretended to find targets to aim at and then shoot at them. He said, "Look at that one! I'm gonna get it!" making pretend shooting noises (*pow pow!*). I smiled with delight. This was a joyous occasion. I had never seen my father like this. It was if he was a little boy again. I loved it. It was almost as though he had forgotten, if for only a moment, what awaited him inside his home.

This entire day it was like my father had forgotten he was sick. We sat and chatted and giggled about anything and everything. I said, "Daddy, wanna know what my all-time favorite movie is?"

"What is it?" he asked.

"*Fight Club*" I replied.

He continued, "You know that soap he makes in the movie? I always wondered if he ever adds any fragrance to it." Something to ponder, I guess.

After a while we headed back up to the house. We sat on the back patio around a wrought iron table with four chairs. By this time my Uncle Gary had shown up and joined us outside. It was too great of a day to spend it indoors. My uncles and I did most of the conversing. I looked over at my father as he sat quietly. He had the sweetest smile on his face as he sat there and listened to us. His countenance was very peaceful; there was an inner joy about him.

After an hour or so, my dad and I went back into the house to see how Gloria was doing. My dad sat in his recliner close to her as I took a seat next to him. As reality began to sink back in, my dad's inner joy began to dissipate. Fear and grief came over him as we sat silent in the dimly lit room. He placed his elbows on his knees and hung his head, saying, "What am I going to do? What am I going to do?" He rocked slowly back and forth while wringing both hands together. I hung my head to the floor and just sat there in support. What can you say to somebody during a time like this? Nothing. There was nothing anyone could do to make any of this better. So I just sat there with him. All I could do was just be there.

A little later, I went out to get dinner for Daddy before leaving the house. (I had to work in Nashville the next day.) I said my

142

good-byes to everyone and kissed Daddy and Gloria good-bye before I left.

Later that evening, when no one was left at my dad's but Dad, Gloria, and Dad's nurse, Hope, my dad stood up from his recliner, about to head back to his bedroom to turn in for the night. He shuffled his way over to Gloria, who was lying on the couch to his left, to tell her good night. He bent over, softly placed his hand on her forehead, and lovingly slid his hand over her brow up to the top of her head before placing a kiss on her cheek. He continued to look at her face and smiled. "I love you, Gloria. I think you're beautiful." Tears welled up in his eyes, and then he stood up straight. He turned to his left to head back to his room. He shuffled a couple steps toward the door that led from the living room, up one step, and into the kitchen.

Before he reached the step-up into the doorway, he stopped. He stood there silently and hung his head. Then my father began to weep. Hope sat silently with nothing left to do in this moment but to helplessly watch a man who had lived his entire life providing for those he loved—and now at the end of it all, he could do nothing to save them. After a moment or two, without a word he lifted his head and quietly walked back to his room, closing the door behind him. Hope said that this was significant because he would usually leave it slightly open at night.

———————————

The next morning around eight o'clock or so, Hope peeked her head into my father's room, same as usual, and said, "Good morning, Mr. James." Most mornings she would hear a sweet and soft reply from him: "Good morning, Hope." She said she loved when they did this every morning; it was the one part of the day when my dad was soft and gentle in his demeanor. The rest of the day he was grumpy and short with everyone. (I would be too, if I were him. He didn't feel well, and his wife was on her deathbed. Who could really blame the guy? I'd be ticked off too.)

But this morning was different. My father said nothing. She said he usually slept on his back, straight as a board. He lay there, same as always, so she thought nothing of it. The only difference was that his right arm was hanging off the side of the bed. She thought maybe he just needed the rest and decided to let him alone so he could sleep in a bit. She pulled the door almost closed and then went to Gloria's room to tend to her for a bit.

About thirty minutes later she had still heard no rustle from my father, so she went to check on him again. "Good morning, Mr. James." But again, nothing. She took a closer look at the sheets covering my daddy and noticed that there was no movement; his chest was not moving up and down. She then walked into the room and approached his bed. As she got closer to him, she could tell that his body posture seemed too rigid to be normal. She took a close look at his face. "Mr. James?" She reached out to touch him, and when she did, she realized he was dead.

Hope ran out of the room to find her phone so she could call 911. After making the call she waited at the front of the house, looking out the window and waiting for the ambulance to pull up. Before the paramedics even had a chance to arrive, a car pulled up. It was the chief of police. He had heard the call come in over the CB radio that Mr. James was not responding, so he ran over to the house as fast as he could, beating the ambulance to the house.

Before Hope even knew what was happening, the two French doors she was standing near suddenly burst open with great force as the police chief pushed them open. He barreled through the house and ran back into my dad's bedroom. He proceeded to do CPR, trying his best to resuscitate my father, but to no avail. It was October 9. My father had a heart attack while he slept.

My stepsister Rebecca showed up to the house shortly thereafter. She watched as the paramedics prepared to carry my father's body out on a gurney. Just before leaving, they stopped outside of Gloria's bedroom across the hall. With the help of her nurses, Gloria stood to her feet, walked over to my dad, and bent down to give him a kiss before the paramedics took him away.

— — — — — — —

I wasn't scheduled to go into work that day until one o'clock, so I took the opportunity to sleep in a bit. Around ten o'clock, I lay in my bed daydreaming about Leo. No matter what had happened between us, it couldn't change the fact that I still loved him. We had known better times—it wasn't all bad—so I would go back into my memory bank to relive some of those. He was my escape from reality; if only for a moment, it made me feel happy again.

Without warning, my mother suddenly burst into my bedroom. She was crying hysterically. Alarmed by her intrusion, I immediately slid away from her to the furthest corner of my bed. She stopped and stood right up against my bed. I watched her face in my disbelief and desperately waited for her mouth to produce words. Through her uncontrollable crying she finally let out, "They found your daddy dead this morning!"

Shocked, trying to fathom this moment as though it was really happening, my mind began to sort and process the information that had just been handed to me. Gloria had been given three days to live a day ago, and then my father dropped dead?

This was quite a change in events; I never imagined my dad would be the first one to go. I was preparing for Gloria.

My brain continued to twist as I let the news sink in. I didn't want Gloria to go, but if anything, to look at things in a more positive light, I'd thought my dad's health was possibly on the upswing; maybe there was a chance that he would recoup and spend a little bit more time here on Earth. This would give us some extra time, a chance to heal some things—give me a chance to spend some quality time with my dad before he left. But it was over.

My mother stood next to my bed and continued to cry hysterically. It was if she was a small child looking for comfort. She waited for my reaction. She expected me to fall into hysterics with her, but I knew that now was not the time for that. I couldn't let myself break; there was so much left to be done. Gloria was still alive, and she needed to be cared for; I knew if anything, I had to stay strong for her. I also had to get up and drive to Murfreesboro. I couldn't drive if I was crying and in hysterics.

I stood up beside my bed. My mother stepped back as I put my feet on the floor. She looked at me, bewildered that I didn't react. I thought to myself, *I've got to go downstairs and make coffee, then get dressed and make the trip to Murfreesboro.* I went downstairs to the kitchen to make coffee. After it brewed, I grabbed my cup and headed out onto the back patio. My mom took a seat across from me. She continued to sob, never looking away from my face. As I took a sip, she cried out, "Gabriel, it's OK to cry!" I stared off in a daze into the atmosphere next to her chair. Calmly I said aloud, "My daddy died today." I put my coffee down and went inside to get dressed.

The drive to Murfreesboro seemed to happen in slow motion. I felt I was in a hazy bubble. I was so in my head that at times

I forgot that I was driving, and I caught myself several times before accidentally veering off the side of the road.

When I arrived at my father's house, the driveway and yard were full of parked cars. I went around to enter the house from the fence that led into the yard off the back patio. I stopped short before crossing over the threshold, the line that separated the pavement from the backyard, and looked down at the tips of my toes as I prepared myself to cross over. Two of my aunts approached me, standing on either side, each with a hand on my shoulder. I stood there weighing out the options in my head, whether I should step over or not. Then I quietly said, "Everything is about to change as soon as I cross over this line." In unison, both of my aunts said, "It's going to be OK."

I backed up and left my aunts standing at the gate. I walked toward the front of the house and chose to enter from the two side doors we used as the main entrance. No one was in the den, nor in the dining room directly past it. There was a door at the far back right corner of the dining room that would allow me to slip through the house unnoticed and step into my father's bedroom door, which stood adjacent to the hallway. The kitchen on the other side of the dining room wall was full of people. I quickly ran through the den and then through the dining room and appeared before them in a flash—in the time it took to take a couple steps through the hallway that separated the two rooms.

I ran into my dad's room, closing the door behind me, then into the bathroom that connected to his room. Finally, I made a right through the double mirrored doors that led into a walk-in closet. To my right were his dresser drawers. I stood in front of them and then pulled the top drawer open toward my chest. This is where my daddy kept his socks. I reached both arms out and slid them under the heap. I turned my head to the side and laid it on top of my dad's clothes and began to weep. I wanted to smell him. I wanted to feel him.

I heard the sound of someone opening the bedroom door; then the sound of multiple footsteps drew closer. I wanted to be alone. I didn't want to be comforted. I just wanted a moment alone with my father. I wanted to tell him good-bye in private. I never rose up or turned my head to see who was coming in the room. Suddenly I felt a multitude of hands on my back and arms. My space had been invaded. I abruptly stopped crying, stood up, and reassured the concerned faces around me that I was OK.

I slid my hands out of the drawers and walked out of the room, hoping that by doing so the people around me would follow suit. Everyone filed out of the room except for my step-sister and me. We sat next to each other on the edge of Daddy's bed, both of our feet touching the floor. I knew she had been at the house earlier that morning, so I had a couple of questions I wanted to ask. I wanted to know what it was like. I wanted to know what he looked like, if he looked peaceful. She said he looked happy, as though he was asleep.

After this, I shared with her a scripture that came to my mind right after I'd heard the news of my father's death. It was John 14:3, "And if I go and prepare a place for you, I will come back and take you to be with me that you also may be where I am." She said the same scripture had also crossed her mind when she heard he had passed away. She went on to say, "My mama always felt comfortable and safe wherever Mr. James was. I feel like he went on ahead of her, to encourage her. She's put up one heck of a fight and won't let go. It's like she doesn't want to leave all of us because she worries who will take care of us. If Mr. James were to go ahead of her to prepare a spot for them in heaven, she might be more inclined to stop resisting and leave this earth, knowing he would be there waiting for her."

This, to me, was the measure of what kind of man my father was. I was so proud of him for his selflessness and for how much he loved. It was rare to witness this kind of love between two people, the kind of love that lives on beyond death. I want to be loved like that. I think we all do.

— — — — — — —

When the funeral home presented me with the opportunity to do my dad's hair, I jumped at the chance. I was told to meet the funeral director in the building behind the home on the day of my father's wake. This is where they prepared the bodies to be viewed. I took one of my aunts with me for emotional support, just in case I got weak in the knees.

When we arrived at the funeral home, the director led us through the building and out the back door to a smaller building directly behind the home. The exterior was brick with white trim and white doors. It looked more like a garage connected to someone's house. We entered into the facility; to my left was a hearse. The temperature of the room grew colder with every step we took.

Finally, after a few more steps, to our right we saw a separate area where the bodies were prepared. On a silver embalming table lay my daddy. He had already been dressed in his suit. There was a white blanket covering most of his body. I had spent most of my life preparing myself for this dreaded moment, seeing my daddy's body lifeless. The very thought of it would bring tears to my eyes, so I would always do my best to cast out the thoughts as soon as they came. Shocked by how well I was taking all this, I looked over at my aunt and then the director and asked, "Why am I taking this so well? I thought I would be tearing things off the walls."

The funeral director replied, "Your dad had a hard year. It's difficult to not feel glad for him, knowing that he is in a better place now."

I stood beside my father's body, peering down at his face, taking in all the details of his new state of "being." I began to talk to him. "I'm so proud of you...you did good, Daddy." I placed my right hand gently on his head, caressing him until my fingertips slid down over his cheekbone. I smiled as I thought about how much I loved this man and always had. In this moment I finally understood the kind of peace God spoke of when He said, "Then you will experience God's peace, which exceeds anything we can understand. His peace will guard your hearts and minds as you live in Christ Jesus" (Phil. 4:7, NLT).

━ ━ ━ ━ ━ ━ ━

I stayed with my aunt and uncle that night. When I woke the next morning, I heard my uncle leave his house around eight o'clock. He seemed to leave in a bit of a hurry for a man who rarely left his home before ten o'clock in the morning, but I shrugged it off, got dressed, and then drove over to my dad's.

When I pulled up into the driveway around nine o'clock, there standing before me was my uncle, posted up like an armed guard at the entry of my father's home. Paying him no mind (some people get a kick out of feeling like they're in charge), I walked past him and entered the home.

Later that afternoon, at the visitation, I stood by my father's casket and spoke to his friends, coworkers, and family members as they came to pay their last respects. An older gentleman approached, shook my hand, and asked if I remembered him. He had lived next door to us when I was a teen. He said the last time he spoke to my father, he'd asked him if I had settled down—if I was still a "wild child," rather, and if I'd found

God yet. What he said next blew me away: "Your dad said not only had you found God, but you could probably recite the Scriptures to me." Standing there next to my dad, I felt great joy in my heart knowing that my father spoke of me in such a way.

———————

I stayed at my aunt and uncle's house for the duration of the week as we planned for my father's funeral. The morning of the funeral, I pulled up to the house after taking breakfast to my mom, who was in town for the funeral. I went inside and started to get ready for the service.

I could tell that something was amiss. People, including my aunt and uncle, were starting to act "funny." I sensed a nervous energy about them as I passed by to go to the guest room. My uncle was outside pacing by his truck; he seemed busy in his thoughts. I already had enough on my mind, so I didn't stop to ask what was up.

Just before I finished getting dressed, there was a knock at my door. My dress still unzipped in the back, I opened the door to find my aunt and uncle standing there. Their faces and body language showed evidence of worry, concern, and nervous, bottled-up excitement.

My uncle said, "I was at the bank today, and one of the ladies that works there told me there were some CDs and IRAs there that belonged to your daddy worth about $250,000." He paused for a moment as his eyes welled up with tears. "Your dad did take care of you after all, Gabriel." He seemed to bat his eyes at me while holding back the tears. He said this as if he had done me some heroic favor by "just happening" to be at the bank after my dad died and "just happening" to run into this lady. It didn't seem like such a favor from where I stood; it looked more like he was in there snooping around.

I didn't feel like it was much his business—at that moment, I didn't feel like it was any of mine either. Money was the furthest thing from my mind in light of my father's death. I always knew he had money, but even while he was sick it never crossed my mind that I would inherit anything if he *were* to die. It was now becoming clear to me that I was the only one hanging around him who didn't think this way.

Without even the slightest hint of an attitude, I straightforwardly replied, "I never doubted for a moment that my dad would take care of me. Now, do you mind letting my daddy's body cool off before we start talking about money?" Then I turned around to finish getting dressed.

My uncle didn't like this at all. He rushed toward me as I turned back around. He got right up in my face and yelled, "I'm so sick of your attitude!" My aunt, a tiny thing, got in between us and tried to stop him from getting any closer to me.

I turned away and started gathering my things around the room and putting them into a bag. "I'm not staying here," I said.

He stormed out of the bedroom, then out the back door, and left. I didn't know he was gone, so I just kept gathering my belongings as my aunt begged me to stop packing and stay. She cried, "Your uncles aren't the type of men that are used to women standing up to them!" Besides the funeral that proceeded, this would be the last time I saw or spoke to my uncle and my aunt.

— — — — — — —

The following day, before my father's casket was closed for the last time, before he was loaded into the hearse, the family was given a moment to pay our last respects. After his brothers and other members of the family said their good-byes, I walked up and stood by his side. I was the last person that would say good-bye before the casket was closed.

I bent down, kissed his cheek, and stood up to look at him once more. During the past two days, I had been very mindful not to leave lipstick on him. However, this time, my clear lip gloss left evidence of my kiss right there on his cheek. Before wiping it off his face, I remembered times when Gloria, Rebecca, or I would leave lipstick on him—we would go to wipe it off, and before we even had a chance to touch his face, he would stop us and say, "Leave it there! Some men don't have lipstick on them because they don't have anybody to kiss 'em!" I smiled down at him as this memory played over in my mind. I decided then to leave my kiss there on his cheek. Before I walked away and his casket was closed, I softly whispered my last words to him: "Some men don't, Daddy."

Everyone loaded up into their vehicles, preparing for the funeral procession. Several family members asked if I would like to ride along with them. Instead, I chose to drive myself. During this time of my life, I could be considered a loner at best, so I liked the idea of being by myself for this trip.

The hearse pulled forward as the funeral directors instructed the other cars to wait until I pulled my car directly behind it. The car that would follow me was my stepbrother and his children in my father's truck. It was an honor. This was the first time since my father had remarried that my place in his life was finally being acknowledged. After years of feeling out of place and pushed to the back, I was finally given credit for being my father's daughter. And who would have thought, after all this time, that the men at the funeral home would be the ones to finally make my stepsiblings stay in their place and acknowledge that I belonged there, that I came first. They had no idea how much this meant to me and what, in actuality, they had done for me. At last, after all the years of being pushed to the side, I got the reminder I needed: that I did, in fact, belong to him.

It was a beautiful, crisp October day. The sky was blue—not a cloud in the sky. The sun was shining bright. The leaves were a multitude of colors, as the seasons were starting to change. We drove out of Murfreesboro and onto a two-lane highway that led to College Grove, Tennessee. When I was a child, about eleven or twelve years old at best, Daddy and I would drive this road out to his parents' house in his bright red Chevrolet pickup truck. We would turn the music up loud. With every twist and turn down that old country road, Dad would take the hills and curves just so, and when we went over them, you would get that butterfly feeling in your tummy. We would laugh and enjoy each other's company as we joyfully headed down the road.

One of our all-time favorite CDs to jam to was *Neil Diamond's Greatest Hits*. As I drove on, behind the black hearse, "Sweet Caroline" came on the radio. I didn't know yet if this trip just might kill me. The reality was, I was following behind a car that held my dad's body. But when this song came on, I knew that I was going to be all right. I rolled my windows down and turned the radio way up. I stuck my arm out of my window and dipped my hand into the cool breeze. I didn't care what anyone in the cars behind me might think. Maybe it would seem a bit odd for me to appear so happy at such a time as this. I wondered if they would they get the wrong impression if it seemed like I was celebrating. Then I thought, "Oh, who cares?" And for their information, yes, I was celebrating! I continued to sing out loud just like Daddy and I did back in the day. We had come full circle; it was just the two of us together again, singing "Sweet Caroline"! Then I said out loud, over the music, "Come on, Daddy. I'm takin' you home!"

My father was from College Grove, which was a short distance, right outside of Murfreesboro, out in the country. He would be laid to rest in a small cemetery there next to his parents, grandparents, and great-grandparents. The cemetery was next to a little white church on a hill, right up the road from the house where he and his siblings were raised. Next to him there was a plot where Gloria would be laid to rest, when the time would come.

Upon arriving, I walked into the church with Rebecca to show her where the restroom was. We stepped though the double-door entryway. Above us was a stained glass window that my father made. His mother drew the design for the piece. She painted the artwork on canvas using watercolors before my father made a replica using stained glass. We stepped into the large area where the congregation meets, and instantly I was transported back into time. A time when I was much younger and life seemed much simpler, and innocent.

I walked down the aisle between the pews and stopped for a moment to take it all in. I even loved the way the church smelled. The sun shone brightly throughout the room through other stained glass windows that lined the walls on every side. I placed my hand on the back of a pew and then glided my fingertips over the dark wood. I looked over at one of the hymn books on the back of a chair and smiled as I thought about how beautiful my grandmother's voice sounded when she sang those old-time gospel hymns. I looked up to the front of the church at the large painting hanging right above the pulpit, where the choir sang. My grandmother painted that. It's a painting of Jesus kneeling to pray on a rock; light from heaven shines down on His face. I smiled as I thought how truly proud I was to belong to this family.

I snapped back into reality as Rebecca breezed by me in a hurry. She turned her head from one side to the other to take a few short glances as she rushed through. "Well, isn't this a cute church!" she said as she crinkled her nose. I watched her as she walked toward the end of the room. As she got closer to the door that leads to the hallway where the restrooms are, she looked back at me to make sure she was going the right way. I pointed toward the door and nodded my head.

Later that afternoon, I was back at my father's house, about to leave there and return to Nashville. As I breezed through the kitchen heading toward the door, my dad's nurse, Hope, grabbed me by my arm, pulling me in so she could talk directly to my face. She said, "I know you don't wanna stir up no trouble, but just hear me this... "—a look of guilt covered my face as I turned my eyes to look away from her. I knew what this was about—"and then you can go," she said. I looked her in her eyes as she continued to speak. "If their mama had five dollars, they should split that with you three ways. Do you hear me?" I nodded my head and said, "Yes, ma'am," and then I was out the door.

CHAPTER 15

PENNIES FROM HEAVEN

*What is the price of two sparrows—one copper coin?
But not a single sparrow can fall to the ground without
your Father knowing it. And the very hairs on your
head are all numbered. So don't be afraid; you are more
valuable to God than a whole flock of sparrows.*

—MATTHEW 10:29–31, NLT

AFTER MY FATHER's death, I kept noticing numbers sequences *everywhere.* This phenomenon had never occurred to me before. I would notice numbers on digital clocks, receipts, billboards, road signs, license plates—you name it: 2:22, 333, 11:11, 1234, etc. In my carnal mind I thought it was my earthly father who was now on the other side calling my attention to numbers so he could communicate with me. In my ignorance, the best excuse I could come up with was that my dad was now one of my "spirit guides." *Ooh, ahh* . . . it sounds clever and deep, doesn't it? I couldn't have been more wrong!

I hadn't a clue how important numbers are to God. Among many other options, He will sometimes use them as a tool to communicate with us. But before learning this for myself, I started to do all I could to learn more and find out their significance and what these numbers could mean. However, none of the answers I was finding at this time led me to the Almighty God. But that all changed one day.

I was pulling out of the mall parking lot, and the tags on the car ahead of me caught my eye. The numbers on the plate stood out above everything else and jumped out at me: 24 15. I took a mental note to remember "24 15" and then went back to whatever other random thoughts were going on inside my head. Then I heard that still, soft voice suddenly become not so still and not so soft: *"If you aren't going to find out what these numbers mean, how are you going to know what I'm trying to say to you?"* The urgency and tone of His voice sounded like a dad getting on to his daughter. He had my undivided attention now. I thought, "Yes, Sir! On it! Sorry... sorry!"

I will spend the rest of my life trying to learn all I can about God, His ways, and His methods and still reach the end of my life not even coming close to knowing a thing. That's why we search for God and pray that He continue to reveal Himself to us. As long as we live, we will never know all there is to know about God. That's why we need to *run* after Him and learn as much as we can while we're here, getting to know Him more and more each day. The more you learn, the more He is revealed to you, the more intimate your relationship with Him becomes. Every day you fall deeper and deeper in love with Him. As a result, your hunger to know even more about Him grows, so you keep searching! A life with God is certainly not boring! He'll take you places and tell you about things beyond anything you could have ever imagined. Like the Bible says in Jeremiah 33:3 (NLT), "Ask me and I will tell you remarkable secrets you do not know about things to come." Did you notice the chapter number and verse was 3:33? This is one way I learned that God uses numbers to speak to us. Recently, I kept seeing 2:22 everywhere I looked, so much so that I decided to start in Genesis and read every scripture in every book of the Bible that was chapter and verse 2:22 or 22:2. Talk about searching!

Around the same time that I started to notice numbers, I started to experience something else "out of the ordinary." It started one day when my mom and I were returning home. As I pulled the car into the garage, I looked over at her and asked, "Did we hear the song 'Pennies from Heaven' sometime today, or did it come up at all in any kind of way?" I had heard this song going round and round in my mind all day but I hadn't a clue why, or even when I would have heard this song last. My mom also agreed that she couldn't recall us hearing that song at any point throughout the day.

Later that evening, my mom unfortunately went on one of her tangents. I remember she went upstairs to take a bath, and in my despair I sat next to the dryer, put on my headphones, and listened to music, trying to make the world just go away. As I sat there, I kept hearing a clinking noise in the dryer as it dried some clothes. I tried to ignore it, but even over the music in my ears and the hum of the dryer, I could still hear the *clank tink clank*.

Finally, after I could take no more, I stood up to take a look inside the dryer. I opened the door and fumbled through the clothes a bit, looking for the culprit. I grabbed the entire load, holding it out of my way with my arm so I could inspect the walls and floor of the dryer. And there, against the eggshell-colored contrast, lay one shiny penny. I walked out of the utility room and into the den, going over it in my head, wondering if this was just a coincidence or if perhaps it had anything to do with the song I had heard all day.

I approached the couch, and before taking a seat, I noticed a penny sitting on the back of the couch on top of the blanket. I thought to myself, "Well, that seems like a strange place for a penny to be...I did spill my purse while I was sitting on the couch earlier...but why would a penny land there? It was next to me on the couch cushions where I sat...I thought I picked up everything that fell out anyway."

Baffled by these two consecutive occurrences, I decided not to sit down. Instead, I walked over to the stairs to go up to my bedroom. And there, on the third step—you guessed it—lying slap-dab in the middle was a penny. All these pennies had one thing in common: they were all facing tails-side up. From that day forward, I kept seeing pennies everywhere. I wasn't yet sure why, but I knew they were being left for me on purpose. Every time I saw one, it would make me smile. Again, I suspected it might be my dad that was doing it, but the wrong "dad"; it was, however, from my Father—my heavenly Father.

Sometimes I would find a penny on the floor or sitting right outside my car on the ground, right next to where I placed my feet as I stepped out of the vehicle; these times just seemed happenstance. But there were other times that seemed to hold more significance, letting me know and reminding me that in that moment, God was with me. Like a wink from above saying, "I'm right here! Be strong! Keep moving forward. It's going to be OK. Remember, I love you!" Something as small (both in size and value) as a penny suddenly held more weight and meant a great deal to me. In a world (and a life, for that matter) that can be difficult at times to maneuver and understand with its many twists and turns, it was as though I now had a copilot with me to direct me and encourage me with every step I took. Whenever those steps made me question myself, wondering if I had miscalculated and made a wrong turn somewhere, I would then look down and see a penny; then all of a sudden what felt like a mistake was suddenly replaced with a "knowing" that I was exactly where He intended for me to be.

— — — — — — —

In the midst of all the chaos, loss, changes, and confusion, I wanted something to relieve the pain. Pills weren't doing the trick; alcohol wasn't either. I even tried to smoke some pot. The only drug I wanted was Leo. The only thing that could make me feel better now and completely forget how bad life felt was the ecstasy only he could deliver.

I was an adult; I figured if I wanted to get laid then I should just be a woman about it and reach out to him and keep it real. "I'm stressed, and the only thing that can relieve it is having hot, passionate sex with you." So I texted him. I figured I could let bygones be bygones at this point. Seeing him was the only thing that would make me feel better, so I took a chance.

I was up-front, and after we texted each other for a day and a half, I asked if he would be down to get a room for a night at somewhere like Embassy Suites. Of course he was. What dumb boy wouldn't be down for just full-on sex? My excuse was, even if this turned out badly, I'd rather think about that than think about my dead dad.

I met Leo at the hotel and walked into the hotel room. I looked him up and down, trying to see if he really added up to the image I kept of him in my head. He was what tormented me. Was he, in fact, worth it? I played it cool while Leo fumbled his words, unable to sit still.

"What?" I laughed.

"I'm just excited to see you!" he said. I was too but did my best to hide it.

Sex was great, of course—just what the doctor ordered. After it was over, we lay in the dark of the night. Leo looked at me and said, "You've always been beautiful, but tonight you're more beautiful than ever." He vowed to do better and even cried telling me how much he loved me. How could I resist? He was all I wanted in the first place. So we would try again. Maybe this would be the time we could make our relationship work.

▬ ▬ ▬ ▬ ▬ ▬ ▬

That Halloween, Leo and I joined the rest of his family at his cousin's house, just as we had done the previous year. "It's our second Halloween together, baby," I said to Leo when the thought occurred to me. We both smiled. Maybe this love could stand the test of time.

Not long after our arrival, I received a call from Rebecca saying Gloria had just died. Not wanting to interfere by putting a damper on Leo's family's spirits and draw attention to myself, I quietly made my way out the front door and crept over into the yard on the side of the house. It was dark, and the shrubbery around the home aided in making this the perfect hiding spot.

I sat Indian style and removed my kitty cat ears, placing them in the grass beside me. I started to come to grips with my new reality. Life as I had once known it was now over. Now that Gloria was gone, it was official. That whole part of my life, consisting of her and my dad, ceased to exist—no more returning to Dad's house to see them; no more holidays together; no more going down to the shop to hang out with my dad; no more sitting across from my dad at the kitchen island watching him do his impression of Julia Child as he made pancakes; no more giggling with Gloria over the silliest things. No more.

I heard someone come out the front door. Then I heard Leo's voice: "Baby?" I heard his footsteps in the grass behind me as he walked through the yard looking for me. He found me lying on my side, curled up in the fetal position. He knelt down, then he lay on his side and wrapped his arm around me. Forcing myself to pull it together and quit crying, I whispered to Leo, "I'm so tired. This has been the absolute worst and most amazing experience of my life." I was so very glad to have known two people like Gloria and Dad; even better still, I had the privilege of calling them my parents.

I rolled over onto my back, as did Leo. Lying there side by side, we peered up into the night sky. It was a purple, lavender color. It was radiant with illuminated hints of a deep fuchsia pink. To our right, as out of nowhere, what looked like a white, puffy sheet of clouds came rushing toward us. It was as if someone had dropped a roll of wrapping paper and the sheet was rolling toward us, stretching out as far as it could go.

Leo said, "Look, babe." He had noticed it before I did. I was unaware of any storm that might be approaching; I hadn't recalled the forecast calling for such weather. Until now it had been a still, clear night. This long, wide sheet of clouds continued to roll over top of us. It was as though it was covering us. It reminded me of how a mother throws a blanket over her child to comfort him.

The stars beneath the clouds began to blink, glowing big and bright. Then they faded back into the night sky only to return shining even brighter, growing larger while they glowed. They appeared to be dancing before us. It seemed as though the heavens above were rejoicing!

Not taking my eyes away for a moment from the wonders above, I asked Leo, "Are you seeing this? Is this really happening?" He smiled a reassuring "Yeah." His answer came across so sure and calm, almost as if he had been in on the surprise. I got the sense that he had somehow known about the show even before it started.

As I lay there in wonder, I saw in my mind a vision of Gloria and Dad dancing together again. With an arm wrapped around Gloria's waist, Dad held onto her hand. They both smiled, elated and joyful as they reunited. Their smiles were so big and bright— I had never seen them smile this way before. The cares of the world no longer weighed heavy upon their shoulders. Carefree and fancy footed, they would be celebrating together, now for eternity. I delighted as I watched them circling 'round and 'round in the heavens. I didn't need to cry for them. They were OK now. The only tears I could justify were the ones I cried for my loss. The Bible says that we as humans have it backward anyway; we should cry when they come in and rejoice when they go out.

> A good name is better than precious ointment, and the day
> of death than the day of birth.
> —ECCLESIASTES 7:1, ESV

In the silence of the night, I whispered to Leo, "I'm so glad you're here to experience this with me."

━ ━ ━ ━ ━ ━ ━

The next day was a Sunday. I drove down to Dad's to be with the family and help out with any funeral arrangements. By the time I got there, there was nothing left to do but wait for the funeral, which would be in a couple days. Leo and I had only been back together for two weeks at this point, so I returned to his place because I wanted to spend some more time with him.

We were lying on Leo's couch resting and watching TV when he received a call from Damien. He said, "Yeah, see you in a minute." I looked at him questioningly because he hadn't asked me whether I felt like having company or not. I had come back to Nashville to spend quiet alone time with him, not to hang out with his cousin while they smoked weed.

His cousin arrived, and Leo acted as though I wasn't there, trying to ignore any opinion I might have. Hurt by this, I went outside while they hung out. I sat on the front porch of the little clubhouse that sat just behind his place. Leo came outside to check on me a couple times but said nothing to suffice, each time being quicker than the last. The way he talked and his body language suggested that he had better things he could be doing. He told me to come on inside and join them, but I turned down his offer. I felt confused. I was at a loss as to what I should do. I would feel like a dummy if I went back inside, and I felt like a dummy for sitting there too. I couldn't jump in my car and go back to my mom's house—I had just run away from her and her antics earlier that day. I couldn't go back to my dad's—I didn't feel very comfortable there either. So I just continued to sit there.

Leo and Damien were watching an episode of one of their favorite shows. I could hear their small conversation about it and their laughter in the distance. At one point, later that evening, Leo's dad came home from work. I watched from afar as he opened the back door of his home and was greeted lovingly by his wife. Even from where I sat, I could tell they were both excited to see each other. His wife looked past him and over into the distance to catch a glimpse of me. Mr. Ramiro looked back for a moment to see what she had spotted. After they both looked to see who was "out there" and realized it was me and not a threat, they both turned their attention back to each other and went into the house, closing the door behind them.

As the night went on, with no better resolve, I went back inside where Leo was. I passed by him and Damien as I walked through the den, and then I crawled into Leo's bed and went to sleep.

At my mom's the next day, I received a call from Leo after he got off work. He asked me if I wanted to come over, pretending like the night before had never happened. I wanted to go to his house more than anything, but at the same time I didn't feel right just "letting him get away with it." Long story short, we got into a fight and he stopped picking up his phone for the rest of the evening.

The following day was the funeral. Gloria's children had asked me to do her hair, so I needed to head to Murfreesboro early that morning. I texted Leo and called his phone, but nothing. I figured we'd had the previous night to cool down and he knew what I had to do that day. I never thought that he would continue to ignore me, not on a day like today. But he did. He blew off my texts by texting me saying he was too busy to answer.

At one point, I sat behind my dad's house crying, texting everything I could think of, begging him to talk to me, if only for a moment. "Not today, Leo. Please! Not today!" Desperate at this point, I lost all my bearings and finally sent out a desperate plea: "WHHHYYYY LEO?? WHY??????? NOT TODAY! PLEASE, LEO, PICK UP THE PHONE!!" But nothing.

I did my best to pull it together. I had to go in and see Gloria lying there, so I gathered myself and tried to do a decent job. My hands shook as the same funeral director who was there when I did my dad's hair looked on. I wasn't the same this time around. My demeanor was definitely different. The pain I felt inside was unbearable. Leo had fooled me again. You know the old saying, "Fool me once, shame on you; fool me twice, shame on me"? But this seemed to go far beyond that. I couldn't believe this was happening. I couldn't believe I had been such a sucker, letting myself be so vulnerable in such an already vulnerable state. I finally stopped trying to reach out to him and promised myself, after today, never ever again.

Jackson drove my dad's truck to his mother's viewing and to her funeral, family in tow. I thought it seemed a bit inappropriate at the time, especially as I drove behind them to their mother's final resting place at the graveyard. I could see his daughter's blonde head sitting in the middle amidst a large group in the front and back seats. It almost felt like a takeover, but at the time I just decided to let it go.

After both funerals, we all went to my dad's house the next afternoon. Jackson had a couple friends at the house, plus his children. Rebecca was also there with her two daughters. My stepsiblings had always been control freaks. They were quick to silence my voice so I would dare not go against them or challenge them about anything. It was hard enough with just one of them around, but a full house? It was them against me.

Jackson sat at my dad's computer showing one of his buddies something on the Internet. A moment earlier, I had added up all the signs and concluded that Jackson was planning to take my dad's truck back home with him the next day. I walked through the den and breezed by him, then stopped short before continuing into the back of the house. I turned in Jackson's direction and asked him, "Are you taking my dad's truck back with you?"

Without looking away from the computer screen, Jackson leaned back in the chair, folding both hands behind his head, and said, "Yep!" Without waiting for my reply, he quickly went back to what he was doing.

I turned toward the door and headed through the house and out the side back door. I took a seat on the swing under the old oak tree and called one of my uncles for advice. He said, "If he

tries to drive that truck out of the driveway, you call the police!"
"Yes, sir," I reluctantly replied.

This was all so confusing. Who was in the right? Did they have the right to do however they pleased? I called my Uncle Gary to get a second opinion before doing something so drastic. I hadn't talked to my uncle since the incident at his home. I felt uncomfortable making the call, but he had been one of my closest confidants in the past; besides, he was the executor to the will. "No, no, no. Don't call the police. Just let him take the truck. It's all gonna be OK," he said.

I put the phone down and continued to swing and stare off into the air. I did as my Uncle Gary said, but something about it didn't feel right. I felt like I needed to get a backbone and stand up against my stepsiblings, but I hate altercations, so I just sat there and continued to swing. So much had transpired in the past few days; I just decided to leave it well enough alone. I should have listened to my first uncle. I should have called the police.

I returned to Nashville for a few days and called the attorney over the estate. I had known this man my whole life. He was one of my father's best friends. I caught him at lunch one afternoon right before I was supposed to go in to work. I inquired about the progress of the estate—any information I needed to know about, any questions I could answer, any hiccups, whatever; just doing what I thought was normal. I hadn't heard from anyone. I kind of felt in the dark, so I thought to at least ask.

To my surprise, he raised his voice and began to yell at me. He told me that he was trying to look out for me; my father had written me out of his will and didn't want me to get anything. Then he told me to stay where I was and keep busy at work, and said he would call me when this was finished.

My heart sank. I felt sick. Then I felt anger. "*Why?* Why would you end it this way? *Why?*" I let out several bloodcurdling screams.

It felt like no matter how hard I pushed, I couldn't scream hard enough. I couldn't get it all out. I wanted all of these feelings out of me—the rage, the anger, the rejection, the abandonment, and the hurt. I cried as I called out to my dad, "Why didn't you ever love me? Why?" demanding an answer I knew I'd never get. Even still, I cried out another desperate plea, *"Why?"*

This was the ultimate slap in the face, the all-time greatest letdown in the history of my life. My heart had just been ripped out of me. I had told myself over the years that after my dad's passing, the truth would be made known—the truth that he did in fact love me. I told myself a story about how he had a trick up his sleeve that would finally be revealed during the reading of his will. I guess it was my way of holding on to hope and dealing with the fact that he didn't want me in his life anymore; to excuse him for not being a dad to me.

I just knew that when he told Gloria he had left her everything, the truth was that he had actually set aside a huge chunk just for me. That would show 'em all! Then they would know what I knew all along, that my dad *did* love me! The joke would be on them. Somehow, when the notion of my dad leaving me nothing would cross my mind, I couldn't ever bring myself to believe it. What—he wouldn't care what was to happen to me after he was gone?

I remember one time Dad brought this up in front of me. He, Gloria, and I were watching TV in the den. He put an arm around her and swayed back and forth. Then he said, "When I die, it all goes to you—isn't that right, honey?" and they both grinned. I waited for Gloria's reply, but she said nothing and kept watching the TV. I just thought my dad said stuff like this in front of me to make her feel better; I never imagined he would gloat about such a thing right in front of me. I never thought it could actually be true.

CHAPTER 16

AFTER THE SECOND funeral, I returned to Nashville and went right back to work. I didn't have anywhere else to be. There was nowhere I felt comfortable or relaxed even if I did want to take a day or two just to do nothing but lie on the couch and watch cartoons. My mother's house was always stressful and tense, like walking on eggshells, so I didn't take my chances being there, even while she was away at work. I thought work might do me some good, or at least keep me busy and help to keep my mind off of things.

While on break one day, I received a text from my stepbrother saying that he was taking all of my dad's guns—twenty-five thousand dollars' worth—back home with him for "safe keeping." Choices about things that belonged to my dad were being made left and right without my consent. It was beyond my control. My hands were tied; there was no way I could stop it.

One of my uncles called me that same day and said, "I was at the house, and they talk like you don't even exist! I'm sorry, Gabriel, I don't know why your daddy left things like this."

When I would receive such texts or calls at work, I would disappear outside and handle all matters before coming back inside and being around clients or customers. No one was aware of

171

anything that was going on with me. My clients had been with me for the better part of a year, so many knew the details of my story, but when they came in to get their hair done I didn't come across like I was upset. I believe I handled myself very well, considering. As memory serves, I was all smiles in front of my clients—many of them even mentioned how well I seemed to be "taking it."

After I'd been back for two weeks, I got a call from the owner of the corporation asking me to stop by his office. I didn't think that anything could be wrong, so I very gladly obliged and headed his way.

I stepped into his office, and we greeted each other with big smiles. He offered me a warm welcome and took a seat at his desk across from me.

Suddenly his mood changed; he hung his head and went silent. He appeared to be mulling over the words in his head, deciding which ones would be the best to use. Finally he told me that he just kept getting calls about me—that the complaints wouldn't stop, and there was nothing more he could do at that point.

I looked away and down at the floor. I hate to cry in business, especially in front of men in a setting like this, but in light of recent events I thought, *Oh, who cares?* I asked him, "When did the complaints start up again?"

He answered, "About two weeks ago."

I said, "Do you know what just happened to me in those two weeks?"

He said yes, he knew. Then, as though on cue, his assistant breezed through the door and took a seat next to us with a pen and pad, ready to take notation.

The owner continued, enthusiastically telling me that he could move me to the downtown location and send out an e-mail blast letting all of my clients know. Then in two months, when the new midtown location opened, I could go to work over there.

Joining in with his enthusiasm and excitement, his assistant chimed in, "And you can go to the grand opening party!" Then the owner jumped in: "Yeah! You can go to the party!"

Still looking down at the floor (I had yet to raise my head to look at him as he spoke), I thought to myself, "My parents just died, I'm being pushed out of my job because of a group of insecure naysayers and backbiters, and you're telling me I can go to a party?"

I blinked a few times trying to shake myself out of my thoughts, then suddenly I looked up at my boss and said, "I do not except your offer." I looked back down at the floor, almost bewildered, as though the answers I was looking for were somewhere around my feet. "I need time to think." I wasn't so sure I wanted to work for people who would fire you for being "a bother" after just losing your parents. I knew the managers I worked under were "low," but to wait and catch me at my lowest, just to bring me down? Their kind of "low" gave the word a whole new meaning.

Not yet knowing what the right decision would be, and not even sure if this was all really happening, I said, "I'll call you tomorrow and let you know what I've decided."

I left his office and sat in my car for a while, letting reality sink in a bit. I was balling now as I thought about all that had taken place in just a matter of two weeks: "Leo hates me and doesn't want me. People at my job hate me and toss me! My mom hates me—she's always telling me everything that's wrong with me! My dad didn't care for me—he even wrote me out of his will! *All* of this... and *guess what*? The common factor is me! It *must* be me! All these people can't be wrong! I must be what they say I am! I must be worthless! And what am I supposed to do for money if I decide not to go back? Look at my life! I hate me too!"

Then I heard the voice of God in my spirit say, "Suck up those tears!" Immediately I tried to quit crying, taking deep breaths. He continued, "It doesn't get this bad unless it's about to get really good! Now dry your eyes!"

Out of nowhere, I received a text on my phone. It just happened to be the attorney in Murfreesboro informing me that I could come by his office soon and pick up the first round of checks from my father's estate, totaling almost three thousand dollars.

I called the owner of the corporation a day later; I still wasn't sure what to do, so I told him I'd call him in a week.

In a week's time I called him and said, "I'm going to take this as a sign that I need some time off...I'll see you at the new location in two months."

CHAPTER 17

For I can do everything through Christ, who gives me strength.

—PHILIPPIANS 4:13, NLT

FINDING MYSELF WITH a lot of free time on my hands, I spent a lot of it at my dad's house. I would contact my stepsister and let her know that I would be there. We still had three of Gloria's cats to tend to at the house. Since Rebecca lived in Murfreesboro, she and her grandmother would take turns stopping by the house two or three times a day, alternating shifts, to feed the cats. I thought it might please Rebecca to know that my being there would save her the hassle of having to run by the house.

I had not seen Rebecca—or any of the family, for that matter—since Dad and Gloria had died. I thought she would at least drop by with the girls at some point during the week to say hi. But nothing. Instead, when I texted her to ask why they were too busy to find the time to stop by, she would come up with every excuse she could. I thought to myself, *If I hadn't been there, she would've had to stop by to feed the cats, right?* I reasoned in my head that her grandmother could have fed the cats for her, seeing that her schedule was so busy. But for some reason, deep down I knew better than that. After going to the house for days with no one stopping by, I finally gave up on the hope of seeing anyone.

A couple weeks went by, and I returned to my dad's house to stay for a few days. I walked back to Gloria's bedroom, and as I stood in the doorway, I reached over to flip on the light switch. I looked at Gloria's bed and noticed a plastic powder puff container sitting there. This seemed like an odd place for someone to leave it, but I thought nothing more of it. I picked the container up to put it back on top of Gloria's dresser only to find cat vomit underneath it.

Wow, I thought. *Someone noticed the vomit, and instead of cleaning it up, they placed something over it...Hmm, weird.* It seemed disrespectful at best, especially since Gloria had taken her last breath here on this bed. *Why in the world would someone do that? Someone couldn't possibly be that busy, could they?* I cleaned up the vomit and tried to give whomever the benefit of the doubt.

Afterward, I also cleaned up around the rest of house. It was filthy. Gloria and Dad would have never lived in a place that looked like this. With three cats still in the house, as you could imagine, there was cat hair everywhere. I went to get the vacuum from the front closet, but it wasn't there. *Someone must have moved it,* I thought. So I went back to Gloria's walk-in closet, but no vacuum. I looked all over, no vacuum. Someone had taken it. *Wow, are you kidding me?* I thought. *There are cats still in this house, and you're going to take the vacuum?* The vacuum had been purchased right before Gloria and Dad passed. It had all the bells and whistles, one of those five hundred dollar gems, and someone had decided to take it. Classy...very classy.

No one had touched the yard either, so leaves had piled up. I'd never taken on such a task, but I decided to give it a shot.

Since my dad's yard took up three and a quarter acres, I went down into his shop to get the leaf blower I had seen down there before. It was one of those awesome heavy-duty things with the shoulder straps; it had a backpack and all. I looked around, and wouldn't ya know it…it was gone. Someone had taken it too. *Great! So not only are people taking things, they are taking things that we need to use to keep the house up.* I wondered if I was dealing with dumb people or greedy people, or both.

I looked around Dad's shop for something else to use. There were several rakes, but with that much ground to cover I needed something that would get the job done faster. After looking around a minute, I finally spotted a small handheld leaf blower. I took it out into the yard and cranked it up. I pointed it toward the leaves, and it barely did anything—the leaves were piled too high; what's more, they were wet and all stuck together near the bottom of the piles, so the "force of gusto" that blew out from the machine barely pushed the leaves even a few feet.

After working for an hour or so, I stopped to take a look at my progress. After all that work, I hadn't done much. I had barely made a dent. I took a look around and felt overwhelmed by the surrounding leaves that covered the yard. I said out loud to God, "I've never done this before. I need Your help. Will You tell me how to do this?" Then I heard Him say, "How do you eat an elephant?" I took a look around at the task before me, and suddenly I didn't feel so overwhelmed. I cranked the motor on the leaf blower one time, really hard, pointed at the mounds of leaves, and shouted, *"One bite at a time!"* God was simply saying to me that it was possible if I did it little by little. And I knew that with His help, I could do anything. Above the roar of the leaf blower's motor, I shouted, *"I can do all things through Christ who strengthens me!"*

I spent many a day after that working in Daddy's yard. I loved the feeling that I was looking out for my dad and taking care of his house for him. Since this was my first time having the responsibility of keeping up a home or a large yard, I had a new appreciation for what my dad and Gloria had done over the years to keep it so beautiful. It was a lot of work! I used to think Dad and Gloria would get out and work in the yard because they were bored. Well, not anymore! There was more that went into this than I had known. I had never done a lot of the work before, so just like I had done with the leaves, I would pray to God and He would walk me through every step to get the job done. The manual labor was great stress relief, and I loved spending that quality time alone with God.

— — — — — — —

Late one afternoon, I returned home to my father's house after spending the day out of town hiring an attorney. As soon as the door shut behind me, I fell to my knees and began to cry as I said out loud, "I'm so sorry, Dad! I'm so sorry, Gloria! Please don't be mad at me for hiring an attorney! I'm not trying to cause problems or make things harder than they already are! Please forgive me if I've disappointed you! I just don't know who I can trust right now! I didn't want to do this alone; things have gotten way over my head!"

I continued to cry there on the floor, and then I heard these words in my spirit: "There is no judgment on this side. We aren't mad at you—we love you! We are just here to support you. This is something that you, Jackson, and Rebecca all have to go through. It's just a part of your story during this lifetime. How the three of you choose to handle it is completely up to you. It is not for *us* to say whether your decisions are right or wrong. We are just here to love you and support you through it."

Later that evening, I found the key to my dad's safe in his closet. When I opened it, I found his original will (which didn't read quite like the one he had made eight years later, right before he died), divorce papers that he had filed to separate from Gloria several years earlier (which I knew nothing about), and manipulative letters from Gloria to my dad, most of them about me (in one letter she even wrote, "And you call that daughter of yours that could care less about hearing from you.") And to top it all off, I found envelopes of check histories from the bank, cash receipts, and whatever else could be used to keep tabs on how much money my father spent on me, all dated from the year Gloria came into my father's life up until I was out of his home completely at the age of seventeen.

I heard in my spirit, "How do you feel after seeing that?" And with all sincerity I thought, "I feel nothing but love for Gloria." I smiled as I recalled the love I had for her now. I finally knew what it felt like to truly forgive someone. If I had found these letters a year earlier, I would have been riotously mad; but all thanks be to God for the time she and I got to spend together before she passed away.

Unfortunately, Gloria and I had spent most of our time knowing one another under false pretenses, fighting an imaginary war between us that never even existed. Out of fear and what we assumed to be true about each other, we kept our defenses up. Instead of letting our guards down, we each drew a line in the sand, keeping our relationship just above the surface.

At the end of it all, we finally realized that we were two females who lived like strangers under the same roof together for years. She and I were ultimately just the same—two sweet women who needed love and support. We found out that what we needed was right there in front of us all along; we could have found this in each other. Unfortunately, after years of being hurt by people, we both went into survival mode. Instead of making our family stronger by having healthy relationships, we tore each other down by creating an environment more like "survival of the fittest."

— — — — — — —

I received a text from Rebecca letting me know that some of the money from my dad's IRAs and CDs would be dispersed that following Monday. She said that the three of us (Rebecca, Jackson, and I) didn't have to be at the bank at the same time, so I should just go ahead and be there that morning. She went on to say that she and Jackson would be going at separate times, but they didn't know when.

That Monday, I decided not to get up and rush over to the bank early. I sensed Rebecca had told me to be there at that time with some hidden agenda, so I waited until later that afternoon to go.

Around three o'clock, I headed that way. As I got closer to the lot, I noticed Jackson leaving the bank and then getting into my dad's truck. I pulled into the parking lot across the street, and I watched as he talked on the phone and backed the truck out of the parking space. I noticed he had put a sticker on the driver's side corner of my dad's truck. *How nice*, I thought, *he's already personalized it.* I wondered who he was talking to. Was it his wife? Was he telling her that he "got it" and was leaving the bank now? Was he feeling like a big shot? I waited until he pulled out of the bank's parking lot and was completely out of view. Then I drove across the street and parked in a space next to the bank.

I walked into the bank from the side door and saw Rebecca across the room, sitting at a desk opposite from one of the bankers. I walked toward her as she continued to talk with the lady. Rebecca then turned her head and watched me as I continued to walk her way. When I finally approached her, I smiled and said hello, extending my arms to hug her. She looked up in horror to see me standing there and shrugged her body away from me so I couldn't give her a hug or even make contact.

I looked over at the lady sitting across from her, and she looked just as displeased to see me. Standing there awkwardly with both arms still out, instead of putting my arms down I opted to pat Rebecca on the head. Looking back, after this juncture, it seemed more fitting than a hug anyway. Not feeling a warm welcome, I turned around and walked toward a couch on the opposite side of the room.

When Rebecca was done collecting her dividends, she stood to gather her things, thanked the woman at the desk, and walked out of the bank. The woman behind the desk then motioned to me that it was my turn to take a seat in front of her. I walked over and sat down.

I said nothing as she shuffled through papers and placed them one by one on the desk. When I had been sitting on the couch waiting for my turn, my eyes watered up with tears as I did my best to hide my emotions from anyone in the room that might have seen that embarrassing debacle. I thought about what I would say to this woman when it was my turn to sit down with her. I thought about cursing her out, but instead I said, "So, you knew Gloria before you knew my father?"

She looked up at me, shocked that I could have known this, and replied, "Um, yes. Rebecca and Jackson actually grew up in the house across the street from me."

It all made sense now. There was no other reason why this woman, who knew nothing about me, would look at me in such a way when I walked up to Rebecca. I thought, *She has to be on their side. But why?* Everybody who knew my dad loved him, and usually I was shown favor because of it. I knew there had to be a reason why this lady had chosen the stepkids' side instead of "team Dad."

After this revelation was made, her animosity started to recede. She began to place before me the checks that I was to sign in order to transfer my dad's funds over to me. As I signed the first one, I saw my daddy's name and my eyes welled up with tears. I promised myself I could do this and stay strong, but I just couldn't help it. This was awful. I started to forget the reasons why I should "keep it together." My daddy was gone, the family was falling apart, and all I had left of my father were these few pieces of paper—that was it. All that was left of my dad lay there before me.

Thinking of it *this* way, I couldn't hold back anymore. I just lost it. The tears streamed down my face like a dam had been broken. Whatever the lady had against me before I took a seat, it no longer existed. Seeing this sincere emotion for my dad, she completely softened to me. She handed me tissue after tissue, not knowing what to do to help. I nodded my head to thank her and put a tissue up to my nose with checks in hand; then I stood up and made my way over to the teller.

I placed the checks on the counter and slid them over her way. In front of me was more money than I had ever seen before; you'd think I would have been excited, but I didn't feel like I had just won any jackpot.

The teller cashed the first check and counted out several one hundred dollar bills before me. I cried even harder as I watched each bill being placed atop another on the counter. Those pieces of paper represented something totally different to me. Each one just reminded me of every hour my dad had spent at the pharmacy; every hour that he spent away from his daughter and wife while they were at St. Jude because he had to work; every hour

I walked in to see him at the hospital or behind the counter at a thankless job, miserable and angry because he hated being there; the years of school to which he dedicated his time and efforts, and for what? So it could all come down to this, a bunch of thankless people who could care less about someone's legacy, just picking apart what he had worked so hard to successfully amass?

A lifetime of pictures, events, times, places, honors, diplomas, first houses, achievements, victories, and accomplishments of a man who had accomplished so much by overcoming the odds flashed before me. I stood there desperate to make this all stop so that my dad's life, at the end of it all, wouldn't have been lived in vain.

As she continued to count, the teller softly whispered to me, "It's going to be OK."

I looked up at her and said, "Nobody will talk to me."

She replied, "I noticed some tension when you walked in."

Then I said, "Maybe I don't want this." I started to shake my head slowly from side to side, contemplating, as I took one step back. "If this is how this makes people act, then maybe I don't want it...I'll just walk away and leave it here with you."

She replied, "Don't you do it. You'll regret it."

"I thought when people came into money, they felt happy," I said. I had spent so many years striving for lots of money, the thing that supposedly would finally make everything all right. But it didn't feel like that. I looked at the teller and said, "Do you have my side of happy back there?"

She smiled gently and looked down to count the last few bills, then she handed them over to me. I stuffed this large amount of cash into my purse along with the remaining checks, thanked her, and then turned to leave.

CHAPTER 18

AFTER THE DEATHS of my father and his wife, I tried to spend as much time as possible in their home. I had a feeling it wouldn't be too long before that would no longer be possible. The vultures were swirling overhead, so to speak.

In hindsight I've come to understand that what my father had of value, in my eyes and those of many others, couldn't be bought or sold. I never thought the greatest part of him was weighed in a dollar amount—to me, a dollar sign was the last thing I thought of when I thought about what I loved most about my daddy. It seems strange to me now, but thankfully "strange" just meant I had character.

When my father was ill, it never crossed my mind that I might come into some money if he died. Looking back over the whole time he and his wife were ailing, I can honestly say that it never occurred to me that I would come into an inheritance. It never entered my mind. My only concern was the well-being of my father and his wife.

I said earlier that it seemed strange to me, because little did I know at the time, money was the first thing on everyone else's minds around us. It makes me shiver and creeps me out to think now that everyone was just there for them waiting on their payout.

I'm sorry, Daddy, and I'm sorry Gloria—it should not have been that way. I love you, and I know so many people who love you too. People who miss you every day like I do. People whose eyes well up with tears just at the mention of your name. People who know that your memory isn't made of money—money isn't mentioned when people share their stories, their admiration, and their love for you. I've never heard anyone say, "Ooh, that Mister James was a good man! He had a *la'ge* bank account!"

The moral of all this is, ashes to ashes, dust to dust. Be sure you make something of worth in this lifetime—and I'm not talking about how much paper you manage to gather until you make it out of here either! They say you can't take it with you. It's pointless, if you ask me—the love of money and money being your only goal, guide, reason to live, work, your true north—it's pointless. God even paves the streets in heaven with gold. Money is so meaningless and worthless to God that He walks on it!

I did my best to hold on to all of the cash and not spend any of it before I came up with a plan. I even bought books like "Investments for Dummies," trying to learn all I could. I wanted so badly to figure out what I should do to make it last, and also to figure out what God would have me do with it. I had a few ideas, including opening a salon of my own, but this still didn't feel right; it was as if something in me knew that just wasn't the plan for me. So I hesitated and procrastinated, not knowing what to do.

I figured I could at least go back to work at the salon to try it again and see if it could work. I thought that if anything, they could spend their money to run a business; I could work for them and save all of mine. I decided to try this first before spending my cash.

As I toiled over and over in my mind what I should do, God put it on my heart that no matter what I did or didn't do, this money was not going to last. I heard Him say this and always tried to brush it off, thinking, "Nah, it will be OK! It's going to last, You'll see!" I knew deep down that what He was telling me was fact, but I just didn't want to think of how awful it would feel when that day became a reality. So I just kept moving forward like this wasn't in my near future.

God did say something about this that I couldn't deny, though. He said, "If you become successful after receiving this money, then everyone will think it was because of your earthly father. Gabriel, did he ever bless you or love you the way I do?"

I answered, "No, God, he didn't."

Then God went on to say, "When you do rise above your circumstances and become what the world considers to be 'blessed,' people will not say it was because any man had done it. It will make everyone that witnesses it say, 'If it had not been for the Lord that was on her side!' No one—not even you, Gabriel—will be able to take *any* of the credit for what I'm about to do in your life!"

Instead, God chose things the world considers foolish in order to shame those who think they are wise. And he chose things that are powerless to shame those who are powerful (1 Cor. 1:27).

━ ━ ━ ━ ━ ━ ━

I rented a small house with a fenced-in backyard. It was perfect, especially since I had a new dog. I had rescued a puppy a week earlier and named him Raymond James Cash, respectfully. I called him Cash, for short. My kids were all safe now—Bliss, Reese, and Cash—we were all together in our new home. We didn't have to worry about fights or threats of anyone harming us or kicking us out. We were finally home.

I sat enjoying my front porch one evening, when I thought to myself, "Well, Gabriel, you can buy anything you want. What would be the one thing you could buy now that would make you happy?" The only thing that came to mind was Leo. He was the only thing that was missing from my life, the one thing that would make me feel complete. But he couldn't be bought. I guess money really can't buy you happiness after all.

━━ ━━ ━━ ━━ ━━ ━━ ━━

The first week of January 2014, I woke up to the peace and security of living alone. As I sat up in the silence and placed both feet on the floor, though, I felt tired and unmotivated. Since I had so much free space and there wasn't much action or drama going on, I thought to myself, *It's time for me to go back to work.*

I received a call from my best friend, Jacob. I commented on the fact that I felt forlorn, and he suggested, "Well, then, let's go get the bike! Go get the cash out of the bank and then I'll meet you at your house."

I met Jacob and another friend at the Harley dealership. Leo's truck was there. I took a deep breath and then walked inside. We asked to speak to someone in the finance department, and immediately someone directed us to the back of the lobby, down a short hall, and into a small office.

I told the girl behind the desk the situation, and she picked up the phone and dialed the finance department. When she got someone on the phone and explained that I wanted to pay for the bike with cash, the man on the other end said that this couldn't be done. She then handed the phone over to me. I lay into the guy, saying, "You guys want money for these bikes, right? Then why won't you take my money and let me pay off this bike? This doesn't make any sense."

Suddenly, as if out of nowhere, I heard God say in my spirit, "It's not time." I had done this on my own accord. I hadn't talked to Him before I went there, and He had never told me to go up there in the first place.

It had now become quite clear to me why paying this bike off was an impossible feat. It was like I had hit a wall, an impenetrable force. *And I had.* This force was God. Everything should be done according to His plan—in His timing, not in our own. I acknowledged this truth just as I was opening my mouth again to protest to the woman sitting across the desk from me. I very quickly closed my mouth and handed the phone back to her. I slid back from the edge of the chair and relaxed my back against the chair, as if to surrender. I looked down at the floor as my mind-set and perception shifted. I lifted my head up and kindly thanked the woman for her time. I stood up to leave, giving a look over to my left and then my right shoulder at both my guys, and they caught the cue that it was time to go.

Of course, as I'm sure you very well know, I didn't just go there for the bike. I went there, more than anything, trying to get Leo's attention. I wanted him back but didn't know how to go about it. My life was in a much calmer place now—I didn't have any stress—so I figured maybe we could give it a try; it might work this time. I thought about joining the gym he went to. I went to night spots that I guessed he might frequent. But still nothing. I had blocked him on my Facebook, but on the twenty-sixth of January, before going to bed that night, I unblocked him.

The next morning, I woke up with a message from him: "I have been trying religiously to get in touch with you!" And again I tried to play it off like the interaction was no big deal. He asked, "Did you get the letter I sent you? I couldn't find you so I sent it from another Facebook page." I hadn't received anything, so he sent it via Facebook Messenger. My heart was all aflutter. He sent me a three-page letter, and it was everything I'd always dreamed I'd hear him say. In times past, I had made the mistake of letting him come around too soon, but I didn't care about all that right now. I had lost people and wasted time not loving them while they were here on Earth—I didn't want to waste any more time. Leo loved me and I loved him.

He asked me to stop by his job while I was out running errands that day. He took his sister to the gym, and then he went to my house later that night. In his letter, he even offered that we go to church, counseling—whatever it would take to get us right. I was down.

With Leo back in the picture, my life felt perfect. It was complete. This was the first time in my whole entire life that nothing was missing from it. I had money, Leo, a job, and peace of mind. *Wow.* I tried to relish in this new state of being and just enjoy it. It's so cool, actually, if you don't have anything to worry about or be sad about...so what do you think about then? This was all new for me. Never before had I experienced not having *one* problem in my life. Life was finally good...no, it was better than good—it was *amazing*!

— — — — — — —

Leo had been back in my life for a week. I *loved* it! I was so happy, but still there was a "knowing" that God was watching and He wasn't pleased. I tried to ignore it.

One day after work, I was back in my bathroom while Leo was up front. I heard God say, "Whatcha doin'?"

I thought, "Oh, not much. How are You? Good to hear from You! Talk later, OK?" trying my best to brush Him off, for now. I loved being back with Leo and didn't want to hear God say that I couldn't be.

God continued, saying, "You didn't talk to Me before you brought this boy back into your life." The jig was up. I knew I couldn't go any further without talking to God about it. I knew I was doing something on my own accord and not His, so I stopped what I was doing and paused to listen. God then told me, "If you want to keep this guy in your life so much, I'll let you...but *only* under My terms. Now go in there and tell him that you have a call on your life and if he can't support you in that, then he can't stay."

After hearing this, I sighed in disappointment. I knew Leo would never go for this. What's more, Leo was probably not at all turned on by the fact that I was some "Miss Suzy Super Christian."

I wanted so badly to do God's will, but at the same time I wanted to keep this other life—to somehow be able to juggle both of them simultaneously. On the other hand, I knew the truth that one foot in and one foot out never works. God's Word says in Revelation 3:16 (ESV), "So, because you are lukewarm, and neither hot nor cold, I will spit you out of my mouth."

I loved my Leo, but I loved God more. I knew there was no getting around this. I had to go up there and tell Leo what God had just said.

I took a deep breath and walked slowly toward the den. I drug my feet, with my shoulders slumped forward—I looked like a little kid being sent to her room. I was not thrilled at all about what was about to come out of my mouth. I stood in front of Leo and took another deep breath, and then let out a sigh. "I gotta tell ya something."

He looked at me and smiled big, waiting to hear. Finally, I just spit it out: "I have a call on my life, and I need you to be supportive of that. You don't have to believe what I believe right away, but God said that if you can't support me in this journey...then you can't stay." And just as I had suspected, the fight was on. We fought all night. We even let the sun go down on our anger.

— — — — — — —

It seemed like almost every night for more than two weeks we came home and fought about something. There was no peace—not for long, at least. No matter how hard we tried, no matter whatever conscious effort we both put in, the atmosphere in the house was one of war and conflict. However, we got along really well if we were having sex.

One day I told a fellow employee, "It's like there's something in the house that's *making* us fight. When I moved in, the house didn't *feel* like it was haunted, not like it did in the last house I lived in."

Every morning Leo and I would vow to do better. We would spend the entire day thinking of ways and preparing our minds to come home to each other. Both of us determined to make it through an evening without getting into some kind of dispute or yet another stupid argument. We would finally return home so excited to see each other and spend a couple good hours together, but before we even knew what was happening, the house would suddenly turn into a war zone. Most nights, after fighting for hours, we would be exhausted, not really knowing what we were fighting about and how it all began in the first place.

As the days went by, it seemed like no matter how hard we tried to refuse to give in to the anger and bitterness that surrounded us, it would always prevail. Somehow it would manage to outsmart us and eventually get the better of us as it continued to gradually get worse. After so many days, the bad in the house had systematically grown so large that it pushed out all the good we had left.

I remember one night, during one of our skirmishes, being down on my knees, crumbled over on my bathroom floor. Leo had gone up to the front of the house so we could get some space from each other. Exhausted and at my wits' end, all I could do was hang my head and cry. The agony from all of this—wanting so badly just to be with Leo and to love him, and at the same time dealing with the constant, uncontrollable conflict that kept us from just enjoying one another—was overwhelming and had become unbearable. The anguish I felt turned my sobbing up a notch higher. I cried harder and louder as I searched in my mind for a way, an answer—some kind of resolve to this matter.

It seemed an injustice now, but we had no one to blame but ourselves. *If the two people involved were taken to court, only to be found guilty of such charges, then who would be left to stand trial as the prisoners were both led away? No one. Why did the only answer that made any sense have to be the one that ultimately meant that we would no longer be together? How could this be? How? If two people love each other, shouldn't it just work? Well...shouldn't it? Tell me!*

All I wanted was there in my house—the one person who consumed my every thought for months; my reason for living; the person I longed for; the reason I cried myself to sleep every night; the one and only thing that I daydreamed about constantly because he was all I knew to be my one true happy place. He was here now, the one I dreamed of, like an answer to my wish come true...and yet it was still torture. I thought about what would happen if this didn't work out and he left once again. As I counted the cost, I considered how much worse it would feel to miss him, just hoping and praying to be able to see his face again.

These thoughts and revelations suddenly turned my crying into bloodcurdling screams as I tried to push the pain that resided deep within me out onto the bathroom floor. *Why must love equal pain? I thought it meant harmony!* I didn't want to be a part of this anymore. At the same time, I never regretted the day we met, because I would have never known him or experienced a love like this. Suddenly it became clear to me: it *is* better to have loved and lost than to have never loved at all. Yet there was a casualty of this knowledge lying there on her bathroom floor—in distress, defeated, and crying out for a solution that would not come soon enough.

Everything around me in that room seemed to disappear as I found myself crying out to God, "Why do You keep taking everyone that I love away from me? Why?" I rocked my body back and forth, wrapping my arms around myself, and began to cry and scream louder. My desperate need to find an answer and break free from this vicious cycle, a cycle that seemed to keep me trapped, increasingly superseded how I may have looked to anyone at this point. Saliva fell from my mouth as I gasped for air, trying with all of my might to push out the torment I felt inside, but still to no avail.

I didn't hear Leo come into the room, but I became aware of his presence when all of a sudden I felt his hand on my back. He gently rubbed up and down, doing his best to comfort me. He then crouched down beside me and continued to soothe me with gentle words: "Shh...baby, it's OK. I'm here. I'm not going anywhere. I'm right here."

One night we went to go do some grocery shopping. In the parking lot a couple called out to him, "Leo!" He turned and went completely silent. I could tell he was at a loss for words, like he wanted to pretend that he didn't know these people. They went on, "Yeah, by the time we see you, you're usually wasted anyway!"

I assumed they were talking about the pool hall he frequented when we were broken up. I played it off cool and never let on to Leo that I could see right through him as he fumbled over his words, hoping that these two people would just go away.

They walked ahead of us, and right before we reached the door, I said, "What were you up to while we were broken up? Was there a girl?" And then finally, after I had inquired for the past two weeks, he finally admitted, "Yeah." I would soon find out there were several; one had even been his "official girlfriend" for the past few weeks.

I just wanted to go home now. I could barely drive considering how angry I was. While I spent months being sad and alone, he was out having a ball, enjoying himself. Leo busted up my house and was the reason I had to stay with my mom (who threatened to take my dog and cat to the pound if I left the house for two minutes, leaving me with no social life at all); he bailed on me and didn't pick up the phone while my dad and his wife were dying; he had me pining over him for months— and during all this he was out there chasing skirts while riding the motorcycle he wouldn't have had in the first place if not for me! Nah, I was *not* OK with that. I reached for my rear view mirror, and it came off in my hand, I threw it in the backseat, barely missing his head.

When we got home, I could not sit still. I paced the floors as I asked him for details. "How long were you and this girl together?"

"Three weeks."

As I tried to digest this, he said, "And I slept with her too."

I covered my ears and walked back to my bedroom as I called out, "Oh my God, Gabriel, it's going to be OK! Oh my God! Oh my God!"

Then he called out again, "It didn't mean nothin'! I used a condom!"

I walked back up to the front of the house and stood there looking at him. With everything I had been through, his life had never stopped. Before I even had a chance to try to stop myself, I lunged at him, coming through the glass coffee table that stood between us. I flipped it out of my way and cold-cocked him three times. Wailing, crying, and in a rage, I stopped, got off of him, and went back to my room. I tried to keep my distance from Leo.

Later that night Leo lay on the couch and went to sleep, but I just couldn't wind down; I didn't know what tomorrow would hold. There was no going back from here. I wanted to erase it all. I went up to the front room and squeezed my way beside him to lay down on the couch. I said, "I can't go to sleep. I don't want to go to sleep, because then I'll have to wake up tomorrow knowing—" Before I could say it, he finished my sentence: "...what kind of piece of garbage I really am."

The next morning we woke up and there was no peace between us. I was off that day, and he headed to work. He didn't text me, and when I finally reached out to him it was like pulling teeth trying to get him to answer. "Wow," I said, "when you switch, you *switch*." I could tell he was already gone.

He stopped by the house after work to get his things. I opened the door thinking he was home and we were going to work it out.

I opened the door, smiling, when he said, "I need to get my stuff."

With tears in my eyes, I said, "What? No, Leo, please don't." But it was like talking to a wall; he had already made up his mind. Of course I was mad about what happened. But I loved him far more, so I thought we could work it out. It was *him* that did me wrong, right? So why is *he* the one who's leaving and I'm the one begging him not to go?

I wanted him to talk to me before he left, so I closed the storm door and wouldn't let him come in. I knew if he got his things, that would be the last time we talked, and I didn't want that to happen—not after all we had been through. I just knew it would start the same old cycle, and we would end up back where we were pretty soon, sad and missing each other. But how could we make it stop?

He even went so far as to call the cops. When the police arrived, I stood at the door and watched the interaction between Leo and the cop. Suddenly the cop pushed Leo, and hard. Then the officer walked up to my door, and I let him in. The policeman said, "If he talks to *me* that way, I can't imagine how he talks to you! Now where is his stuff? Just give it to him so he'll get out of here." I complied, and then Leo was gone.

That was the week of February 13, the three-year anniversary of Ethan's death. And of course, Valentine's was the next day. *Oh joy!* I made it through, though. That following Sunday, my friend Alexis took me by the bar that Leo always went to, the place where he had met this girl he'd dated. She wanted to show me what a slum it was so I wouldn't worry. She promised that whomever he had met there wasn't much of a prize.

We went in about an hour before the bar closed. I ordered a beer and sat in awe looking at the people around us. These definitely weren't my kind of people. I went to the restroom, and while I was in there I read the writing on the walls. Now, it's not out of the norm to see writing on bathroom walls—but here, you didn't want your name on these walls. These roughnecks weren't playing. Again, these were not my kind of people. I went home feeling dirty. Even still, he was getting laid and I wasn't; he had a life and I didn't.

I was sick of having strife with him. If things were going to end again, I wanted to at least try to make them end on less of a bad note. So late Monday night I sent him a text telling him that I was sorry how things went and that I loved him very much. I told him that any girl would be lucky to have him.

The next day, I texted him at work to see if he had gotten my texts from the previous night. We talked until it was time for him to get off work. I thought things had gone well and misread the signs as usual, reading his texts and hearing what I wanted to hear instead of what he was really saying (i.e., I said, "How do we move on and be happy?" [I meant with each other]; he answered, "I know, I want to move on and be happy" [he wasn't talking about moving on with me]).

I told him that I was about to get in the shower and he should come over and join me. (I know, I know. I can see the error of my ways *now*. *Sigh.* Love makes people so dumb!)

He replied, "Really? I'll be there after I leave work."

Everything seemed fine that night. We ordered pizza, watched a movie, and took that shower. We had sex a couple more times.

At one point, as he was drying off from the shower, Leo asked me, "Baby, are we too far gone?"

I answered, "No, baby! Now, if you're asking that, that's what you really believe." I tried to pay all the signs no mind. I knew in my gut that he was on his way out, but I wanted him to stay so badly that I tried to ignore the truth.

The next day, I ran home from work on my break thinking that he would still be at the house like in weeks past. I grabbed two coffees and ran home to see him. I texted him, and he said he wasn't there. I said, "Please come over!" I could sense his hesitation.

When I get to my door, the key I made for him was hanging in the door. He had left it that way after he left that morning—sign number 81,000 that he didn't have any intent of coming back. Before I got to the house, I had sent him a text, "I love how it feels to be happy," but I heard nothing back.

When he got to the house, we sat down and enjoyed our coffees. I asked him, "So are we back together?"

He said, "We can't just go on like nothing even happened the other night. You hit me, Gabriel."

Tears welled up in my eyes. "I know, and I'm really sorry. I just thought we could move on from there."

He let out a sigh. "I knew I shouldn't have come back over here. We can't live together. We can still be together, I'll still text and call you and stuff, but I'm not going to live here."

I knew what "I'll still text and call you" meant. It made me sound like I would be a "jump off" (somebody just there for his convenience while he still did his thing, not a real relationship). I wasn't going to sit around and wait for him to call like I had done so many times in the past.

Then he said, "It's already done. I've already moved in with my boy Jay."

I was a wreck again. I was in a panic. I felt like there was not enough time to get this resolved. I wished I didn't have to go back to work. I paced the floors trying to think, but there was nothing for me to grasp. There was no going back; he was already gone. I wanted the guy back who had been there two weeks earlier, the one who had written me the letter, but he was long gone.

"I do not accept your offer," I told him.

I had to go back to work; I had a client coming in fifteen minutes. Distraught, I didn't know what to do. I thought to myself as he walked me out to my car, "Gabriel, you know how bad you've missed him—do you want to go through months of that again? Drop your pride! Tell him, no matter the cost or how desperate you look. Who cares? You know your life is even more miserable when he's gone. Three months from now when you're crying because you miss him, what would you wish you had done right now in this moment to keep him from leaving? Do it!"

I turned to Leo and grabbed his hands. Sobbing, I cried out to him, "*Please* don't leave me! I'm so sick of missing you! *Please* don't go!"

He said, "Shh...it's OK, baby. OK, I won't go. You have to go to work. Don't worry, I'm not leaving."

I did my best to pull it together, and I headed back to work.

▬ ▬ ▬ ▬ ▬ ▬ ▬

I called Leo in the middle of the day, and he didn't pick up. I called him when I left work, but still nothing. Finally, he sent me a text that was so not like him: "I'm busy, I'll call you in an hour."

Oh my God, it's happening again! I thought to myself. I dialed him over and over and texted him, "Leo, don't do this!"

He sent me a text, "Turning phone off now, I'll call you in an hour!"

I pulled my car over to the side of the road, too upset to drive. I cried out, anxious and panicked, "*Why* is he getting away with this again? *Why? I can't believe this is happening!*" I can't describe the pain I felt. Add that to the pain of being rejected and abandoned by him once again—I was starting to lose count.

I got to my house, and all I could do was wonder when I would hear from him. I was consumed with it.

Finally, the phone rang. When I answered it, Leo said, "I can't do this anymore." Then he hung up. I cried and panicked, trying to ring his phone and text him so he would pick up and talk to me. But nothing. I sat and cried, feeling exhausted and brokenhearted, among many other emotions. I didn't know how to calm myself down. *How am I going to survive after this? Is it possible?* I sent him one last text: "Leo, *please* pick up the phone or we will never have another chance to talk again."

In my mind, I recalled a teaching of T. D. Jakes that I used to listen to all the time titled "Nothing Just Happens": "I don't want you to beg another person to call you, love you...hang it up! Remember...*nothing just happens!*"[1] Then I made a vow to stop trying to contact Leo. This was over. It was time to stop. I blocked him from my Facebook, and I blocked him from being able to text or call my phone. I put my phone down, wrapped both arms around myself, and rocked back and forth, saying, "Break the ties that bind...Break the ties that bind."

---

1 Bishop T. D. Jakes, *Nothing Just Happens*, "Nothing Just Happens," DVD, https://store.tdjakes.org.

CHAPTER 19

RUN AFTER YOUR DESTINY

So Elijah went from there and found Elisha son of Shaphat.
He was plowing with twelve yoke of oxen, and he himself
was driving the twelfth pair. Elijah went up to him and
threw his cloak around him. Elisha then left his oxen
and ran after Elijah. "Let me kiss my father and mother
goodbye," he said, "and then I will come with you."

—1 KINGS 19:19–20

IN MARCH, I believed within my heart of all hearts that God wanted me to lay down my job so I could pick up my cross and follow Him. As it was explained to me, He didn't want me to miss out on an opportunity to do His will because I was instead making the "world's economy" my god and not Him.

In 1 Kings chapter 19, Elisha was plowing behind a group of oxen when Elijah rode past him. He felt that this man was tied to his destiny somehow, so Elisha burned his oxen and plow and left everything behind to follow Elijah. He chose to run after a man he didn't know yet, leaving behind everything he did know to follow what he believed to be his destiny.

After giving it another try at the new salon location, I was met with the same trials and difficulties—some even worse than the time before. This led me to believe that God wasn't going to allow me to feel comfortable in this environment (or any, for that matter), a place where I didn't belong anymore and where He hadn't put me in the first place. I knew that my season here was done. Over. *Finito.* He was leading me—rather, *pushing* me—into another place so that His will would be done and not my own. I felt like an eaglet being pushed out of the nest.

> Like an eagle that stirs up its nest and hovers over its young, that spreads its wings to catch them and carries them aloft.
>
> —DEUTERONOMY 32:11

To add to my already confused "fish out of water" state of being, God didn't even give me a chance to try out my new "land legs" before laying another one on me. He put it on my heart that I needed to tithe 10 percent of the money I had received from the inheritance. I crumpled to the ground knowing there was no way around it. A year ago He had told me to tithe ten dollars out of the last one hundred dollars I had to my name. This was hard enough to do when I *didn't* have money. Now that I *did* have a large chunk of change, would I bring Him the 10 percent?

As I rationalized and weighed out all the options in my head, He asked me, "So you can believe everything else you read in the Bible, but when it comes to this... you want to ignore *this* part? You can't just keep the parts that work for *you* and toss out the rest!"

I knew that anything and everything I had was only because of God. I knew, like always, that He was right. I also knew that if I wanted to continue walking with Him and receive *everything*

He had in store for me during my time here on Earth, I had to fully commit and bring Him the tithe.

> "Bring the whole tithe into the storehouse, that there may be food in my house. Test me in this," says the LORD Almighty, "and see if I will not throw open the floodgates of heaven and pour out so much blessing that there will not be room enough to store it."
>
> —MALACHI 3:10

I didn't belong to a church at the time, so I wasn't sure where to take all this money—seven grand, to be exact. There was a huge church I had gone to a couple times in the past. They had an office with someone there all day every day, and you could go there to pay your tithes or to sow a seed. It seemed like the best, quickest solution at the time, so I *forced* myself to stop by there one day before work. Almost a week had passed since God had put this instruction on my heart, and every day since then He had reminded me to do it. Something in me sensed that I didn't have much time because something in my life was about to shift. This sign of obedience was important before this shift would take place.

On a Friday morning, I ran through the church with an envelope filled with seven thousand dollars cash in hand. I wanted to get it over with before I could change my mind. I ran forever, it seemed. This place was more like a compound.

After making my way down three long hallways, I turned a corner and finally caught sight of a lady sitting behind a desk. I made my way toward her and down the final stretch—the only thing between she and I was a long wheelchair ramp. I had on a small-heeled boot, which made it hard to run (plus, I smoked cigarettes).

Just as I reached the bottom of the ramp, she and I locked eyes. I stopped and put both hands on my knees, pausing for a second, trying to catch my breath. The lady sat there and watched me, amused, not sure yet what was going on. I stood up, gasping for air, and took off running again—dragging myself at this point—trying to make it up this small hill. I made it up to her desk (it was surprisingly tall, almost past my chest) and plopped both arms on top of it, gasping for air. I handed her the envelope. I could barely speak. "Here. Just take it."

The woman looked so confused as she took the envelope from my hand. "What is this?" she asked. "Do you want to tithe this? Do you need a receipt?"

I shook my head and waved my hand no. "Don't open it until I'm gone," I said. Then I turned around, and after taking one more big breath, I ran as hard as I could away from her and back out into the parking lot to find my car.

━━ ━━ ━━ ━━ ━━ ━━ ━━

By the first of April, things had finally come to a head between me and the people (corporate and managerial alike) at the salon. I was making more enemies than friends, it seemed. Once again, they all hated me; only this time, they hated me as soon as I walked through the door. I didn't stand a chance, because my new managers were aware that I had been pushed out of my former salon. This knowledge only served to further fuel the fire and their disdain for me, giving validity for their hate. *If the other place hated me, then it had to be all me, right? I get it.* If I were them, I probably would have thought the same thing.

During the grand opening party, I had to see all the people that I used to work with. One by one they took their jabs. I smiled politely and just took it. One guy walked in, and as soon as he saw me, he said, "There she is! There's the hooker!" These are grown people we are talking about here. What's even more disturbing is that some of these people have kids.

When my coworkers' behavior began to affect my clients, that was the final straw. I was uncomfortable, and so were my clients. It was not the kind of environment that any of us wanted to be in (let alone *pay* to be in).

After one of my clients and I were both treated very poorly, my client told her husband, and he became livid. She called me later that evening to tell me that he wanted to talk to corporate himself—how dare they treat either of us that way!

The following Monday, I was called into corporate myself yet again to "talk" about what was going on at work. In the days and weeks that led up to this, I had been trying to decide if I should stay at this job or not. I saw a story on the news about how our state representative was hoping to protect adults against bullying in the workplace, so I sent a brief e-mail to the representative to get his two cents. I kept trying to figure out if it was me, if I was making this all up, if I was in fact the problem and not them. I thought a second opinion from someone who had never met me would help me see things more clearly.

Less than fifteen minutes after I sent the e-mail, I received a response from the representative via text. He said that I was exactly the type of person that he was trying to protect by putting this bill into place. I knew then that it was time for me to stop second-guessing it and make the decision to leave my job.

After being pulled into the office, I sat and listened to one of the owners of the corporation as he tried to convince me that the sky outside was red (I had been more than sure, when I took a look at the sky before coming in, that it was blue). This is how badly their manipulative bubble had affected me in such a short amount of time. I couldn't tell which way was up or down. Nevertheless, he had brought me into his office for no other reason than to just *tell me* what was happening at work instead of hearing my side and then hopefully talking it out with me so we could eventually reach some kind of resolution. In a matter of words, all he had to say was that it was just a figment of my imagination.

Without coming to any conclusion on how to resolve the conflict other than to keep my mouth shut when I felt I was being treated unfairly, he then showed me the door. "Have a good day," he said. I went to open my mouth, but before I had a chance to speak, he continued, "...OK, that's great! See you soon. Buh-bye."

I went home later that afternoon, and Alexis met me at the house. I paced the floors in front of her as she sat on my bed facing me. I stopped in front of her and started pleading my case, trying to hear myself talk it out and to get her advice on whether I should go through with it and quit my job or not. She said nothing, so I started pacing again, talking out loud, going over all the pros and cons. I stopped in front of her again and asked a question. I could see "that look" on her face—the one where she goes into her cave and there's no coming back. The more I pressed for an answer—or for her to just to speak a word, *any* word at all—the further she retreated. She even pulled the neck of her shirt up to cover her face.

"What are you doing here, then, if you're not going to talk?" I asked. At this point I was used to this girl coming over and doing nothing more than taking up space. It annoyed me, mostly because her presence served no purpose; she would just sit and watch me live my life—I might as well have been home alone! I had a huge decision to make; I couldn't afford any distractions. Another day, maybe. But right now I didn't have time to go over this again with her. I knew all too well the usual game of "Why are you so quiet and awkward?" followed by *me* talking endlessly about how *she* felt and what I had done to make her like that. Oh *no*! I had become all too familiar with this 'round and 'round we go scenario. I couldn't let it get in the way of what I really needed to focus on.

I usually tried to be as nice as I could when she started to get on my nerves, but not today. I just asked her to leave. "I don't mean to hurt your feelings, but I'll have to deal with this later!" I said as I escorted her to the door. She walked slowly down the hall in front of me. I grabbed her coat and purse and handed them to her as we got closer to the door.

Before walking out she turned to look at me with tears in her eyes, like a lost puppy. I said, "Don't call to check on me or come back to see if I'm OK. I need tonight to be between me and God, no interruptions! We'll figure this out tomorrow. Bye!"

I spent the rest of the evening with God. I hung out, cleaning my house and whatnot, as I listened and talked it out with God, asking for His divine guidance and direction. I knew what I had to do. When I could no longer escape the clear answer of the Almighty God, I ran outside on the back patio so that I could look up into the heavens above as He continued to put instructions on my heart. Then He said, "Gabriel I don't want you always looking for miraculous signs and wonders to know that it's Me. Now go back inside and pray to Me in your bedroom; where there are four walls, carpet, and a ceiling. Can you see Me there? Can you see Me in normalcy?"

When I asked Him for the next instruction, the next step—what I was supposed to do after I quit my job—He said to me, "I'll tell you where you're going, once you get there. Now go."

> If you fully obey the LORD your God and carefully follow all his commands I give you today, the LORD your God will set you high above all the nations on earth. All these

blessings will come on you and accompany you if you obey the LORD your God.

—DEUTERONOMY 28:1–2

The following morning, after I left the corporate office, in my exuberance I said with a big smile, "What now, God?" He replied, "Well, Gabriel, why not just go enjoy the rest of your day?"

CHAPTER 20

It's in the House

I will put My Spirit within you and cause you to walk in My statutes, and you will be careful to observe My ordinances.

—Ezekiel 36:27, nas

B RIGHT AND EARLY one morning, I rose up in bed. I looked over at Alexis, who was still knocked out. I pushed the covers off of me and headed toward the kitchen to make my coffee. Still half asleep, I opened the pantry, and to my dismay there was no coffee in sight. "Grrr!" I grumbled out of frustration, letting out some steam. I'm just not what most people would consider a "good person" until I've had my morning coffee.

Begrudgingly, I accepted my fate and grabbed my keys. I headed out the front door and got into my car. *Why does the sun always seem brighter on days like this?* I drove out of my quiet neighborhood and into the hustle and bustle of the world. I then headed toward the nearest McDonald's. Still feeling groggy and not yet awake, I could barely keep my eyes open. I wondered, *If I were to be pulled over in this state, would I be charged with DUI? Oh well. Must...find...coffee!*

I made it to a Mickey D's at last. When I pulled up, I saw the longest line I'd ever seen at the drive-through, wrapping around the entire building *twice*. After waiting for almost twenty minutes, I ordered some dressed-up blended coffee drink over ice, dazzled up with whipped cream. At this point, I didn't care what it was; dress it up however you want—as long as it has caffeine in it and the taste somewhat resembles coffee, we are good!

The line took *for...ev...er*, and the employees weren't exactly glad to see customers. They begrudgingly took my order, not caring what any of us thought about "customer service."

I finally got my coffee and drove back toward my house. I went to take my first sip of what I had worked so hard for, and wouldn't ya know, it was watered down. It was merely something that resembled coffee. I took three more sips and then it was all gone, seeing how the ice inside the cup took up more room than the coffee itself. A mirage! I felt like I had been hoodwinked! I had barely gotten out of the parking lot, and the one thing I had worked so hard to attain was now outta sight.

I drove ten minutes or so back to my house, defeated. I was left wanting. I went inside my home, and Alexis was now awake. "Where'd ya go?" she asked. She was awake and perky like a brand-new cocker spaniel, which added to my already annoyed state.

Under my breath I said, "To get coffee." I went on to say, "It was awful...a waste of my time...ugh."

I walked into the kitchen, opened the pantry, and tossed my "empty" cup full of ice into the trash can. For some reason, my curiosity led me to double check the drawer where I keep the Keurig coffee pods. I slid the metal drawer toward me, and there before my very eyes were three pods of coffee. I looked at them in disbelief. I knew I had checked that drawer before I had left the house—the coffee was not there before. If it had been, I would have never left the house. Oh, the time, the effort, and the trouble I could have saved myself if I had just seen those earlier! Then I heard the voice of God, deep in my spirit, say to me, "What you need is in the house."

Oh, I thought. *God just used this as a teachable moment.* You don't have to struggle, nor do you have to suffer through a lot of unnecessary self-effort. *What you need is in the house.* You don't have to search far for God, nor do you have to search far to find His path, purpose, and will for your life. *It's in the house.* It's already been prepared for you. "Before I formed you in the womb I knew you, before you were born I set you apart; I appointed you as a prophet to the nations" (Jer. 1:5).

God doesn't want us to go out searching for the answer or to come up with our own "wise ideas" on how to accomplish His will for our lives. Remember, it's God's will, not your own. Let Him lead you and guide you, step by step. Don't search for the answers. Search for God, and then the answers will come. "But seek first his kingdom and his righteousness, and all these things will be given to you as well" (Matt. 6:33). Trust Him. His way is always easier than our own.

When in doubt, just remember, "What you need is in the house." The house is His temple, your body; your spiritual house that belongs to God. Submit the control over to Him, let Him take the reins, and life will flow. Things that once seemed difficult will be achieved with ease. "Let go and let God." Besides, your life is not your own; it belongs to Him. Until you come into agreement with that fact, your life will always seem like a struggle, an uphill battle. Nothing will ever make sense until you fully commit your life into God's hands. He loves you and wants what is best for you. He is calling; why don't you answer and say *"Yes!"* to God today!

"For I know the plans I have for you," declares the LORD, "plans to prosper you and not to harm you, plans to give you hope and a future."

—JEREMIAH 29:11

▬ ▬ ▬ ▬ ▬ ▬ ▬

During the next month and a half, I was amazed that I didn't think about or pine over Leo like I used to. Instead, I was spending most nights home alone with God. In months gone past, I used to be miserable sitting at home—crying, missing Leo. But not this time around.

I remember sitting out back one night just gazing at the moon, hanging out and talking to God, when for a quick moment my mind went to Leo. I thought that at the same exact moment, he was probably having sex with some girl. But it didn't hurt to think of such things, and I didn't stay there and dwell on it for long. I just took my thoughts back to God.

Even songs that came on the radio didn't remind me of Leo like they used to. Instead, they made me think of God! Every love song made me think of Him. It was as though I was singing them out loud to Him. Only this time, I was smiling and dancing when I sang, not crying and moping like I would have been thinking about Leo. Two songs in particular that made me think of how much I loved God were Amerie's "Why Don't We Fall in Love" and Stevie Wonder's "Signed, Sealed, Delivered, I'm Yours."

I was falling deeply in love with God, and every day that love grew deeper and deeper. He stayed on my mind. This new life with Him and the deep connection I now had with Him was so exciting and all so satisfying; nothing in this world could compare to it. All I wanted to do was be with Him and hear every word He said to me. My eyes, ears, mind, heart, and understanding had all been opened to a whole new world. The veil, so to speak, had been lifted. He was all that mattered to me now.

— — — — — — —

After dinner one evening, God instructed me to go outside and to bring Alexis. Recently I had discovered that behind my house was an open meadow lined with trees. I hadn't ventured very far off into the depths of it, so I was unaware of what might be back there.

I said, "God, what if we go back there and nothing happens? What am I supposed to do when we get out there? How am I supposed to show her You?" He said, "Don't preplan anything, and have no expectations. Just go."

So I told Alexis that God had instructed us to go outside. We put on our rain boots and headed out the door. We made a right and headed toward the dead end of my street. We stepped across where the grass meets the pavement and then made our way up a small embankment. We crept up and over the bank and then turned to our right as we made our way through trees, vines, and shrubbery. Leaves and broken limbs crunched and crackled beneath our feet.

We made it to a clearing and stepped out into an open field full of tall grass. We made our way through and then continued down a large hill until we finally came to a crossroads. Before us was a cleared pathway without any tall grass, shrubbery, or trees in our way; but to get over to the other side of it, we would have to go through some mud and murky water. As I inspected this option, I heard the croaking of toad frogs, so I decided against it. To the right of us was a densely forested area. There was a small opening in the trees, a cleared pathway it seemed, that led deeper into the woods. After considering both options, we decided to go through the trees.

After we walked down the path a ways, the forestry and shrubs got thicker, and it became harder to see where we were going. We had brought a flashlight with us, but God had instructed us earlier not to use any artificial light. Up until this point, we had kept the flashlight off. Alexis decided to turn the flashlight on and shined it around in front of us, hoping that we could get a better idea of our surroundings. She shined the light to our left, and there, amidst twisted vines and branches, sat one red cardinal. Upon our intrusion, he didn't move at all. He just sat, staring back at us.

"Wow," Alexis and I both said aloud. "Have you ever seen anything like that?" I asked her. "No," she said. I started to walk ahead, saying, "That must be a sign that we are exactly where we are supposed to be. Come on."

We stepped over and onto branches and foliage, pushing vines and trees limbs out of our way, doing our best to see our way clear through what looked like it had once been a cleared path. Then I heard God say, "Come find Me."

At this point, Alexis was a few feet behind. I started to make my way up a hill, and at the top of it, over to my left I could make out what appeared to be a large circle made out of roots, in between two trees. As I got closer so I could see it in better detail, it almost looked like a sculpture. It was magnificent in size and somewhat mystifying, this large, round, circular root; unending, winding, as though independently suspended in between the balances of these two trees, there on either side of it. After seeing this, I knew for sure I had not heard wrong; this was God talking to me. It reminded me of something I had come across earlier that day: "God's love is like a circle, no ending can be found..."

I went down the other side of the hill and walked a bit until I could go no farther. Standing there at the edge of a huge ditch, I started weighing out my present options. The only way to go on through the woods now was to cross over one of two logs that stood between us and the other side of this large ravine. There was no way around it. It was as though we had stumbled upon an obstacle course made just for us. *Who could have ever imagined that all this, off in the middle of nowhere, was behind my house?* Being back here, you forget that you are actually in the middle of the suburbs. I peered over into the large hole in the earth. It was dark; I couldn't tell how far it dropped off or what might be down there. I chose to not be a wimp and just go ahead and get it over with, giving it my best go.

I stepped onto one of the logs, gathered my balance, and then proceeded with one foot in front of the other. I stretched my arms out straight on either side to help keep me from teetering. I began to speak aloud, "When you walk in faith, you will not wobble." My stance was impeccable, my balance was centered, and I walked smoothly straight ahead. Then suddenly something came over me—the fear of "What if?" entered my mind. "What *could* possibly happen if I fell? What if this is really high off the ground? What if I fall and break something?" I started to tremble and almost lost my balance. Then I got my mind back centered, and said aloud, "But when you put your faith in God that He will get you to the other side..."—my balance quickly returned and my footing became sure—"you will not fall or fail. As long as you move forward without the fear of the 'what ifs,' God will carry you through..."—I got to the other side and put my feet on solid ground again—"landing safely, no matter the challenges you face."

I stood on the bank and celebrated by doing a victory dance. I thanked God and cried out to Him, "I can do all things through

Christ who strengthens me!" Then I looked over at Alexis, still on the other side. "Come on! It's your turn!" This reminded me of Matthew 14:28–33 (NAS), when Jesus walked on water:

> Peter said to Him, "Lord, if it is You, command me to come to You on the water." And He said, "Come!" And Peter got out of the boat, and walked on the water and came toward Jesus. But seeing the wind, he became frightened, and beginning to sink, he cried out, "Lord, save me!" Immediately Jesus stretched out His hand and took hold of him, and said to him, "You of little faith, why did you doubt?" When they got into the boat, the wind stopped. And those who were in the boat worshiped Him, saying, "You are certainly God's Son!"

Alexis crossed over, and we continued to walk through the forest. We were in deep now. Determined to not turn around and go back the way we came, we pushed forward, trusting that God was with us and would not forsake us on our journey. Even in the wildernesses of life, when we feel alone, He is there and walks with us, helping us until we find our way out and see our way clear.

We came to a place where the trail seemed to abruptly end. We were surrounded by trees, thorn bushes, and limbs; we could no longer see our way clear. From every angle it was think and dense all around us. We had somehow stepped off of the path, and had even lost sight of the distant lights from the houses that surrounded us in the neighborhoods nearby. The forest seemed to swallow us. We had lost our way. We couldn't make sense of which direction we had just come from and in which direction we should head. Feeling scared, I let Alexis take the lead. I wasn't thinking clearly. My thoughts scrambled rapidly with the fears of "what if."

I heard a noise over to our right; I jumped and shined the flashlight in that direction. I saw a plastic chair sitting under some brush next to what seemed to be a drop-off to some kind of a riverbank. The thoughts went through my mind: *There might be other people or another person out here with us... What if somebody's hidden away somewhere in the brush?*

I turned off the flashlight, and in my panic I tried to jump clear over Alexis as she patiently cleared a way for us to travel through the thorn bushes. "Go, go, go!" I shouted and scrambled to push her forward, trying anything to get her to move. I pushed us right into a bunch of branches full of thorns. The thorns grabbed us by our clothes. The sharp points pressed into our skin.

We stood still, trying not to move, now stuck in submission. We were covered in these prickly beasts from head to toe. I had made a mistake by trying to move faster because my imagination had gotten the best of me. This only hindered our process even further. If I had only been patient earlier and followed Alexis's lead, gathered my thoughts, and *slowly* made a way through the thistle by pulling each branch away, one at a time, like Alexis did, we would probably have been out of the woods by now. But no—because of my bright ideas, we were stuck in here like two flies trapped in a spiderweb! We could barely move an inch.

"Wait! Hold on! It's OK," Alexis reassured me. I stopped and cowered behind her, grabbing onto the back of her coat. She stayed calm and moved patiently, methodically, moving each limb of thorns away from us and finally clearing a path so we could move forward. *Whew!* I was glad she was there! In my panic I had made things worse. But she stayed focused, and by doing so she was able to resolve the problem without causing us more trouble. We were able to make it through this dense area into a clearer part of the woods.

We keep walking, trying to judge which way would get us out of there the fastest. Then we hit a wall, literally. Before us stood a tall dirt wall. There had to have been ten to fifteen feet of dirt between us and our way back home. We stood, staring at the top of it, as we weighed out in our minds what we should do next. It appeared to be all that was left of what had once been an old riverbank. Huge roots from the tree above us protruded out from the dirt and almost reached from the very top of the wall to the bottom.

Alexis decided to go left and find a way to get around it. I knew that could take forever, so I went with my first instinct. I ran straight toward the wall of dirt and jumped up, grabbing onto the large roots of the tree. I dug my feet in and systematically went branch by branch, pulling myself up like I was on a rock wall. As I questioned my strength and capability, I shouted, "I can do all things through Christ that strengthens me!" I made it to the top, and with both arms I lifted my body up and over the edge. I stood up and turned to look for Alexis. She was still standing down at the bottom, looking up at me in disbelief. She hadn't even begun to find another way out. I said, "Do it! You've got to, if you want out of there!" Not thrilled at the notion, she found a less steep and more slanted part of the bank with roots from a smaller tree. She grabbed hold and slowly pulled her way up and out. By this time, I was so ready to go and eager to find the rest of the way out. I stood there watching, just wishing she would hurry it up.

She finally reached the top, and we both turned away from the embankment to assess what our next challenge would be. This part looked less intimidating. We had to be close to an outlet by now. We were surrounded yet again by bushes and trees; there was no clearing to indicate in what direction we should go.

Then I remembered something God had put on my heart earlier that day: the star. I looked up and was reminded of the three wise men who followed the star that led them straight to Jesus. I looked up through the limbs of the trees and into the night sky. I spotted the North Star and pointed up toward it. I yelled out to Alexis as I took off running, "Follow the star!"

I pushed past the brush and limbs in my way and finally saw a clearing. *Yes! This must be it!* I ducked as I ran under the limbs that were above the opening I saw, then I stood to take a look around. *Have we made it?* Nothing looked familiar. Then, to my left, far in the distance, I saw dim lights coming from the houses in my neighborhood. And to my left I heard frogs croaking, coming from the muddy water at the bottom of the path, the one that we hadn't chosen earlier. *Yes! Victory!* I ran down the hill and toward the mud and water. I jumped over it, clearing it. After making our way through the challenges we had just faced, the frogs and mud didn't seem so intimidating this time around! I thought, *Piece of cake!*

CHAPTER 21

"My grace is all you need. My power works best in
weakness." So now I am glad to boast about my weaknesses,
so that the power of Christ can work through me.

—2 Corinthians 12:9

After receiving several harassing phone calls from "the children" (my dad's stepchildren), I had to meet the attorney over the estate in his office to sign some paperwork. I kindly obliged. While I was there, I asked him about the status of Gloria's estate. I was then told that it was none of my business.

Just as he said this, his secretary walked in and placed a document on the desk in front of me. I took a closer look; it was a quick claim deed. I had no idea what that was. I kept reading, and it mentioned something about a house. I looked at the address, which was completely unfamiliar to me. This document included Gloria's name and the names of both of her parents. I still had no idea what this was. *A quick claim deed? What's that? I guess I gotta google.*

I could have sworn that less than two minutes earlier the attorney had been telling me that I had no business sticking my nose into Gloria's estate. But if that was the case, then why was

I being asked to sign something that appeared to be a consent form, signing my rights away to something with her name on it? If they were all telling me that there was nothing in her estate, well then wouldn't zero equal zero? Why would nothing equal this? I was confused. The attorney offered no explanation, so I told him that I would be glad to sign it, just after I took it with me to get a better look at it.

Before I got up to leave, the attorney told me that I should be very grateful to Jackson and Rebecca—I was lucky to be getting even 10 percent. He told me my father resented me for all the money he had given to me over the years. The attorney told me I should be nice to Jackson and Rebecca, or they could take what I *was* getting away from me.

I looked down at the briefcase sitting next to his desk. Both sets of numbers on the top of it were on 555. The number 5 represents God's grace. I looked back up at the attorney and calmly said, "I don't believe you," before getting up and walking out of his office.

Not even an hour passed before I received a call from Rebecca. Throughout all this, God instructed me not to fight with them nor open my mouth to say a word, so I let the voicemail pick up. My stepsister went on to say that she didn't know what kind of game I was playing, and that I was to stay away from her family because I was dead to her. She was also nice enough to include that the house from the quick claim deed was certainly not meant for me, and as God is my witness, she was going to make sure that I didn't get it.

One thing I did know, after hearing all of this—I certainly felt all warm and cozy inside. I wasn't sure, though, which god she was referring to—without a doubt, it wasn't *the* one true God I know.

CHAPTER 22

AFTER MY ROAD to Damascus experience, God laid it on my heart that something was about to happen—the next "breaking." "How could this be?" I asked Him. "I'm Your child... if You really love me... Lord, I've been through enough as it is. Why would You allow something *else* bad to happen to me? What could You possibly take this time? I don't have much left for You to take... so it would have to be something *very* important to me, something I would hate to lose. Why would You put something so heavy to bear on Your servant, Lord? If I am highly favored in Your sight, then why would You make the load greater? Haven't I suffered enough?"

Then the Lord went silent. For an entire month, I heard nothing from Him. "We've been through so much—me quitting my job and stepping out to follow You, my gift of sight, and everything You've revealed to me. I used to hear from You continually day and night, even with seemingly small instructions—'Hey, Gabriel, turn left... turn right... open the door... pick up your shoes...'—and now, *nothing*? *Really*, God? You mean to tell me You're just going to leave me hangin' like that, left to my own accord... with no further direction?"

━ ━ ━ ━ ━ ━ ━

One afternoon, Alexis and I sat across from each other at a picnic table on the patio of a local bar and grill. I asked her, "I was doing fine without Leo, wasn't I? For a minute there it seemed like I was…don't you think? Now, all of a sudden, I can't stop thinking about him." As tears welled up in my eyes, I asked, "What happened?"

She shook her head and said, "I don't know…yeah, you seemed to be doing great at first."

I grabbed a napkin from the container in the middle of the table and wiped the mascara running from my eyes. Then I said, "I'm scared for him." No longer able to hold back my tears, I continued, "…why does he have to die? I don't want him to die."

Alexis stood up, put one leg on the other side of the wooden bench, and started to gather our phones and her keys. I looked up at her through tears, with one hand still holding the white cloth close to my face. She seemed worried and distraught; it seemed as though she was trying to find a way to make the conversation stop. Her body language suggested to me that it was time to go. With a concerned look on her face, she said, "Girl, something bad is about to happen to him on that bike. I don't know if he's going to get hurt or killed, but something is about to happen…We gotta stop talking about this. Come on, let's go."

▄▄ ▄▄ ▄▄ ▄▄ ▄▄ ▄▄ ▄▄

A few nights later, Alexis and I sat at my house watching TV. I sat in the recliner next to her on the couch, reading a book about numbers. I was reading a chapter that discussed the number six. I read the last paragraph out loud, which included a scripture from the Book of Revelation. It read: "This calls for wisdom. Let the person who has insight calculate the number of the beast, for it is the number of a man. That number is 666" (Rev. 13:18).

Suddenly, out of nowhere, all of the lights went out. Alexis and I looked over at each other, wondering what had just happened. We both thought it strange because there was no inclement weather that evening and no signs of an impending storm.

I stood up and looked out the window. The entire neighborhood was without power—for no apparent reason, it seemed. Within me I sensed what—or who, rather—the culprit was. Suddenly I bolted out of my front door and ran down the street. As I ran I shouted, "No weapon formed against me shall be able to prosper!" There was an eeriness about the sky above. I looked to my right and I saw ominous storm clouds start to form; they had a smoky, hot pink tint to them mixed with dark shades of gray. My running had now turned into a skipping, sideways gait. I called out to Alexis, who was trying her best to catch up with me. "This is it! He's going to let you see one of the signs in the clouds with me!"

I turned my attention from Alexis's face and back to the clouds overhead. I slowed down, coming to a stop, facing the houses over to my right. I stood there quietly, in disbelief, as Alexis approached and then turned to see what I was looking at. There, above the row of houses, a dragon had taken shape. He was magnificent in size. His long body was almost as tall in diameter as the houses below him, stretching over at least three or four homes. It appeared as though he was lying on his belly stretched across the rooftops. His legs seemingly wrapped beneath him, revealing only his paws and claws. His body ran parallel to the street beneath him, but his beastly head was turned facing toward us, so we could see all of his face. Although it was an image of a dragon, it appeared to be less menacing than you would think. But there, slap-dab in the center of his forehead, he bore a black cross.

> The great dragon was hurled down—that ancient serpent
> called the devil, or Satan, who leads the whole world astray.
> He was hurled to the earth, and his angels with him.
> —REVELATION 12:9

▬ ▬ ▬ ▬ ▬ ▬ ▬

The following Monday, I lay awake in my bed. It was early morning, around six o'clock. I hadn't had much sleep. The tornado sirens, which had started at three o'clock in the morning, were still going off. The light violet, pastel yellow haze from the color of the sky seeped into my windows. There was a strange sense in the air—a calm, a stillness—of an approaching storm, some kind of imminent danger on the horizon.

My thoughts went to Leo. I hoped he was OK. After you've broken up with someone, you want to ring their phone in times like this just to make sure they're safe from the storm. No alternative motives, no agenda—just sincerely making sure that they are OK. No more, no less; a five-minute call at best. But I decided that wouldn't be a good idea, so I just lay there.

News reports showed that tornados had caused massive damage just across the river in a small community called Mayflower, Arkansas. It crossed my mind that I would like to go help. I called Alexis and asked, "Do you want to collect some things for the people in Mayflower?" She excitedly said, "Yes! I've always wanted to do something like that!" I said, "I don't know how to go about it, but let's just do it!" I could hear her smiling through the phone as she said, "Cool! I'm excited!"

We agreed to meet at my house. Her stepdad said we could borrow his Chevy truck, so we headed to his house to switch vehicles. He had left a note instructing us to raid his pantry and take everything we wanted. Also, he had set out clothes and blankets for us to donate. I had also posted on Facebook that we were collecting goods to take down the next day.

New to this, Alexis and I headed to Wal-Mart to see if they would like to donate anything. We approached three female employees as they unpacked boxes and put new products on the shelves. I said, "Excuse me, we were wondering who we would speak with about donations to take to the tornado victims in Arkansas."

The oldest lady, who happened to be a manager, told us that we would first have to apply for a charity permit, come back, and present it to Wal-Mart customer service. I thought to myself, "Yeah...we don't have time for all that."

Then one of the younger employees replied snidely, "Wal-Mart will send a truck down there." Her attitude seemed to say, "Someone else will take care of it. Those people don't need any other help. Now...back to *my* day."

Alexis and I bought white poster boards and large markers and headed back to the truck. We both agreed that the employees would have a change of mind if the tables suddenly turned and *they* were the ones that had just lost everything. We pulled to the very end of the parking lot at a corner where traffic enters and exits. Not knowing if we would be run off or not, we took a minute to make a couple signs, letting people know that we were collecting donations. I thought it would be great if people saw our signs, went inside to shop, and also collected a few things to bring outside to donate to us. People honked and waved in support. One man stopped and gave us thirteen dollars.

A police cruiser circled the lot and then pulled up beside us. "We appreciate what you ladies are doing, but you have to have a permit to do that," the officer said. We jumped down from the tailgate and kindly obliged, throwing our signs in the back of the truck, and then left the parking lot. We were there for fifteen minutes at most, but hey, we tried it. That was all we could do, not knowing how to go about this. At least we gave our best try.

We returned to my house and pulled out things around my home to pack up in the truck. When I had first moved in, I'd bought a twin bed and box springs to sleep on for a few nights before I was able to have my big bed delivered. I didn't have any use for it now, so we loaded it up in the center of the truck bed. On either side we packed bags of groceries, blankets, clothes, and household goods. We decided to get some good sleep and leave first thing in the morning.

The following day, when we were almost there, only an hour outside of Mayflower, we stopped at the Wal-Mart right off the interstate. I wanted to grab at least a couple hundred dollars' worth of nonperishable goods and supplies, just one more load, before we dropped everything off. After shopping, we loaded the bags into the truck.

My dog Cash had come along for the trip, and Alexis took him out to the grass on the side of the lot. I sat on the truck's tailgate swinging my feet back and forth underneath me. In my mind, I thought about peanut butter sandwiches. *They are so good!* We had bought bread, jelly, and peanut butter for the families in need. I thought about how good those PB&J sandwiches would taste to the kids. I wanted one! I resisted the temptation to go into the bags and make one, though.

As I sat just thinking, kind of staring off into nothing, a car parked a couple spots down from the truck. A blonde, middle-aged gal stepped out with royal blue scrubs on. She was wearing a wedge heel, and had pep in her step. I thought to myself, *How cute she looks!* "I like your heels!" I said.

She turned her attention toward me and smiled. In that brief moment, I could already sense that this was one sweet lady.

She walked toward me, and with an inquisitive look, she asked, "What are you guys doing? Are you moving?"

I said, "No, ma'am. We're taking things down to Mayflower."

Then she asked, "Are you from around here?"

"No ma'am," I said. "I don't even really know where I'm at." I looked over both shoulders. "I'm from Nashville."

She smiled wide. "You guys need cheerleaders! Can I take your picture?"

I stood on the tailgate and waved to Alexis to hurry back. "Sure!" I said. "That's my best friend, Alexis, and my dog Cash. Wait for them."

As Alexis got closer, I told her, "She wants to take our picture." Alexis picked Cash up and put him on the tailgate with me. Then she pulled herself up and sat beside us on the tail bed. With Cash between the two of us, we each placed one arm around him and leaned our bodies toward him and smiled.

The woman said, "I'm going to post this on Facebook and say, "Two angels with a truck full of blessings heading to Mayflower."

I asked her if she wanted our names. As soon as I said the words, I wished I hadn't asked her that; a quick sense of regret flashed over me. She looked over at me and smiled, with a "knowing" look, almost as if to say, "Now, you know better."

I said nothing and smiled back at her as though we'd had a full conversation in the silence. I like that she got that and caught me on it, not allowing me any "proud bragging rights," so to speak. If I had done so, this whole trip would have been a waste—for me, anyway. The Bible says we are to do for others in private and want no reward in return. Like it says in Matthew 6:1–4 (NLT):

> Watch out! Don't do your good deeds publicly, to be admired by others, for you will lose the reward from your

Father in heaven. When you give to someone in need, don't do as the hypocrites do—blowing trumpets in the synagogues and streets to call attention to their acts of charity! I tell you the truth, they have received all the reward they will ever get. But when you give to someone in need, don't let your left hand know what your right hand is doing. Give your gifts in private, and your Father, who sees everything, will reward you.

━ ━ ━ ━ ━ ━ ━

I had never seen the destruction left in the wake of a tornado in person. I had only seen footage on the news. The rubble left behind in its path of what used to be homes, churches, businesses, RVs, and cars looked like someone had taken a shoebox full of toothpicks, closed the top, shook it up, and then turned the box upside down and dumped the toothpicks all over the ground.

One image that will forever stick with me was the remains of an old church building protruding from amidst all the rubble. All that was left standing was the rear wall and one adjacent to it. In the corner of these two walls was a wooden cross with a purple sash draped across the top arms. You could see it stand out prominently from the freeway. Its rich tone stood out against the contrasting white walls it leaned against, there on top of the piles of rubble. Its silent but loud statement was heard by all: "With man this is impossible, but with God all things are possible" (Matt. 19:26).

This cross valiantly stood alone, speaking out for the entire community. Little did we know it at the time, but what we saw with our eyes would be what affected us the least that day. What would ultimately reside in our memory banks was this community and the people of Mayflower, Arkansas. Never before had I witnessed so clearly the meaning of having grace and strength under pressure as I did on this day. Before, I'd thought we were coming to bless them, but it would turn out to be the opposite.

We exited the interstate and drove through several road blocks. Fortunately, they allowed our truck to enter their community and our feet to tread on their land. In hindsight, I feel honored that we were allowed to pass their city lines that day. The roadways where the tornado had done the most damage were blocked to incoming traffic. The I-40 freeway was gridlocked from rubbernecks gawking at this small town that now lay in ruins. It deserved more respect from the people just driving through, trying to get a better look, like it was a tourist attraction. So the mere fact that we as outsiders were able to come in was a very big deal to me. I'm thankful for that.

The lessons I learned from this people and what I took from this life journey would come in handy a lot sooner than I expected.

After unloading the truck and spending what turned out to be a rather surprisingly awesome day, around 3:20 or so we made our way back through the town and headed toward the exit ramp that would take us back to Nashville. Before we hit the interstate, suddenly I couldn't sit still. I became so anxious that I just needed to get out of the truck. I saw a tattoo shop with a couple of motorcycles in front of it. I decided I'd feel comfortable there.

We pulled in, parked the truck, and then walked over onto the sidewalk in front of the tattoo shop and peered into the windows. There on the wall was a tattoo that looked *just* like Leo. It was a skull with the same exact haircut as him, a bandana tied around the top of his head and all. There was even a

Mexican flag over the top, a motorcycle...everything. I laughed in amazement at how close this was to being *exactly* Leo.

After we'd hung out for a minute, we decided to try again and get back on the road. While we walked back over to the truck, I told Alexis, "There was this one time Leo said, 'Baby, I did something so stupid. You're gonna be so mad at me.' He told me he was riding the bike one day, and he let go of the handle-bars with both hands and did devil horns at the car passing in the opposite lane." We laughed a little as I shook my head, still thinking about Leo telling me this story.

When we got into the truck, I looked at the clock and it said 3:33. I took a deep breath and let out a sigh. "Everything's going to be OK...Everything's going to be OK." Alexis began to repeat it with me as we headed down the road.

A couple miles down the road, I couldn't find my cell phone. I looked in the rearview mirror and strangely enough I spotted it lying on the tarp in the back of the truck. I pulled the truck over on the side of the freeway to retrieve it. I got out and walked along the side of the vehicle, then I put one foot on top of the rear wheel, leaned over, and reached as far as I could, using my fingertips to coax the phone over to me little by little. Finally, I was able to grab hold of it.

I jumped down and walked back toward the cab of the truck. Alexis had also gotten out of the truck when I did and matched me step per step on the opposite side of the vehicle. All of a sudden, I turned toward her, we both stood facing each other on either side of the truck bed, and I shouted, almost pleading, *"But I love him! I love him! I don't care what anyone says or thinks about it! I love him!"*

There was an urgency in my voice, an insistent plea, as though I was begging someone for just one more chance. As though I was finally admitting, let the truth be told, no matter how I tried to play it off, I couldn't stop loving him. I couldn't make it stop; I didn't want to. All I wanted was to be with him. I was tired of pretending that he didn't consume my every thought. Alexis looked me in the eyes and calmly replied, "Let's just stop talking about it for now."

The next hour, as we journeyed back to Nashville, it was quiet between the two of us. We stopped at a rest stop just outside of Nashville so we could walk Cash and let ourselves regroup for a bit. I opened the back door to the truck and dug through one of my bags. I'd brought a change of clothes, just in case. I found a bandana I had packed and proceeded to fold it a couple times longways until it looked like a rectangle. Then I tied it around my head. I remember on the drive home I fidgeted with it in the rearview mirror, adjusting it over and over again, trying to make it look perfect—the way Leo would have worn his.

CHAPTER 23

Now when Joshua was near Jericho, he looked up and saw a man standing in front of him with a drawn sword in his hand. Joshua went up to him and asked, "Are you for us or for our enemies?" "Neither," he replied, "but as commander of the army of the LORD I have now come." Then Joshua fell facedown to the ground in reverence, and asked him, "What message does my Lord have for his servant?"

—JOSHUA 5:13–14

THE VERY NEXT day, I woke up to a text from Jacob that read, "I can't imagine how you must be feeling right now. I know you must be hurting so bad." I called his phone, but he didn't answer. Annoyed, I texted him back, "What are you talking about? I better not have to check my Facebook to see if someone is dead."

I sat in my salon chair up against the wall next to the station and mirror to wait for Jacob to respond. I sat and pondered what could have happened. Could someone have died? If so, who? My mom? Leo? As soon as it crossed my mind, a hot flash came over me from the top of my head down into my stomach. It resonated inside of me. I felt a sickness and a wave of nervous butterflies send a quick *shock* in my belly. I stared off into space, waiting. Finally the phone rang. I picked up and said, "What is going on?" Without even a hello, Jacob said, "Leo is dead."

I called my mom at work. "What's wrong?" she asked.

"Mom, I need you to pull up Facebook to see if this is true."

I told her which page to look up, and she read a post to me: "We are so sad we have lost one of our own." My mom said, "I can't tell if it's him or not. He doesn't look how I remember. He has on glasses. Did he wear a bracelet?"

"Yes," I answered.

She read the first post under the picture and said it was from someone named Donna. I said, "That's his mom's name!" Mom went on reading her post: "We are so heartbroken by this news. We appreciate everyone's condolences. Turning phone off now."

"Oh, God!" I screamed through tears. "Oh, God!" My mom said, "I'm sorry, Gabriel. Now pull it together...you've got clients coming today." I wiped my tears and made a call to Alexis. With no answer, I texted her, "I need you to get over here ASAP!" I paced in circles, back and forth, all over the kitchen, the living room, and the dining room floors. I went to call Lisa, my best friend from Nashville, who still lived in LA. As it rang, I saw Jacob pull up. He walked up to my storm door, and I opened it to let him in without saying a word. He said nothing and walked toward the dining room table. He pulled out a chair, turning it to the side so he could face me, and sat with his back toward the wall.

Lisa still hadn't answered. I continued to pace. I called one of Leo's cousins. "What is going on?" I asked him, desperately pleading for answers. He said, "I'm sitting here with Leo's sister now. He was killed yesterday on his motorcycle. It happened around 3:30 yesterday. We tried to call you; I figured he would have wanted you to know."

I sat on a stool in front of my desk and put down my phone. Jacob still sat quietly by. I was silent. I stared off into nothing, not sure what thoughts to think. I was suspended in disbelief. Then suddenly, I thought of God. My first reaction was to rise in anger, as I had done in the past. I sat straight up, ready to lash out at Him, but before I had the chance to, a rush of memories flashed through my brain. Just as quickly as I had felt this anger come over me I now saw every sweet, intimate moment I had spent with God over the last two months. I quickly put a lid on my rage.

My posture dropped as I slouched down again with both shoulders hunched forward. I just sat there and continued to think. The things God had shown me before this happened—there was no doubt in my mind that He was real. There was no going back now. I couldn't try to push Him away or scream at Him in anger. I *knew* Him now. I loved Him, and I knew now for a fact that He loved me. I couldn't possibly try to walk away.

Leo dying was the worst thing that could have happened. I was so ready for some good news, and now this? I couldn't wrap my brain around it yet; a God that loves me so and tells me He is for me, yet my life feels like a living hell? I wasn't ready to talk to God about it. At this moment, truthfully, I wasn't even sure if I wanted to talk to Him at all.

When I'd first heard the news that Leo was dead, there was one fact, however, that had become very clear to me. I knew now, without a doubt, that I had been chosen by God. I no longer had to wonder whether or not God had a call on my life. In a sense, I felt like I needed to throw my hands up to surrender, take a step back, give God the reins and get out of His way. I knew then that I could no longer call my life my own. It didn't belong to me. For the first time in many days, I finally sensed the presence of His Spirit. I started to hear that still, small voice again like someone had suddenly turned up the volume on the radio.

My thoughts also recalled the people I had just encountered less than twenty-four hours earlier. I was reminded of the brave people I encountered, struck by disaster, and their will to carry on. Now faced with my own personal tragedy, I had no excuse to disregard this recent "life class" I had been in only a day earlier. I could no longer just *say* how amazing these people were. Everything always seems so poetic and heroic when you're not the one it's happening to. You can stand and watch from the sidelines as if you were watching it all on a movie screen and say, "Oh, how awful!" No longer could this visit to Mayflower *just* be another heartwarming story recounted with a moral ending for a life lesson. In less than one day's time, I had gone from wondering how I would tell people about what I learned from this journey—what they could learn from this as well—to now. I was left with the responsibility to not just *say* I had learned something but to actually live that very truth.

I reminded myself, *Things could always be worse. You're not the only one that goes through hard times.* At the time I would have preferred to sink into my oblivion of "Woe is me" and "Bad things only happen to me" type of selfish thinking—but then I remembered the mother who stood by her house that now lay flattened by the storm. Not only had she lost her home, but what's worse, her daughter was killed in the storm too. When asked how she felt about all this, she responded, "This experience has only strengthened my love for God and my relationship with Him. I trust His plan." Today, I think about that mother. If she can make it through with such grace and dignity, how dare I think that I can't?

Then the story of Jesus being raised from the dead after three days and the rolling away of the stone suddenly appeared in my spirit. I saw a vision of the stone being rolled away from the entrance of the tomb.

> On the way they were asking each other, "Who will roll away the stone for us from the entrance to the tomb?" But as they arrived, they looked up and saw that the stone, which was very large, had already been rolled aside.
> —MARK 16:3–4, NLT

I didn't know what to do with myself for the rest of the day, so I had Alexis drive me over to Urban Outfitters. Maybe menial tasks would be better than none at all, I thought. But I knew no matter what I did, even if it were to sit staring in the mirror all day putting on makeup in a daze (which I did for three hours before we left the house), I was going to be a nutcase.

Alexis parked right outside the shop. I opened the passenger side door and slid forward a bit to get out of the truck. Just before I did, Alexis said, "Girl, look." I grabbed hold of the bar above the window with my left hand and turned back to look at Alexis's face. Her eyes looked at mine, then down at the seat behind me. I turned my head slightly to look down behind my shoulder. And there, lying on the seat behind me, was a penny—tails side up. When I saw this, my left hand gripped tighter onto the handle above me. I thrust my body weight and ejected myself out of the truck. I turned to look at the penny once more and shouted, "Not right now, God! That's not even cute right now!" I looked up toward the sky as I took a step back, and then slammed the truck door closed. "I'm not real happy with You right now, God! I'll have to talk to You later! I'm gonna need a minute!"

Then a vision came to my mind, from the Book of Joshua. I remembered the story of when Joshua ran up to an angel with his sword drawn high above his head, ready to attack. Joshua yelled, "Are you for me or for my adversaries?" And the angel replied, "Neither! I AM." (See Joshua 5:13–14.)

We went inside the store. I did some version of "looking around a bit," and then I tried on some clothes. I tried my best to do something that would make me happy, but it didn't help at all. Nothing could have helped at this point, but I had to try.

I received a call from Leo's cousin letting me know when the services would be. I told him, "I need to know what I'm walking into. Did he have a girlfriend?"

He answered, "There were women before you and women after you. He was a good-looking cat; women were always chasing him. He had a girlfriend, but he broke up with her the day before he died."

I thanked him for letting me know when the service would be and got off the phone. I changed out of the clothes I was trying on and headed out the front door. I walked around the corner of the building and behind a dumpster behind the store. I started to scream at the top of my lungs—so hard now that I didn't care if the force made me pee on myself or if anyone heard or saw me. I got on my knees and continued to scream until I couldn't anymore.

— — — — — — —

This was a huge blow. God fell silent to wait for my response. Would this be the "hit" that would make me lose all faith? Would I turn from God? Would I continue to trust and serve Him? Was I still all in? Could I believe that He loved me, even still? Would I think that God had somehow forgotten that I existed, not realizing that one human being can only take on so much pain? Could I love Him even still? And the answer was *yes.* Yes, I could. And *yes,* my *God loves me! Highly favored.*

> Because the Lord disciplines the one he loves, and he chastens everyone he accepts as his son.
>
> —HEBREWS 12:6

CHAPTER 24

ASKED ONE OF my closest friends, whom I knew I could trust in my most vulnerable state, to join me at the wake. The following Sunday, she drove us to the funeral home late in the afternoon. We got out of the car and walked toward the building. There was a mêlée of people and motorcycles everywhere.

Leo had always been taken aback by how many people I knew when we went out. He even mentioned to me one time that since I was so "popular" then maybe I would love him more if he knew more people too. From the looks of it now, he had done a great job at doing so. One could only hope that this many people would show up at your funeral. It wasn't surprising though; as much as I loved him, it was easy for me to see why so many other people would too.

I made my way through the crowd and toward the front door of the funeral home. I spotted Leo's cousin and his fiancée on the sidewalk in front of me. I couldn't stop crying, so I held my head slightly down, trying to keep people from seeing my face completely. My tears made everything around me a blur. The crowd's attention was directed over to our right, where a guy stood on top of a motorcycle raising a toast to Leo—good thing, because it diverted everyone's attention away from me, the only one crying so loudly that people were starting to look. I couldn't help it. This was awful. I didn't want to be there. I didn't want this to be happening. I didn't want to go to Leo's funeral. He wasn't supposed to be dead.

I finally made it over to Chris and walked straight into his arms, pressing my face into his chest. Chris was a big guy, real sweet, like a teddy bear. He felt so comforting, especially at a time like this. I asked him where Leo's parents and sisters were, and he said that now wouldn't be a good time for me to see them, that it would be best if I waited until after the service. I understood; they were dealing with their own pain. A sobbing girl was the last thing they needed to get through a day like today.

After the toast was finished, I grabbed my friend Candace and we proceeded to move with the crowd into the building. Candace took the lead so I could keep my head down, also freeing me from any further responsibility of trivial details that would require me to use my brain, like walking in a straight line, not running into people, or trying to figure out where to go next. She took me by the hand and guided me, moving slowly to get through the people, through the lobby and over to the room to the right. When we walked in, the seats were already full from front to back. She found us two of the last seats available in the back of the room on the front aisle next to the walkway, close to the door where we had come in.

After the deaths of my dad and his wife, my body held on to so much suppressed stress that I developed a tic. I didn't know that you could "develop" tics until it happened to me. When I sat still or idle in any way, my head would bounce up and down. I pointed my chin in toward my chest to try to lessen some of its effects, but it did no good. I had to just go with it and allow my body to do as it pleased in order for it to cope. As soon as

Gloria's funeral was over and life had simmered down a bit, the tic eventually went away—that is, until the day I found out Leo was gone. I had even forgotten about the tic until the moment it showed up again. As if someone had flipped on a switch, my chin started to bob up and down uncontrollably. So there I sat at Leo's funeral, leaning over, hanging my head down close to my chest, sobbing uncontrollably, my head tic-ticking away. I'm sure I looked like a mental case. I sure felt like one.

As the people standing in front of us started to disperse, the walkway cleared. I lifted my head, and there standing before me was Leo's sister. (The one who had been on the phone when Leo was cooking at my house before we got in that huge fight. Remember? Her.) I didn't know if she hated me or not, so I waited for her to say something first.

She stood there, looking at me. She had on her brother's military-style Harley Davidson jacket, and one of his purple bandanas tied around her head. She was a gorgeous girl, about seventeen now. Without a word, she came toward me and dropped to her knees, began to cry, and threw her arms around me. We held on to each other for dear life, saying nothing, only sobbing. In this moment, we let go of any "he said, she said" or "who wronged who" to come together for the one thing we would now forever have in common—our pain. "I'm so sorry that you lost your big brother," I said to her. She cried harder and said, "He loved you so much."

After a moment, our tears began to subside. She let go of me and pulled back a bit, resting her hands on my knees so that we were looking at each other face-to-face. She has the biggest, most beautiful eyes, and the fullest, longest eyelashes you've ever seen, which were still wet with tears. We paused, looking into each other's eyes—sometimes silence can say the most. She blinked a couple times, never taking her eyes away from mine.

She appeared to be trying to process all the information her mind had taken in over the past few days. She's a smart girl, more mature than most seventeen-year-olds.

She continued to gather herself; we both knew she couldn't stay long because she had to go up to the front before the service started. She stood up, gently holding on to one of my hands as she gradually took one step at a time, slowly backing away. I watched her as she went. I gave her a reassuring smile as she let go, took one more step back, and then turned around and walked away.

Leo's parents and two of his sisters stood up to speak. There were so many people in the room that I couldn't see what was going on up front; it was standing room only. The large aisle in the center of the room between the pews was packed with people too.

Halfway through, Leo's mom interrupted because people were still trying to come in but the funeral director began turning people away. She insisted that they allow everyone to come inside. She told the newcomers and the ones that were already in the room, standing, to sit on the floor all around, wherever they could, to make more room available.

As the "Celebration of Life" continued, I decided to move a little closer to the front so I could not only hear but also see what was going on. I carefully stepped through and around people sitting on the center aisle. I finally came to a small clearing; there was just enough room for me to plop down and take a seat on the plush burgundy carpet. I had on a black dress that was pencil-straight and reached my knee—not the most ideal for floor seating, but I made it work. I sat sideways, facing the front of the room, both legs out to my right, slightly bent at the knees. I put most of my weight on my left arm, stretching it out straight beside me, holding myself up with my hand as I rested my head on top of my shoulder.

On the back wall I saw a large screen with pictures of Leo being shown one by one. I was still crying and ticcing. I hadn't a clue who the people surrounding me were. I tried my best to look up at the pictures while still keeping my head down, for the most part. I think at some point I was rocking myself as I cried too.

I noticed a couple people look over at me like, "What do we do with it?" Someone over in the pews passed a tissue box to the person sitting on the floor next to me. I saw this happening in my peripheral and also saw the awkward look on the man's face next to me as he extended his arm to hand me the tissues. I guess he thought I might bite if provoked—or even worse, detonate and explode if aggravated in the slightest way. *Nah…I wish.* I took the tissue box and set it on the floor beside me.

I continued to look at the pictures, still trying to convince myself that this was, in fact, all really happening. I stared into Leo's face in one of the pictures as it went by. *How did we get here…a funeral? Really? Dead? Are you sure? Leo…is…dead.* It was like I was watching it all play out in front of me. In my mind I was still somehow separated from the reality of all of this. It was like I was standing on the other side of a plate glass window peering through, seeing a parallel universe take place somewhere in my imagination, like I was watching a television screen. At times it felt like I had been transported into the future, seeing a scene from my life that would take place maybe some twenty, thirty years from now. But then I would see a picture of Leo and look around at the faces of the people in his family, seeing that no one had aged, crushing my theory and all the hope I had of coming up with any other version of what was taking place rather than the truth.

I had been to funerals before. I had already done this once in my life, at Ethan's funeral. But that was then; that was Ethan. It already happened. It wasn't supposed to happen again. I'd already been here. This wasn't supposed to happen. Those pictures of Leo weren't supposed to be up there. These people around me wouldn't be here at a funeral home talking about Leo if he really wasn't dead, so...this has to be real. Right? I tried to piece it all together as I watched his pictures go by. He was so young and vibrant, full of life. There was too much life left in him for him to be dead.

As I watched the rest of the slideshow, I hoped that nothing would pop up that I didn't want to see—like pics with other girls or anything else like that. Then an image appeared of Leo standing next to a girl in a tight, black pleather leotard with a plunging neckline...with kitty cat ears on her head. Then it hit me. *Oh my gosh... That's me!*

My face flushed red with embarrassment at first. *Of course... wouldn't ya know it. That's just like me...I made it into the pics but somehow managed to take things one step further.* I always was the type to have a flair for the dramatics, always wanting to make an impression and turn heads when entering a room. But I hadn't planned this one myself. There I stood, tall, from the ceiling to the floor...in a tight, black, shiny pleather leotard. There was barely room in that thing for me to breathe in air. I was so thankful, though, that these photos of us turned out great; that we weren't making any weird or funny faces. It helped me feel less shy about the leotard. I'd never had a chance to see these pictures of us before now. They were taken at Halloween. I never imagined I would be included in the photos.

Another photo popped up, and it was me and him again. There I was, thinking nobody thought twice about me—but I was wrong. There was only one girl in the slideshow that wasn't kin to him, and that one girl was me. I was honored. There were four photos of us; shots taken in succession, so it was the same moment in all four but brief glimpses in different fragments of time. So they were all the same, but at the same time they were all very different.

I smiled for the first time in days as I looked up and saw us. The love I felt for Leo wasn't just all in my head; it did exist at one time, a happier version of us. He held me close with one arm around my waist, both of us posing for the camera with the biggest smiles on our faces. We looked so happy. For a moment I was taken back to that night. Things seemed much simpler then, even though in the background of that photo my world was falling apart. If I had known then that life would only get worse from that night forward, I wonder if I would have enjoyed it more, even through the trials. Would I have loved Leo more? But like his cousin Chris said when I asked him that same question, "More? How could you have possibly loved Leo more than you already did?"

I wasn't sure if the girlfriend was anywhere near me, or if I had seen her, not realizing who she was. I tried my best not to surf the crowd looking for anyone that "might be her." I really didn't want to see her or know her name. Sometimes it's best to not know *everything*. I didn't Facebook stalk or do any research or digging to find out more about Leo's personal life after we broke up or after he died—the life I knew nothing about. The other Leo that I had never met. The one that he kept secret from me; the one that existed when we were apart. Yeah, that guy. It made me feel strange and heavy hearted to be so affected by this one life and yet be surrounded by a room full of people who knew a different version of him than I did.

Which one was the real Leo? Did he hide me and keep me separate, never introducing me to his new friends after he started to work at Harley and ride a bike, because he was ashamed of me? Or was it because he thought I would look down my nose at his lifestyle and circle of friends? Once he got the bike and started to hang out at pool halls and bars that catered mostly to bikers, our relationship became strained. My parents got really sick around that time too, so that kept us apart.

We'd bought the bike in February, and I had broken it off with him in May. So I guess we spent more time together before we bought the bike; maybe him trying to "hide me away" wasn't really the case. Even still, the fact that he had a life that I never felt included in the whole time we were together sure stabbed the knife in deeper through my heart as I sat there on the floor surrounded by the very real truth that I could no longer wash away with excuses and denial: the guy I fell in love with had lived two separate lives—one life that included me, and another that included everything else.

A couple days before the service, I sat in my bathtub thinking about how awkward and unwelcomed I was going to feel when I showed up at the wake. Then after a while it finally dawned on me: *Bing! Oh!* I thought to myself. *You don't have to go. He treated you like crap, he had a girlfriend, you weren't supposed to be with him anyway, none of the family has contacted you or included you in their gatherings with friends and family at their house—you know they probably all hate you anyway. So why torture yourself any more than you have to? It's already going to take some time and major healing to get through the fact that he's dead—why add to it and pile that much more on your plate? Duh. Don't go. Leave it alone.*

Looking back on it now, I wish I had gone with this notion, leaving well enough alone. Even if I regretted missing the wake for the rest of my life and wished I had gone, I think in the long run it would have been in my best interest not to go. The trauma of losing Leo had already done a lot of damage to my soul. When I went to the wake and dove in the mix with his family and friends (and girlfriends), I found out a lot of information about him, his life, and what he did while we were apart, which added to further ripping and tearing away at my already fragile soul.

These wounds just toppled on top of old wounds until my capacity overflowed and burst at the seams. The grief period can typically last six months to a year. In that time it is imperative that you do your best to be good to yourself and allow for the full process to run its course so that you can come out on the other side, stronger. But during this process, as a result of dabbling into Leo's life after his death, on top of my grief I now had bitterness, rage, regret, anger, resentment, jealousy, rejection, depression, oppression, guilt, shame, and loneliness to add to it.

Add all of this on top of all of my previous traumas, which I continued to suppress, and I was a ticking time bomb. Weighed down by so much pain, self-doubt, insecurity, and lack of love, I desperately longed for a support system, the kind that Leo's family had in each other, but I had no one. I couldn't have cared less what happened to me next. For me, there was no next. I couldn't see my way clear. Putting in the effort to try to get back up again just seemed like a joke. Every time I started to believe things were going to be all right, something else would happen, even before I got a chance to fully enjoy any kind of success.

I had spent most of my life being rejected by people, being the butt of the joke, and trying to find a place where I belonged. Now I was starting to feel like a fool to have ever believed that God thought much of me at all. Now it felt as if He was rejecting me too, looking down from heaven laughing at me right along with everyone else. *Stupid girl. Nobody is ever going to love you. Nobody wants you around, get it? Just give up. Nobody cares what happens to you, so why should you? Once a whore, always a whore. You had it right when you used to take money in exchange for sexual favors…because that's all you're worth. That's all you're good for. Your own daddy didn't even love you. You got written out of his will!*

When are you going to "get it" and stop sticking up for yourself like you deserve any better? Has it ever occurred to you that maybe everybody treats you like you're worthless because that's how it's supposed to be? You're the only one that believes you should be treated better. Maybe it's time you snapped out of this delusional fairytale land that you created in your head. People treat you like you're worth nothing because that's exactly what you are…worthless. People like you don't get the "happily ever after" endings. Look at you…Leo couldn't even stand you. He left you for someone else as soon as he walked out the door. You dumb girl. When are you going to stop trying to have a good life? It will never happen for you. Dummy. I hate you. You're ugly. You disgust me.

I walked outside for a minute to get some fresh air. As I was walking through the parking lot to go back inside, the thought of Leo having a girlfriend went through my mind. I heard God say in a whisper, "I did that for you." I had so much information already swirling through my mind; I was doing my best just to process it all, but I was failing. I couldn't possibly try to add to it, especially *that* kind of noise. I couldn't even attempt to come close to understanding how in the world that was for my good, because it sure didn't feel good at the time. I heard His words and answered Him in my spirit, "OK, God, I hear You—but I'll have to figure that one out later."

At the end of the service, I walked to the front to speak to Leo's family. His little sister, who was eight, caught sight of me. "Gabriel!" She stretched both arms out and ran toward me. I got down on my knees, and she ran into my open arms. We both cried as we held each other. Then I pulled back to look at her face and said, "We've got to be strong, Natalie." She nodded her head, trying to hold back the tears. "You're going to make it through this, OK?" I said.

She let out a whimper as I pulled her back to me and ran my hand over the back of her head. I stood up and pointed her back over to where her parents stood. I still wasn't sure how his family would act when they saw me. I felt nervous to approach them because I didn't know if they cared to see me at all. So I stood from afar and waited as people surrounded them to pay their condolences. At times like this, with the shock of it all, most of us were in a daze. If they felt any bitterness toward me, I'm sure they weren't thinking much about that now anyway.

Leo's dad, Ramiro, started to walk by where I stood. I took a step toward him, and he stopped. I said, "I'm so sorry." He looked lost, nodded his head, and said, "Thank you." He continued to walk by. I wondered if he had understood what I meant when I said I was sorry. Of course I meant for the loss of his son, but the first "sorry" I wanted him to hear from me was the one for cosigning on that stupid bike.

One of Leo's sisters, Allison, approached me. I had seen her earlier when we first arrived, so I didn't completely fall apart this time. She looked at me and presented the girl standing next to her. "This is Avery," she said. I completely lost it and sobbed as I said her name, "Avery," and put my arms around her in a hug. His mother lived out of state with her second husband and Leo's half-sister, whom I had not met until this very moment. Later that day, Avery told me that as I was standing there waiting to talk to the family, she caught sight of me and asked Allison, "Who is that? Did Leo ever see *that* girl? He would have loved her, she's beautiful." And Allison answered her by saying, "That's Gabriel."

When I first walked up to the front, I made my presence known to Leo's mother, Donna. She continued to talk to the people around her as she raised a finger to me, nodded her head, and mouthed the words "hold on." So I stood at a distance and patiently waited for her.

After I had met Avery, I backed up to the railing that separated the visitation area from the seating area and watched the pictures go by on the back wall, still asking myself if this was really happening. Standing a few feet away from me, to my left, were Leo's aunt and uncle. His aunt noticed me standing there, approached me, and then said, "He talked to me about you the week before he died. He really loved you."

My head was tilted down, my eyes still looking up at the pictures on the screen as tears continued to stream down my face. A loosely balled-up fist covered my mouth. I nodded my head and moved my hand over just enough to let out a gentle, "Thank you." Then she walked back over to her husband.

A few minutes passed, and I started to feel silly for waiting. I assumed Donna had forgotten about me—or, even worse, was avoiding me—so I decided it was time to go. I tapped her on the shoulder and excused myself for my intrusion to those speaking to her as I waved a little good-bye. "I'm gonna go," I said.

Unexpectedly, she excused herself from those around her and said, "Sorry, you guys, but it's really important that I step aside and talk to this one." She motioned for me to follow her and walked over to a quiet, empty corner of the room. "Come on, we need to talk," she said. "Just you and me."

I'd never expected that she would pull me to the side. I wasn't sure what she was about to say to me, whether it would be bad or good, but I followed her into an empty pew and took a seat next to her. She looked at me and said, "There were thirty ex-girlfriends here and ten girls who *thought* they were dating Leo when he died. But you, boo...you were the *one*. You and Leo—the reason you two weren't together wasn't for a lack of love; you were both just broken in different areas that kept you guys from being able to make it work."

Then a young, handsome Spanish guy approached Donna to ask her about something. After he did, he looked over at me and extended his arm to shake my hand. He introduced himself: "Hi, I'm Tomas."

"I'm Gabriel," I said.

"Ooh," he said. "*You're* Gabriel." Then Leo's mom looked over at me and said, "See? I told ya."

━ ━ ━ ━ ━ ━ ━

The day after the service, Alexis was asleep in my bed. I went outside to call my mom to say hi and let her know everything was OK. My voice was completely gone because I had screamed so much in the past week, so when she answered, I let out a raspy, "Hey."

She started to cry, not even asking me if I was OK. I had played this game with her in years past; she was turning the tables to turn the attention on herself. Usually I would ask her, "Mom, are you OK?" But not today. The sheer audacity that she would pull this card; I'd finally had enough. It had been a week since I had talked to her. The last time we spoke was the day I found out that Leo was dead. She had not tried to call me or come by the house to see if I was OK. *And now she wants me to make sure she's OK?*

This was far too reminiscent of the time when I'd called her after I had stayed a few nights at the hospital with my dad. I was exhausted both mentally and physically. She said, "This affects me too, ya know," and then hung up on me. *No. Not this time. I'm not going to let her do this to me again. For just one day, could she be a mother? Just once. Could she not make this about her, and be there for me? Just this one time?*

When I realized that she was making it "the Linda show" instead of being there for her daughter, I couldn't keep it together. I no longer cared about consequences or people's feelings at this point. In years past, I had tried to consider how she might be feeling too, but not now. I was done. I was so tired of her getting the best of me and doing nothing for me in return. Not today; it wasn't going to happen. In my mind, I demanded that she step up to the plate and accepted nothing less. I had been through too much at this point to baby my mother when I was in a time of need, not her.

I could barely talk as I screamed out over the phone, "Why are you doing this? Not today! What could possibly be wrong with Linda? Not today! If ever there was a day I needed you to be a mother, today would be that day!"

I hung up the phone and went back inside. I collapsed, falling down on my knees and crumpling over. I pushed against the floor with my hands as I screamed as hard as I could, doing my best to get out of me the anger and rage that consumed me, overwhelming me. My voice was literally gone at this point, so I tried my best to get it out. I vowed that from that moment forward, I wouldn't be talking to her for a while. I knew that if I were to have any chance of coming out of this alive and healing mentally, emotionally, physically, and spiritually, I couldn't have her anywhere near me. I knew it was time to break all contact with her, guilt free. For once in my life, it was time for me to put myself first, and to love myself enough to do so.

— — — — — — —

Later that day, Alexis and I went to Leo's parents' home to visit with Leo's sisters and his mom. When we first walked in and stepped through the kitchen, Alexis stopped and said to me, "This is the house…this is the house from my dream. The one where you were sitting on a plaid couch, crying. The one I had back in January, when we first started hanging out—remember?"

I pointed outside to the garage where Leo stayed. "The plaid couch is out there," I said to her. "What was the Bible verse again that God showed you? I can't remember."

Then she said, "He placed a piece of paper on the counter next to me, and written on it was John 1:5." She also told me what the verse says.

After hearing about the dream for the second time, I still didn't understand why God would show her that verse. *What was He trying to say to us?* It still didn't make any sense to me.

After spending time with the family, news was brought to light about this other girl that Leo had been dating. It was the same girl I had punched him in the face over back in February. As soon as he'd left my house for good, he was right back with her, for almost two and a half months before he died. It hurt to hear all of this.

Sometimes it's best to play dumb and not know the truth at all. The girl was not at all what I would have imagined. Sometimes I'm thankful that she wasn't anything great, but at the same time it seemed to hurt worse because she wasn't fabulous. I had spent the last year and a half wondering if I was pretty enough for Leo.

When I first saw this girl and realized who she was, it made me jump. I didn't think she was pretty at all. I know that looks aren't what is most important, but from my stand, I was trying to deal with the pain of rejection, with him choosing to leave me only to go back to her. I had done all I could to be good to him, or so I thought, and to find out that he had chosen someone who seemed less than me made me feel even worse about myself. *Wow*, I thought, *there must really be something wrong with me if he would choose her over me.*

This added to my list of reasons why I should give up on life and quit trying. I had spent so much time trying to figure out, *Am I good enough? Do I measure up?* all in vain. It obviously didn't matter how hard I tried to be the best of the best in life—attitude, personality, career, goals, money, or looks; I did all that, and he still chose to go with someone who wasn't even in the same category as me. All I'd have to do to make this girl feel bad was to step out of my car and show up. It seemed like a no-compete—but obviously it was, since he still went running back to her.

So here I was; I had come to this point in my life. Nothing good had resulted from anything I had tried . . . and now *this. He left me for this?* There are no words to explain the rage and confusion that brewed inside of me. Every day beat me down as I continued to run out of reasons to hold on to any kind of hope.

Of course, after these things happened, I wondered what I should have done differently. After finding out about the other girl, should I have instead grabbed Leo and told him, "OK, that's the past. We're here together. We keep it moving from here on—a new start"?

I thought about the last letter he had written me. He said that the days faded as he realized I still wasn't there with him, with no one special to come home to (even though he was going home to someone and I wasn't). *Was I supposed to be flattered by this? Is that what "most" people would do? What would most people do in this situation? Sweep it under the rug, be passive about things they felt were injustices to them?* I hadn't a clue but desperately sought one.

CHAPTER 25

*And the Holy Spirit descended on him in bodily form
like a dove. And a voice came from heaven: "You are
my Son, whom I love; with you I am well pleased."*

—LUKE 3:22

I WALKED AWAY ON the sidewalk. With my head down, I
stopped and kicked at the grass that grew between the cracks.
Two pairs of feet suddenly appeared, stepping toward me, and
then stopped just at my feet. I looked up to see two of the most
beautiful black women before me with two small children
standing at their sides. One of them said to me, "Where have
you guys been? I've been looking for you! In the paper, in the
obituaries, online... His name was Leo. He said he had five sisters. I was there with him the day he died."

Very softly I said, "There are some people you need to meet." I
took the woman's hand and led her toward the family. I pointed
to the street at Leo's mother, who was lying facedown on the
concrete where he lay when he took his last breath. "That's
his mother right there." Ramiro came walking toward us, and
before he could pass by I gestured for him to pause, saying,
"And this is his father, Ramiro." Through tears the woman said

to him, "I was with him on that day." She walked past me, and then the two embraced.

I left them standing there and walked over to join the family again. I stood next to the sidewalk, on the edge of the grass, and waited for the motorcycles to arrive. Then suddenly Ramiro called out, "Hey, you guys. Look!" I looked over at him as he pointed upward at something across the street. I turned to look, and directly there before us, perched on a power line up high, was a white dove. He sat still and quiet, looking at us as though he had shown up to get the best seat in the house. The bird never moved an inch, never flapped a wing nor turned his head. No sooner than he appeared, the bikes came rolling toward us.

Three of Leo's friends and his cousin pulled up and parked in front of us with their front tires resting against the curb of the sidewalk. Our attention was no longer on the bikes; our main focus now was the dove. We all pointed overhead across the way, calling out, "Look! Look!" All four men turned back to look. When they saw the dove, they dropped their heads and then turned back, facing us, all shaking their heads. Then almost in unison, they all started to gun the accelerators on their bike handles. Their back wheels spun like mad as white smoke billowed behind them, covering the entire street until you could no longer see anything behind them. Cars continued to drive through as the fog enveloped them.

We all cried out as their motors wailed, the smell of hot rubber all around, "I *love you*, Leo!" We all screamed toward the dove, "*I love you!*" The smoke rolled over the area and enveloped the bird and everything around it. He never moved. One of the bikes suddenly made a loud *pop!*, loud enough to make us jump, and still the bird never flinched.

I walked over to where Leo's mom was standing. As I continued to video the bird with my iPhone, I yelled over to her, "What? Are white doves known to live in this area?"

Never turning to look away from the dove, she shook her head and said, "No."

"It hasn't moved at all!" I cried out.

Donna yelled, "I'm not leaving as long as he's there! I'm not leaving until my son does!" We cried and continue to call out, "*Leo!*"

Ramiro passed behind us. As he slid both hands over his head and then down the back, cradling his neck, he said to no one in particular, "I didn't think I was going to make it..." He looked straight ahead, almost in a daze, in disbelief. "I didn't think I was going to live through this...until now...I needed to see that dove so bad. Seeing it saved me. That's my son...my son's OK." He curled his head down toward his chest and began to sob. Then he covered his face with the palms of his hands, his shoulders moving up and down with every gasp of air he tried to take.

The woman (her name was Brianna) who was with Leo the last moments of his life said that she asked him before he died if he had accepted Jesus Christ as his Lord and Savior. I am forever grateful to her, because she was an angel sent from God to ensure that I would one day be reunited with Leo again. I don't know for sure whether or not Leo would have gone to heaven if she had not been there, but now I can rest assured that he was saved in Jesus's name, just like the man who hung on the cross next to Jesus, who acknowledged Christ as savior in his last moments. "Jesus answered him, 'Truly I tell you, today you will be with me in paradise'" (Luke 23:43).

CHAPTER 26

I STOOD IN MY backyard in the dawn's early morning light. I shouted up at the moon, "God, if You want me to make it through this, You gotta help me! I need You, God. I am but a man; I can't do this on my own! I love You, God, but truthfully, I get tired of talking up at the sky to You and hearing nothing back. I need something tangible! You're taking all of my people away from me! I have no one to talk to, Lord! I have no one to go to for advice!"

Days later I was at my dad's, standing in his closet looking through an old file cabinet. I found a file full of letters written by my father, addressed to me, that he had never given to me. As I read the one lying on top, it hit me: God had answered my prayer. This was the tangible I had asked Him for.

I started to cry and made my way down to my dad's shop. I took a seat in the old wooden chair where my dad used to sit all the time watching TV. I covered my mouth with my hand in disbelief and sobbed harder as I continued to read. It was exactly what I needed to hear—the advice and encouragement I had asked God for! I held in my hand a list of reasons why I shouldn't give up.

This letter was so sweet. I didn't sense tension, pointing of the finger, or anger in his words. I wasn't used to hearing my dad talk like this. I wasn't being berated for anything I had done wrong. All it was, was love.

I was grateful for this gift, but my heart still sank. "God, I never knew my dad loved me," I cried out, "not like this. Why didn't he ever tell me he felt this way? I never knew!" I sat and cried, wishing I could tell my dad how much I loved him too. I heard God answer, "Because if he had, you wouldn't have become who you are today. If you had known all along that he loved you this way, you wouldn't have been molded for My purpose. You are exactly as I intended, for My perfect will to be done in your life. You are perfect in My sight."

The following insert is the letter I found from my father:

Dearest Gabriel,

I dearly love you.

How can I prove this? I know you cannot talk to me about your real problems. I know because when I talked to my father it was useless. I would tell him my troubles as clear as I understood them, yet when my father began to give me advice, I knew we were out of tune.

As always, when we want advice, we will not take it...No matter who gives it to us. No one understands our situation...I was lucky. I made it through...

I, and for those who know you (your uncles, their wives, my mother, my father, your nephews, your nieces, your aunts, your old girlfriends who look you up to find out what happened to you...And others you could not believe are watching you. Yes, there are those that admire you and emulate you that you don't even realize.) know you are a blessing for many and have a purpose, therefore are capable of a greater destiny in your life than any person can imagine!

My earthly father fulfilled his role in my life to help mold me into who I was meant to be. When he died, he passed the torch over to me so I could run my course. It was now up to me to finish the race and *run* into my destiny that God had prepared and preordained for me.

Do you not know that those who run in a race all run, but only one receives the prize? Run in such a way that you may win. Everyone who competes in the games exercises self-control in all things. They then do it to receive a perishable wreath, but we an imperishable. Therefore I run in such a way, as not without aim; I box in such a way, as not beating the air; but I discipline my body and make it my slave, so that, after I have preached to others, I myself will not be disqualified.

For I do not want you to be unaware, brethren, that our fathers were all under the cloud and all passed through the sea; and all were baptized into Moses in the cloud and in the sea; and all ate the same spiritual food; and all drank the same spiritual drink, for they were drinking from a spiritual rock which followed them; and the rock was Christ. Nevertheless, with most of them God was not well-pleased; for they were laid low in the wilderness.

Now these things happened as examples for us, so that we would not crave evil things as they also craved. Do not be idolaters, as some of them were; as it is written, "THE PEOPLE SAT DOWN TO EAT AND DRINK, AND STOOD UP TO PLAY." Nor let us act immorally, as some of them did, and twenty-three thousand fell in one day. Nor let us try the Lord, as some of them did, and were destroyed by the serpents. Nor grumble, as some of them did, and were destroyed by the destroyer. Now these things happened to them as an example, and they were written for our instruction, upon whom the ends of the ages have come. Therefore let him who thinks he stands take heed that he does not fall. No temptation has overtaken you but such as is common to man; and God is faithful, who will not allow you to be tempted beyond what you are able, but with the temptation will provide the way of escape also, so that you will be able to endure it.

—1 CORINTHIANS 9:24–10:13, NAS

CHAPTER 27

Hope deferred makes the heart sick, but a
dream fulfilled is a tree of life.

—PROVERBS 13:12, NLT

EVEN STILL, RECENT events proved to be too much for me to handle. In the days that followed, everything changed. I lost hope. I gave up. After losing Leo, I just didn't want to take part in this thing called life anymore. Nor could I find a reason to. In times past, thoughts of suicide and wanting to die had crossed my mind, but they would quickly pass and the thoughts would go away.

This time it was different. I finally understood the conflict that went on inside the mind of a man named Job, the torment he felt between loving God and trying to hold on to his faith while he desperately searched for one reason to keep living. With all the bad behind him, would he ever see the day when any good thing would happen for him again?

I understood what it meant to be frustrated to be alive. I loved God; I knew He was real; I didn't want to disrespect Him by canceling out this gift He had given to me called life. And I didn't want to live separate from Him for all eternity in hell.

I didn't want to die, but I didn't want to live. I felt stuck. The reality hit me that it was not up to me whether I was to stay on this earth or leave.

After Leo passed away, I was overwhelmed; things became too much for me to bear. I didn't understand why so many bad things had happened in such a short amount of time. It seemed like before I had a chance to get over one traumatic thing, another one would happen. Picking myself back up again and pushing forward in faith became redundant. I felt like I was doing it all in vain. And the things that were happening in my life weren't just bad—like kind of bad, like a breakup or something, normal everyday stuff (not to lessen these experiences at all)—these were real-life tragedies. These were deaths. And to add to it, the people I loved most who were leaving this earth left in very tragic ways.

I had amassed years and years of unfinished business and unanswered questions. On top of suffering the loss, I heard about what they had been doing—and the girls they had been doing. While I sat and sulked, they had moved on with their lives.

I was angry. I was tired. I was tired of trying to convince myself that everything was going to be all right. Nothing had gone right in years. I was starting to feel like an idiot for ever having believed that something better was in the future, only to be sucker punched with yet another tragedy.

I threw in the towel. I told God that whenever He was ready to come get me, I was ready to go. I literally gave up. Everything stopped after this moment. I didn't care what happened next. I didn't try to think ahead, because to me there was no "ahead." I stopped paying my bills; I stopped reaching out to my clients; I didn't move forward with starting my new business; I didn't check my bank account to see how much money I was spending. I just stopped. Everything stopped.

I didn't care about anything—especially not myself. It no longer mattered to me what God might have in store for the future. I had been doing that for almost five years, and look where "looking ahead to an exciting and great future" had landed me. It was a bunch of nonsense, I thought. I wanted no part in this. It was hard for me to go to bed at night because I felt no reason to get up the next day, so I found myself staying up until seven or eight o'clock most mornings, and then finally taking a mix of Xanax and prescribed sleep meds. I had to *force* myself to sleep. I couldn't find the point in getting rest. *For what?*

CHAPTER 28

THE SIGNS COME IN THREES

For his anger endureth but a moment; in his favour is life:
weeping may endure for a night, but joy cometh in the morning.

—PSALM 30:5, KJV

I RENTED A STORAGE unit from a facility not too far down the road from my father's house. The looming deadline Gloria's children had set for me to be out of the house didn't allow nearly enough time for me to haul these things back to Nashville. It required several trips running back and forth up and down the road from Murfreesboro to Nashville.

As I finished unloading the last batch of my father's pottery in unit 355, I felt led to pick out one of the pieces and set it aside. I felt that my dad wanted me to take it across the street to his friend, Bryan. Bryan was also an artist. My dad always had an appreciation and love for the works Bryan created, so it seemed to make sense that Daddy would want to gift Bryan with a piece of his own art.

I placed the colorful vase on the passenger seat of my car and drove across the street and then through the parking lot.

I parked my car behind several businesses in a small strip mall. Next to the businesses was a small plot of land with an iron structure that consisted of twisted, bent, and strategically placed metal. Standing almost five stories tall, its length stretched from the front of the parking lot and ran parallel to it for almost a mile. It was a work of art that Bryan had committed most of his life to building. Each piece of metal told a story; it was a biography of sorts. Sometimes, if you looked hard enough, you could spot Bryan amidst the steel's gray contrast suspended by a harness welding another piece to the puzzle. I pulled up next to it hoping that today might be one of those days. Unfortunately, there was no Bryan in sight, so I drove back to Daddy's house.

The next night I found myself on the other side of the structure, trying to sneak my way into this property marked NO TRESPASSING! Bryan resided in a warehouse tucked away among huge piles of metal and large singular metal structures. It was late, around one o'clock in the morning. I didn't want to be rude by coming onto this man's property unannounced, so I turned off my headlights so I wouldn't seem so blatantly intrusive.

Being born and raised in the South, I was no dummy to the very real possibility of being "shot on sight" if Bryan were to consider me an unwanted guest. I had a healthy respect for the men I was raised around. These men lived by the mantra "Shoot first, ask questions later." Don't get me wrong—these are good, kind, God-fearing men; but 'round these parts, if you got your butt shot off, you had no one to blame but yourself, especially if your dumb self was treading somewhere you ought not have been in the first place. With that being said, I still didn't feel a great sense of danger. If Bryan were to approach me and ask what my business was being there, once he realized that I was

James Pearson's child, he'd be as tame as a kitty cat (without the claws). But still there was no sign of Bryan. I backed my car up as slowly and quietly as possible. Then I turned my car around and headed to the other side of town for some late-night grocery shopping at Wal-Mart.

Around 3:00 a.m. I returned to Dad's. I stepped into the kitchen from the back door with grocery bags hanging from both arms. During my shopping adventures, several good memories of Leo and I had crossed my mind—grocery shopping trips together, meals we cooked, future meals we planned, and laughs we shared. I placed the bags on the counter and closed the door behind me. These thoughts that flooded my memory banks, however good, seemed bittersweet... then these feelings suddenly turned to anger. I missed Leo so much. I knew I would never experience these moments with him again. No matter the bad things that had happened between us, we *were* happy once! I remember it!

To experience such moments of joy only to have them disappear, yanked out of your life, suddenly leaving you alone to recall those days gone by: it's enough to make you wonder if knowing that kind of joy is truly better than never experiencing it at all.

I've sometimes thought that daydreams were a gift; they bring a brief moment of solace and escape from the present day. Unfortunately, here's the rub: when you land the plane and "snap" back into reality, these euphoric thoughts can turn on you and become your greatest enemy. They seemed to taunt and tease me for what I longed for the most, cruelly reminding me how empty my life was now. They also reminded me of the fact that no matter how hard I worked to recover, there would always be this ominous void lingering that no one and nothing could ever fill.

The rage I felt from this revelation began to rise up inside of me. Like an outside thermometer on a sweltering summer day, the mercury on my meter went straight to the top until there was no more room for it to rise. I cried hard and put both hands on the edge of the oven, stretching both arms out. In my fit of rage, I began to push up against it, lifting the bottom front of the appliance off the kitchen floor. The topmost part at the back of the range thrust up against the wall. I continued to push with all of my might, crying out to God in my frustration, *"Why, God? Why?* Why did You have to take Leo away from me? Why are these people forcing me out of my father's house? *Why, God? Why?"*

I stopped pushing and hung my head low, standing there sobbing as though I had been defeated. Then, as if out of nowhere, I heard very distinctly that still, small voice ask me a question: "Do you want to come home?"

It caught me off guard. I thought my screams were in vain; I'd never thought He was really listening. I wasn't even expecting an answer from Him. And to hear God ask such a thing? You mean the God Almighty would actually present us with this choice?

I stood up, jumped back, and pointed my finger in the air out in front of me. "Don't You do that! Don't You take pity on me...don't You give in to me! Don't You do that...just because I'm tired! We've come too far! You didn't bring me through all that for nothing! How dare I give up and bow out now!"

Then God asked, "What do you want?"

My body collapsed over the oven. With my forearms supporting me, I tucked my head in toward my chest. "All I want is to serve You, Lord, and with that I will be satisfied!"

Then I heard Him say these words: "Weeping may endure for a night, but joy cometh in the morning!"

This was the pivotal moment that turned everything around and gave me hope again. I made up my mind then that I would press forward, with God's help, so that His will and purpose for my life would be done.

━ ━ ━ ━ ━ ━ ━

The next day, inclement weather rolled into Murfreesboro. Limbs from the trees surrounding my dad's house broke off and fell on top of the roof and into the yard. It struck me that this could be God answering my prayers.

I ran outside and onto the deck. "Haha! How brilliant, God! If the storm were to tear the whole house down…when those people arrived to claim the house, there would be no house left for them to take! How brilliant! Throw Your weight around, God! Show them who's Boss!" Then, not too far from where I stood, I heard a large *crack!* Suddenly, another huge limb came tumbling down and fell right on top of the house. I turned to look up at the trees, saying, "…but before you do, God, let me get out of Your way!"

I got in my car and drove uptown. I ran a couple errands, giving the storm some time to subside. I found myself, once again, next to Bryan's structure. I parked my car diagonally behind the building furthest toward the back. This time, however, I couldn't recall what made me go over there. Looking back on this moment now, without rhyme or reason, I was instinctively drawn to this area.

My car sat caddy-corner, the front of it facing toward the building. After finishing up a call with a friend in LA, I placed an unlit cigarette in between my lips. As I fumbled around looking for a lighter, I noticed a guy to my right spray painting something gold. The rain had stopped. Both of my windows were down. He stood up and asked, "You OK?"

I returned with, "Yeah, I just talk loud!" and let out a laugh. "Hey, you got a light?"

"No," he said as he walked toward my car.

"What are you guys doing over here?" I asked.

He replied, "We're starting a church."

I say, "You're non-denominational, aren't you?"

"Yes," he answered.

Like a lightbulb going off over my head, it became clear to me. I said to him, as I pointed over toward the structure, "I've been by here the past three nights. I thought I was looking for this guy, but it was actually you guys that I was looking for."

"Hold on," he said as he started to back away. "I've got someone you need to meet."

I thought nothing of it and stepped out of my car. I finally found a lighter in my shorts pocket and lit my cigarette. I stood next to the hood of my car, took a drag, and waited patiently for him to return with...whomever.

A moment later, the door to the building swung open and a beautiful black woman wearing a red sweater with a braided French twist on her head walked briskly toward me. She extended her arm out toward me and said, "Hi! I'm LaShondria."

Darryl, now standing beside her, said, "She's the pastor of this church." He and I recounted to her our recent conversation. Then I turned to her and said, "There's a shift happening, huh?"

She invited me to come inside and take a look at the church they were preparing to open. We walked up to the storm door of this small building—it looked like nothing. You would have never known there was a church inside. It was just a box on the far back corner of a small shopping strip. Since I was from Murfreesboro, I remembered that it had been used for many purposes. At one time it had been a hair salon, a bank (hence the small drive-through window to the left of the door), and a pharmacy, and now it was going to be a church. I thought, *Cool, whatever...who am I to judge?*

I followed behind LaShondria up one step and into a small lobby. We turned to the left and walked through another small door and into an open room, large enough to fit two rows of about twelve pews. The room was painted a lavender color. In the corner to the right of where we stood was a guy standing on top of a ladder painting, working on the final touches. A woman stood next to the ladder.

When we entered the room, they both acknowledged my presence and exuberantly said, "Hi!" I smiled wide and said, "Hello!" As the pastor continued with my tour, we walked to the front of the church, through a hallway over to our right into another room that was to be LaShondria's office. In the corner of the room was yet another man standing on a ladder, painting away. This room was also a shade of purple, but this one a darker, more royal shade. LaShondria introduced us, and with the same enthusiasm as the couple before, he said hello by saying, "Praise God!" I smiled and said, "Hi!"

I took a quick look around at all the work that had been done to beautify this place. Then the pastor led me back into the main room of the church. She and I both took a seat on the first pew, and Darryl sat on a stool behind the altar to our left. He casually rested his chin in the palm of his hand as he listened to our conversation.

LaShondria and I talked for a bit, and then she looked over at Darryl and said, "Remember what I told you God told me last night?" She looked back at me and continued on a different topic.

"Wait," I said interrupting her. I looked back over at Darryl. "What did God tell her?"

He replied, "When she was praying last night, God told her that a white woman was going to pull up behind the church tonight, and that she was going to be the beginning of the cultural blending." LaShondria added, "When I saw your lights when you pulled up, I knew it was you."

I looked back at her and asked, "What time was it when you were praying?"

She answered, "3:00 a.m."

I told her, "That's the same time I heard God say, "Weeping may endure for a night, but joy cometh in the morning." I added, "I drove by here last night too."

"What time?" she asked.

"Around one," I said.

LaShondria smiled and said, "I left here last night just before one."

After a quick chat, thinking to myself that I already had enough to process, I decided it was time to go. LaShondria and Darryl walked me out to my car. Before leaving, I opened the passenger side door, reached in and retrieved the piece of pottery my dad made, and handed it to LaShondria.

With one hand holding it from the top, she turned it to inspect it. "Wow," she said. "This is beautiful! Thank you! You know, pottery is in the Bible."

"I know," I agreed, adding, "the Master Potter." I continued, "My dad signed all his pots with a dove on the bottom."

LaShondria took a look, found it, and then spotted two more, one on each side of the piece. She looked up at me. "There are three doves on here."

"I never knew my dad did that," I said. Then I added, "There's some money in there too, just keep it."

She turned the vase toward her to look inside, and looking back up at me, she said, "There's three dollars in here."

I smiled. "Is there really? Oh, I hope there is!" I laughed in disbelief.

She reached in to grab the bills to count once more, just to make sure. "Yep."

Will You Still Love Me Tomorrow?

> They have quickly turned aside from the way which I commanded them. They have made for themselves a molten calf, and have worshiped it and have sacrificed to it and said, "This is your god, O Israel, who brought you up from the land of Egypt!"
>
> —Exodus 32:8, NAS

Sometime during the month of May, I heard that "still, small voice" beneath all the clutter and noise going around in my head and all the busyness around me. It said, "Now it's time for me to remove another idol: money. Will you still love Me when you're broke?"

At the time I still had some money left in the bank. When you have it, it doesn't seem like that big of a deal to *not* have it. I stayed busy all the time; I didn't care what I did—I just couldn't stop moving. I was scared that if I did, I might actually have to face my current circumstances. I remember hearing this and metaphorically breezing past God at a fast gait, and replying, "Yes, God, of course I will. I still trust You after everything that has happened, why would I stop then?" It didn't seem like such a difficult task...until the day came and I had nothing left.

CHAPTER 29

That day when evening came, he said to his disciples, "Let us go over to the other side."

—MARK 4:35

ONE DAY, AT two o'clock in the afternoon, I decided to go to Murfreesboro. When Alexis and I got there, I wanted soul food, so a friend of mine suggested we go to a place, kind of hidden, right off the beaten path. "If it's a 'hole in the wall,'" I say, "you already know they gotta have the best food!"

When we found the little brick building, we went inside and checked out the menu. The owner had her little girl there with her, Vanessa; she was around the age of five or six. As we waited for our food, I invited Vanessa to sit at the table with us and hang out. I thought to myself that she knew all the answers. I said, "You know about a lot of stuff, huh?" She sat quietly, still trying to smell me out, trying to play shy.

Alexis stepped outside for a moment to find an ATM. Not too long after, the moment finally came when Vanessa started to talk. I knew she had all the answers, and she did! She sat to my left facing the window. I looked over at her as her eyes suddenly started to water. "You OK?" I asked. "Yeah," she said, "the sun is in my eyes." I thought no more of it and turned my head to look over at the TV on the wall.

Then the little girl went on to say, "You know when you stand out in the sun...and then you spread mud all over your face?"

By this time she had my complete attention. I gave her an inquisitive look, wanting to know more. I pushed my chair back from the table, enough to turn my entire body to face her. I placed both elbows on my knees and then rested my chin on top of both fists. "Uhh...yes... Tell me more, go on."

With both hands, she started to make circular motions over her face to illustrate what this would look like. "...and the sun is in your eyes...and it feels so good and you go, 'Mmm...mmm...mmm'"—she then moved both of her hands down to either side of her neck and continued to make small circles, then back and forth on her shoulders—"...then you take the mud and you rub it all over your neck and shoulders." She closed her eyes and grinned with joy as she recalled how good this feels.

This chick for sure sold it...I wanted to go find some mud!

Feeling more comfortable around me now, she opened up and told me about another one of her favorite things. She put both of her hands on the side of the table and pushed herself up off her knees, as her tippy toes touched the seat of the chair. She leaned her upper body a bit over the table, then pushed herself back and rested on her knees again. "Do you like to eat bugs?" she asked.

I sat straight up in my chair and cocked my head to the right. "Nooo...Do you?"

She smiled big. "I *love* bugs! I like to eat them with mustard on them!"

"Do what?" I asked. "You put that much thought into it? What about jelly? Do you like them with jelly on 'em?"

Removing her hands from the table, she sat back in the chair and rested on her knees. "No, just mustard."

Processing this information, I looked straight ahead in a daze, my mouth open just a little in disbelief. I lay back against my chair. "Let's hope this is just a phase, OK? I don't want you eating bugs forever."

When Alexis returned, she looked like she had just hiked Mt. Kilimanjaro.

"Girl, uh-uh. Where did you go?" I asked.

She tried to catch her breath so she could speak, but she couldn't even get enough air in to get the words out.

"Girl, uh-uh. Let's go," I said. I took the cash out of her hand, paid for our food, and grabbed our "to-go" bags. As we gathered our things to leave, Vanessa playfully hung off the small swinging door that led into the kitchen, next to the cashier counter. She asked me, "Do you like donuts?"

I put the change in the tip jar. "Yes! With sprinkles!"

She replied, "They're the best when you get them first thing in the morning."

"You're too smart, girl." I placed my hand on her head. "I'll stop by next time I'm in Murfreesboro, K?"

She grinned and nodded. "OK."

— — — — — — —

Around seven o'clock, we drove over to the church where I had first met LaShondria. I had told Alexis about meeting LaShondria and Darryl, and I was excited for her to meet them too.

When we pulled up, we noticed the cars in the parking lot and people inside. This was a Tuesday night, though; most churches had service on Wednesday. Not sure what we were about to walk into, and hoping we were exactly where we needed to be at exactly the right time, we walked up to the door. I grabbed the handle, then I looked back over my shoulder at Alexis and said, "We're not late, we're right on time."

We nodded at each other, and I swung the door open and stepped inside a small square entryway. The door on the opposite wall swung open, and out stepped LaShondria. She immediately recognized me. Her mouth opened wide with surprise, and she said "Hi!" She opened her arms and wrapped me in a huge bear hug. She looked over at Alexis and joyfully hugged her too. *What a welcome!* I thought.

LaShondria headed toward the door just to our left and motioned for us to follow her. The pews were almost full, so we found space on the back pew and took a seat. A woman at the front stood before the altar. She wore a long skirt that reached the floor. With a baby on her hip, she shifted her weight and swayed with the music as she sang the words that she preached. This was one of the most beautiful services I had ever seen. Alexis and I were amazed at what we were experiencing as soon as we walked through the door. *Sold!* I thought. I knew then that this was going to be my church. We both agreed that whatever happened next—or at all, for that matter—in this church, it was going to be great!

I stood at the end of the pew. I had on short white shorts, a racer back tank top, and a pair of gray Air Jordan Flights. My hair color of the week was bright purple. As LaShondria preached, she exclaimed, "You don't have to look a certain way to come to God!" She didn't direct these words specifically *at* me, but with my tattoos, hair, clothes, etc., I knew she had to appreciate the certain flair I brought to the congregation. Considering that she herself had come from the streets to follow God, I was happy I could be another great example of that. We were like lotus flowers; we had both come out of the muck and murk to become God's beautiful creations.

As the service came to a close, LaShondria told everyone to get their "seed" in hand. I tapped the girl in front of us on the shoulder and asked her with a big smile, "What did she say?" She laughed and smiled as her eyes directed me to the money she held in her hand. "Your seed!" Oh! *Seed. Right!* I thought as I ran toward the door and out to my car. We came in empty-handed. All my cash was in the car.

I dug through my middle console and collected whatever cash I found loose in there. Before exiting the car, God caught my attention and instructed me to grab a handful of mints out of a lifesaver bag sitting in the front seat. I didn't know why or what He would have me do with them, but I didn't question it and grabbed a bunch in my hand. Then I heard Him say, "Now grab a couple more and keep them separate from the other pile." And so I did and ran back into the building.

Before I returned to my seat, God instructed me to give the large handful of lifesavers to the row of little girls sitting in the pew across from us. So I did. They all accepted my gift joyfully and passed the mints amongst them all. Then I walked across the aisle, back to my pew.

As I listened to the rest of the sermon, I kept an eye on what was going on next to us. There was a little girl that was sitting a few rows up who had now made her way to the back and stood in front of the girls on the back row. She asked for a piece of candy, and one girl went to hand her a piece. When she reached out to grab it, the girl snatched it away from her. I turned toward the girls, and their eyes meet mine. I said in a low whisper, "Are you sharing?" Trying to cover up their guilt, they all at once shook their heads with an adamant "Yes!" The candy beggar gave up and returned to where her mother was seated. She stood next to the pew with her back facing us.

God then instructed me to take the two lifesavers that I had put to the side and give them to the little girl that was begging for candy. I crept up behind her, so as to not disrupt the service, and swung my arm around her, presenting to her an open hand with her very own candy. She looked down, grabbed the treats, and looked up at me with a big smile. I turned and went back to my seat.

I watched her as she ran toward the back row and stood right in front of those girls who had taunted her. She stood boldly and proud, and stretched her arm straight out toward them, both pieces of candy dangling before them in her hand. It was as if she was saying to them, without saying a word at all, "*Ha! I was given my very own! I don't have to beg you for anything!*"

Then God explained to me, "This is how I am going to bless you in front of your enemies." It reminded me of one of God's many promises to us found in His Word: "You prepare a feast for me in the presence of my enemies. You honor me by anointing my head with oil. My cup overflows with blessings" (Ps. 23:5, NLT).

Just as LaShondria brought the service to a close, she walked up to me to with a word from God. I stood fast and never took my eyes away from hers. Since the night I'd met her, I knew this was a woman of God and what she said held a lot of truth. I swayed slowly back and forth, with my elbows bent, my arms held over my chest as I wrung my hands together. I played it very cool and took in every word she said to me, taking note of what God was confirming to me. Then she got me. I couldn't hold the cool front any longer. At the close of her prophecy, she said to me, "God said the *entire* inheritance will be yours!" My head dropped as I began to cry, and hard. She continued, "He will show you how to have permanent provision so you will never go 'without' for the rest of your life!" By this time, other women were standing around me in support. The girl in front of me had one hand on my arm and cried with me.

LaShondria walked back to the front of the church and brought the service to a close. I did my best to gather myself before walking into the aisle so we could leave. As I did, the little girl that I had given the candy to walked toward me, as though on purpose, so I stood there and paused for a moment. In one of her hands she held the two pieces of candy I had given her. I didn't notice yet that there was something in her other hand. She held out her closed fist, like she had something she wanted to give me. She looked up at me, and without a word she opened her little hand. And there in her palm were two pennies, both tails side up.

━ ━ ━ ━ ━ ━ ━

After the service, Alexis and I stopped by my dad's house before returning to Nashville. It must have been around ten o'clock by this time. I pulled up to the house, got out of my car, and walked around the back to enter through the fence gate. I usually walked faster than Alexis, but as I pushed the gate open, I noticed she had barely even made it out of the car. This annoyed me, for reasons I didn't understand at the time. So I called out to her, "Alexis, come here!" Then I saw her come hurriedly toward me through the cracks in the gate. "Coming!" she said.

As she neared, I paused before stepping into the backyard; I held the gate door open until she was right at my feet. I said, "I'm sorry, I don't mean to come across bossy, but for some reason I feel like you should not be out of my sight right now.

So stay close, OK?" She looked at me without questioning it and said, "OK."

We continued through the yard and onto the back patio. We entered the house from the patio door, which leads into the kitchen. I turned left and walked over to the fridge. I opened the double doors and grabbed a soda. Without looking back to confirm, I sensed that Alexis was standing behind me. Without closing the fridge doors first, assuming she would also want to grab a beverage, I took a step back and then around the fridge door to my right.

I made my way down one step and into the living area. I stopped in the middle of the room, facing the wall opposite the kitchen. Pausing to take a sip of my soda, I quietly stood there recounting the events at church.

Suddenly, I turned my attention back to the kitchen. I looked, and the fridge was still open, its long, black door obstructing my view. I didn't hear any movement from Alexis, so I leaned a little to my left to see if I could catch a glimpse of her standing near the fridge. I didn't see or hear a peep from her. In my spirit, I saw what looked like something holding its hand over her mouth as if to gag her and keep her silent.

Sensing that something was very wrong, I called out to her in a panic, "Alexis where are you?" I immediately ran from the living room into the kitchen. I pushed past the fridge door and stopped abruptly in the middle of the kitchen next to the island, quietly waiting for her response. Then I heard the toilet flush from the bathroom in the hall directly in front of me. She opened the door and quietly came out of the bathroom, walking toward me. "I told you to stay next to me!" I said, "...not to get out of my sight!"

She walked around the other side of the island, and then we stood facing each other. I apologized to her again for my sense of urgency, but still I plead for her compliance. She quietly and sheepishly let out an "OK," again with a nod of her head.

Then, out of my peripheral, I caught a quick glimpse of something peering out of my father's bedroom and into the hallway. The flash of a dark shadow appeared out of nowhere in the doorway and then moved back out of sight. My eyes and attention swiftly diverted from Alexis to this unwanted guest. I turned my head quickly to the right and then looked down at the floor. Almost instantly my eyes filled up with tears. I didn't know what that flash of black was yet, but my spirit knew right away. Whatever this was, it was *very* evil—so evil, in fact, that my first reaction was to turn away from it, and my eyes became full of tears, almost out of instinct.

Without looking up at Alexis, I said, "I just saw something." "I saw it too," she replied. She continued to look at me as I stared at the floor, searching my brain for what to do next. Unfortunately, I fell short as I scrambled through my mind, desperately hoping that an answer would pop up, but to no avail. Alexis seemed less disturbed, but at the same time very aware that what had just made its presence known was not good; like she was used to it; as though she had seen this thing many times before.

I went on to say, "Give me a second—let me check and see what this is." In the Bible it says to "check the spirit by the spirit": "Dear friends, do not believe every spirit, but test the spirits to see whether they are from God, because many false prophets have gone out into the world" (1 John 4:1). At this time, I was unaware of what I was actually doing, but my spirit man knew it was the right thing to do. I had not read this scripture in the Bible yet. (Thank God and Jesus for the Holy Ghost!)

I waited for a moment but still didn't receive a "clear" answer. I hoped and wished for an audible voice to scream out at me what to do next. So I did all I knew to do at the time: I looked up at Alexis and said, "Do you love God?" She quietly said under her breath, "Yes." I said, "No! That's not good enough! If you want this you need to say it loud and proud so the other side will know it! Do you want this or not?" She sheepishly nodded her head and said to me, "Yes." It was as though I was screaming at a meek little girl trying to pull this out of her. I went on and pushed her more by saying, "I've been through this part before. God has rid me of my demons. I'm not going to let you tag along with me if you're not sure. It's not fair—you choose right now!"

I grabbed a Bible I had left in the house sitting there next to us on the kitchen island. I didn't know what verses to read, so I just opened it and started to read out loud. I wasn't going to be bullied by the devil and his cohorts, so I pushed past my fear and walked hard and quickly toward the hall and over to my right into what used to be my dad's bedroom. This is from where the black figure had stepped out and shown itself in the hallway. I didn't know what I was up against and had no previous knowledge or instruction on spiritual warfare, so I just stood in the middle of the room and began to read the Bible loud and aggressively. I wanted whatever was in the house to know that I belonged to God and that it had no place here. I was also riotously mad that this chick who had been following me around the past few months had attachments around that were now coming against me and her both.

I continued to read aloud as Alexis stood next to me. The look on her face was almost one of bewilderment. She was completely silent, as usual, with a sense about her that said, "I don't know what's going on. I'm completely innocent and unaware of what we might have just seen." *Yeah right* was my first thought. I sensed that she knew all too well what was going on. You would think she would have brought me up to speed—but no, she just stayed quiet. Not seeing any more activity, and not at all sure what to do to "evict" this visitor, I decided to call it a night and just go back to Nashville.

A few times during the hour-long drive Alexis mentioned that she was excited to go back to the church and that we had to make it there the following Sunday. I agreed. I couldn't wait to return. I wanted some more. It was the first time, after several years of looking for a church to call home, that I had been to church and actually felt like God was there. I was also excited that I had finally been introduced to people that I felt I could learn from and in a place where I could grow up spiritually.

CHAPTER 30

*Brothers and sisters, I could not address you as people who
live by the Spirit but as people who are still worldly—mere
infants in Christ. I gave you milk, not solid food, for you were
not yet ready for it. Indeed, you are still not ready. You are still
worldly. For since there is jealousy and quarreling among you,
are you not worldly? Are you not acting like mere humans?*

—1 CORINTHIANS 3:1–3

AFTER MONTHS OF spending as I pleased without checking
my account balance, the time finally came when I knew I
couldn't go any further without coming to grips with reality.
Alexis stood next to me in my kitchen as I took a deep breath,
preparing myself before I called my bank to check my balance.
I checked my checking account first—seven hundred dollars—
then my savings—also seven hundred dollars. It hurt to hear
this, of course, but it was no one's fault but my own. Taking
full credit for this, I ended the call, lay the phone down on the
counter, took a deep breath, and instead of telling Alexis how
much was left, all I could say was, "I've made some mistakes."

I was three or four months behind on all of my bills at this
point. I think the only thing I had kept up with was my rent.

After Leo died, I lost my "care," and now that I had found it, it was too late for me to scramble to catch up. I called my car company, but my story fell on deaf ears and they told me I was to surrender the car. I exhausted every option I could think of. I even went by CarMax to see about selling the car, but they only wanted to pay me four thousand dollars—I still owed the company six thousand dollars. I didn't think being without the car and still owing for it was a good idea, so I decided this wasn't the best option.

The ship was going down and going down fast. By the time I wanted to put in the effort to try again, it was too late to repair what had already been done. I sent texts and calls to all my clients to resuscitate my business. I got a few bites, but not nearly enough to make a significant difference.

There was an insurance policy from my father's estate that was supposedly left to me as sole beneficiary. It was worth forty thousand dollars. *Great! Outstanding!* I thought. This would be more than enough to get me back up on my feet again. But after several attempts to retrieve the funds, it turned out that this policy was not left solely to me. I was second in line to Gloria. The money was to be split three ways between the stepchildren and I. The policy information was returned to the attorney over the estate, and now it would be up to them to decide when to disperse the cash.

Grabbing for straws at this point, I tried any and everything. I even took my daddy's TV to a pawn shop so I could buy groceries for me and my kiddos. It seemed the harder I tried to stay afloat, the harder it got. Things that used to work, or should have worked, all fell through.

▬ ▬ ▬ ▬ ▬ ▬ ▬

The following weekend, Alexis sat at the island in the center of my dad's kitchen. It was early yet, about nine o'clock or so, but she struggled to keep her eyes open. Drowsily she said, "I've got to go to bed, I can't stay awake any longer." From the opposite side of the room, I turned from the sink toward her and said, "OK...but just make sure you wake up in the morning with the other Alexis, because this one hates me." She glared at me as I turned back to what I was doing.

I heard her footsteps as she walked by and into the den. I also heard Cash's nails as he shuffled by, following her to the couch. I piddled around the house for a bit until about 1:00 a.m. and then joined them in the den. I decided my bed for that night would be one of the recliners, one that sat adjacent to the couch where Alexis and Cash were sleeping. The furniture in the house was disappearing (the two beds from the back bedrooms had been moved out) so it was slim pickings; you found something you liked, and *voila!*—a bed.

TVs had also disappeared. My usual habit was to land wherever a TV was (I like the noise and light; I guess you could say I'm still afraid of the dark), but tonight I was proud of myself for being a big girl and falling asleep in the dark with no background noise. (*Look at me go!*) I pulled back on the bar on the side of the chair and stretched my legs out. I turned off the lamp beside me and pulled a quilt over my head. "See, I can do this," I reassured myself. "I don't feel scared, and my thoughts aren't going rampant without the distraction of TV noise. I feel...like...I'm about to...fall asleep."

I felt something bump the end of the recliner. Without looking up to see, I told myself that it must have been my cat Bliss jumping up onto the recliner near my feet. I lay there for what I'm sure was a good five minutes, and then I realized I'd never heard Bliss *after* she jumped up on the chair. That's not like her. Bliss was always one to make her presence known. Usually after jumping up next to me like that, she would walk down close to my head and meow—but nothing. "That wasn't Bliss," I told myself.

I threw the cover off my face, sat up, and took a look around me. Nothing—or so I thought. I knew something had hit my chair, but what? I continued to look into the dark around me for the culprit. I sensed there was something to my right. I squinted my eyes trying to make it out in the darkness. It wasn't a solid form; it was a dark figure. It wasn't wispy or like a shadow like most people describe when they say they've seen a "ghost." No, this was different. It was part of the atmosphere. It seemed to be made up of the same air that separated it from me. The only difference was, when it moved, I could see the energy it was made of, like floating atoms, moving fluid in a pool of dense, liquid mass. It was in what the atmosphere is made of. Some might call it the "heavenlies," that invisible, unseen realm around us. Welcome to hell on Earth—literally.

I turned on the lamp and jumped out of the chair and onto the floor next to the couch Alexis and Cash where sleeping on. I felt afraid and alert. I looked past the couch and over into the open area in the dining room. I could make out shapes in the dark that looked like other beings—four, to be exact, of all sizes. There were two small ones that stood about the height of the table. There was a tall one that stood on the other side of the table, near the back of the room; another like he stood in the corner of that room closest to me. I couldn't tell you what they were doing there. All I knew was that they were aware of me as much as I was aware of them.

I didn't know what to do. I wrestled with the idea of waking Alexis up. I knew she was tired, and I hated to bother her. It seemed to me that she might not see what I saw and would think I was silly. Seeing how I had been through a great deal of stress recently, she might just think I was being selfish and waking her because I was dealing with anxiety. No matter if she believed me or not, I decided to try to wake her. I didn't want to go through this alone.

I shook her and she mumbled a little. "Wake up!" I said. She muttered out a "whaah?" and lifted her head as she barely opened her eyes. "I'm scared," I told her as tears started to fill up my eyes. I looked away from her face and around the room. Those things were now gone. Alexis put her head back down and went back to sleep.

I waited a moment before letting down my guard and convincing myself that what had just occurred was nothing but a mirage. Then suddenly they appeared again, and this time they were more aggressive. I could hear thumps and pops in and around the two rooms as though they were saying, "Back off! You don't want to mess with us!"

I shook Alexis again and said, "Seriously! Wake up!"

She rose up, both eyes squinting.

"There's something in here," I told her.

She touched my head and said, "It's OK," not once questioning what I meant, as though she was used to whatever was in the room with us.

I looked again, and like before, they were gone. I didn't want her to go back to sleep. They seemed to go away when she was awake, so I pleaded with her again, "Stay up with me for a minute; I know you're tired, but please."

She sat all the way up, stood to her feet, and said, "I got to go pee."

I slid away from the couch to let her get by me. She walked around the couch and toward the doorway. I said something to her, and she stopped suddenly—the wall next to her wobbled. *Oh my gosh! I've just seen a portal!* In that moment my mind went blank as my jaw hit the floor in disbelief. I no longer recalled the words I was about to say. I looked at Alexis with my eyes wide, as it registered in my mind what I had just seen. *I just saw an actual portal.*

Before this moment I had heard of portals but never knew if they really existed or not. But *this* was undeniable. Alexis didn't wait for me to finish my sentence, never questioning my puzzled look, and continued to walk back toward the restroom. I sat in disbelief looking at the wall that had just wobbled, almost as if she had bumped into it when she stopped, causing it to ripple like waves in a pool.

▬ ▬ ▬ ▬ ▬ ▬ ▬

Later that week, we returned to church for the Sunday service. I wore a long DKNY maxi dress that I had bought for Easter. I had twisted my bright, glowing purple hair into a French twist; my bangs were cut straight across and touched right above my eyebrows.

We stepped into church just as the service was starting. We were met by the usher and directed to a pew about three rows from the front. Alexis and I took our seats and sat quietly as we took in the sights and sounds. I had never been to a church like this where people worshipped freely.

There was a beautiful, young, black pastor at the front. He held an open Bible in one hand and a microphone close to his mouth in the other. He had a white cloth lying over his shoulders. He seemed to sway back and forth ever so gently as he lovingly professed his love for God and encouraged others to praise Him.

Not knowing what to do or how to "praise," I chose to close my eyes and meditate. I went inward and could feel the "goodness" that enveloped the room. I immersed my senses in the sights and sounds of the atmosphere all around me. Then suddenly my head dropped and my hands that I held up and toward the altar seemed to suddenly go limp, as though I had fallen *deep* into meditation—deeper than I had ever gone before (and trust me, I have gone *deep*...or so I thought). I suddenly raised my head as to shake myself out of a trance.

I opened my eyes, got my bearings, and looked up toward the front of the church where the leaders sat. I looked almost frantically for LaShondria, but I couldn't put my eye on her. Sensing something was about to take place, something I had never experienced before, I felt that I might need someone like her with more knowledge about such to walk me through it. Without saying a word to Alexis, I stood up and walked toward the back and out of the room. I looked in the bathroom, peeked outside, went into the kids' area—but no LaShondria.

I didn't know what was about to happen; I was apprehensive, but I knew I didn't want to keep it from happening. I stopped for a moment to catch my breath and gather my thoughts, preparing for whatever would happen next. As I stood out in the dimly lit hallway, next to the small lobby, I suddenly heard that still, small voice. It said, "Take the tank top you have on, under your dress, off...Shimmy it down your legs and put it in your hand. You're going to need it to place it over your head."

I had no idea what this meant, but desperate for some guidance and instruction, I followed suit. Without anyone around me, I went ahead and did so right there in the hallway. I took the shirt in hand, took a deep breath, and then went back to my seat in the pew next to Alexis.

I sat at the end of the pew, closest to the center aisle. I kept looking down at the floor next to me, sensing that I was supposed to get down on that floor. I questioned this for a minute. "What would Alexis think of me? This is pretty much her first time in church in forever. What would the other people sitting around me think? What do I do after I get on the floor? For how long?"

I didn't know the answers to any of this; all I knew was that I had to get down there on my knees and down on my face ASAP. So I did. I got down on my knees and stretched my arms straight out in front of me as I placed my face close to the ground. Instinctually, I took the black tank top, which was still in my hand, and draped it over my head to cover it.

After I had been on the floor for a moment, I felt a soft breeze above me as I was covered over top with a large, white sheet. *Oh, that's what they use those for,* I thought to myself. The pastor at the beginning of the worship service had one of these around his shoulders. Other patrons at the church also had these draped around their bodies as they sat in the pews, and others over them while they lay on the floor in worship.

Being new to all this, I have to admit, when I first saw people wearing drapes with tassels while they sat on the floor weeping, expressing their love for God, I couldn't help but wonder how much of this was nonsense. To me, it seemed to be for show. Now I was having a firsthand encounter with the Holy Spirit. This was not, in fact, all just a put-on. I thought these people were just being emotional. *Who knew?* I thought. *They weren't just putting on after all.* These linens actually served a purpose, and the dramatics of being on the floor was not all for show.

Not really sure what to do next now that I was on the floor, I raised up on my knees, grabbed the cloth from my back, and returned to my seat on the pew. Or so I thought. Like a magnet,

I felt a force pulling me down to the ground. Not wanting to lie on the ground again, I tried to keep my body from being pulled back down. I even placed both hands on the pew in front of me to keep me from going down. I slid my bottom back into the pew and succumbed to the force that was pulling my head and body down toward the floor.

I placed my head in between my knees and put both hands as flat as I could between my feet on the floor. My head hung low; it felt as though my back, head, and hands were being forced to stay down. Like a pull, something was causing this. I couldn't sit straight up if I tried. I didn't feel scared; I was calm, peaceful—almost lethargic. It didn't feel like an angry force; it just felt as though something was trying to make me submit to it.

The force to the ground was finally so strong that I gave in to its pull. I got back over into the aisle and assumed the prayer position down on the ground, as though I was saying, "Uncle!" This time I stretched all the way out on the carpet. Knowing that whatever was pushing me to get down was not going to give up until I gave up, I thought, *How far can I get down? OK! OK! I give!* I stretched my fingertips and toes as straight out as I possibly could. Knowing I was dealing with a force greater than I, I no longer cared what I looked like to others.

How do You want me? What will please You? I give, I surrender! I thought. My body long and outstretched, once again someone placed a linen over top of me, making sure to cover not only the majority of my body, but most importantly, my head. Every part of me touched the floor except for my face. I kept it just barely off the carpet, thinking, *This floor might not be clean. I wonder, when was it last vacuumed?* The tip of my nose barely touched the floor. Then suddenly, like someone was pushing the back of my head, my face pressed into the floor. My face now smooshed into the carpet, I sensed whatever was pushing me down was saying, "Oh yeah? Let go. Surrender. Humble yourself. Let go of what the flesh wants! Give Me what I want! Your flesh is worthless compared to Me! Show Me that I mean more to you than your flesh does!"

I lay there, my face mashed into the carpet, like I was being held down by the LAPD; I finally succumbed to the Holy Spirit. At this point, wanting to do whatever was pleasing to Him, I just lay there until I no longer sensed a heavy force holding me down, almost paralyzed on the floor. During all of this, it was almost as if I was aware but at the same time still so unaware of what was going on in the room around me. I could still hear the apostle as she preached, but somehow it was different. It was as though she sounded muffled, far away. I heard her say at one point, "God will cause a service to be about only one person!" I felt glad she was supportive. I had not come to church planning to be the center of attention; I had to just go with what was happening to me. And I was so glad to be in a room full of people who understood.

Toward the end of the service, I felt OK about getting up, and I returned to my seat. The pastor did an altar call, and Alexis slid up to the edge of her seat, as though she was eager to go and wanted to move, but couldn't bring herself to go up to the front. Sensing this in her, as the pastor went on to pray for those who did stand, I placed one hand on Alexis's back and held the other palm out toward the apostle as she prayed for the others. Again, I went into a trancelike state, and my head, as though it was being pulled by a magnet, slowly rolled to the side, away from Alexis and over to my shoulder. Since this had never happened to me before, questioning whether it was really being pulled or if I was doing it, I pulled my head back over to the other side and then let go to let it rest. Like a strong pull, suddenly, again it was drawn away as though someone was doing it for me. It kept my head away from Alexis until I took my hand off her back after the prayer.

After the service, we got into the car and realized it was two o'clock in the afternoon. *Wow!* We both started to laugh. I had never been in a service that lasted that long. Plus, it only felt like an hour had passed, not four! Excited and pumped about what we had just experienced, I talked gleefully to Alexis about my thoughts on what had just taken place. I looked over at her, and once again, she sat there silent. It annoyed me, and I was tired of feeling bad about being annoyed by it. Why was this girl hanging around me so much? She had no personality and didn't "bring anything to the table." I felt that she was just along for the ride. I wanted someone to hang out with me that would talk back, not just sit there and look at me like a deer in head-lights. It was as though I was being exploited for my personality because she didn't have one.

Finally fed up, I said, "Now that's not normal. We come out of *that*, and you still say nothing?" Then suddenly it hit me: "My dad's house isn't haunted! It's *you!*" She immediately started to cry and covered her face with her hands. Thinking this was way too much for me to deal with on my own (I didn't know how to do exorcisms!), I ran back into the church and looked for LaShondria for some assistance, or at the very least some advice—*anything.* I didn't want this girl to be around me if she was all "demon possessed."

I ran inside and found LaShondria sitting on the front pew in what was now an empty church. I gave her a quick rundown on what had just transpired, and I asked her to come outside and speak to Alexis. We walked out to the car, and LaShondria opened the passenger side door. Alexis had quit crying by now.

LaShondria bent down to speak to her and told her that everything was going to be OK. Immediately Alexis broke out into tears, covering her face with both hands, and continued to sob. I sat on the driver's side and watched. I felt bad for Alexis, sympathetic really, but in my gut I felt like Alexis's reaction was a put-on. It seemed real and looked real, but for some reason I could tell that her reaction was not sincere. It was as though she was being manipulative. Her dramatics seemed to convey, "Please don't leave me," to both LaShondria and I instead of, "I need help. I don't want to live with these demons anymore." LaShondria continued to talk to her for a bit and then sent us on our way. As I drove back to my dad's house, I thought, *Great. I'm bringing demons home with me.*

When we returned to the house, I turned on a gospel song playlist and placed it in the kitchen window so that the music would carry throughout the house and out into the yard. In the wake of our recent revelation, everything—including the house, the atmosphere, myself, and Alexis—felt peaceful. She said she felt like taking a nap, so she lay out on the covered patio on a pallet I had slept on the night before.

After recent events in the house, I was afraid to sleep indoors, especially with Alexis around. The weather was nice, so I chose to take my chances outdoors instead of taking my chances with what might be inside. As she snuggled up with the blankets and pillows I had lying on top of a large comforter, Alexis admitted, "This is the first time I've felt this at peace in years. It's the first time in a long time that they have left me alone." When she said "they," she was referring to the dark shadows that had followed her for most of her life. She lay there in the cool breeze on this lovely Sunday afternoon and closed her eyes. She looked happy; there was a hint of a smile on her face. I felt great. A nap sounded wonderful too, but I decided to get busy and do yard work instead.

Later that evening, I went inside and peered out the kitchen window to check on Alexis. She was still knocked out. As I prepared to go to bed, I decided I would prefer to sleep on the patio again. I went out on the patio and looked around Alexis and my two dogs, who were snoozing away, for a spot to lie down. I found myself lying longways at the foot of the comforter at Alexis's feet.

I rose up and looked back over at her. As I looked at her lying there, so happy and comfortable, it then became clear to me that not only had I been "run out" of my house because of her; now she had also taken over my spot outside. Instead of waking her up and evicting her from my makeshift bed, I decided to just lie down and get some sleep.

— — — — — — —

The next day, I woke up feeling anxious and confused. I went back and forth on whether or not to call my attorney and tell him that I wanted to keep the house. I paced the floors back and forth as I weighed out the pros and cons. "It just feels like this is where I'm supposed to be," I said. "Like this is where God wants me. It seems like I'm in the 'flow' here. I've had so many supernatural events happen here; I feel like this is the place that God needs me to be in order for His will to be done."

Alexis sat and watched me pace, saying nothing as she watched me stew. The only thing she had to offer as advice was, "I think so too. I love it here. Truthfully, I've been looking for jobs here."

After lunch, my dad's nurse, Hope, came over to visit. I told her that I was now considering moving into my dad's house instead of putting it up for sale. I felt as though I could confide in her about anything, but on this day she seemed a little annoyed. "Gabriel, whatever you do, you need to make up your mind! Now you can get mad at me all you want, but I'm just gonna keep it real. Don't take this as a word from me; this is what God has put on my heart to say to you. I'm sorry, but right now you need a little tough love. You have got to stop going back and forth and make a decision and stick with it."

It stung a little, I have to admit, to have her go from being my "bestie" into the "get it together" tone of voice, but she was right. It was what I needed to hear. After an hour or so, she headed out to do errands. I felt confident and less worried after our chat. Alexis was stone-cold silent again. I decided to ignore her instead of letting it get on my nerves. Alexis's silence, most times, felt like an oppressive weapon toward me.

Deciding not to let that ruin my new state of mind, I went outdoors to finish mowing the yard. But it did. The longer I thought about Alexis's weird moods, the more annoyed I got. I started to mow aggressively. Alexis then appeared, coming out from the side door to the house, and walked down the driveway toward me. I stopped the mower and waited to hear what she had in store.

She said, "I have to get back to Nashville. I don't have any money on me, so I need to get to the bank before it closes." She didn't wait for a response and turned to walk back toward the house.

Huh? Really? This was what she was going to use to get to me? Having been around me so much for the past few months, she knew I had abandonment issues. I didn't like it when plans abruptly changed and someone around me took off without first giving me a heads up. This annoyed me, as did the fact that she had been cool and calm all day.

Earlier, I had asked her if there was anything she needed to do that day, and if she had any reason we might need to run back to Nashville. She assured me that she didn't. She had seemed quite content earlier that day as she watched me be anxious and confused. I had noticed that she started to change and seemed less pleased *after* Hope had been there and had given me some helpful advice that lifted my spirits.

Now that I knew that there was something working in Alexis trying its best to get to me, I wasn't going to take this lying down. I turned the mower off and walked up to the French doors on the side entry to the home. I walked through the living room at a fast pace and into the kitchen to find Alexis leaning over the island on bended elbows, looking at her phone. Caught off guard and surprised by my entrance, she immediately stood up like she had just been caught.

(Now, mind you, it was 3:00 p.m. at this time—she said she needed to rush back because her bank closed at 4:00. It takes a little over forty-five minutes to drive to Nashville. Wouldn't you think someone working on that time line would be gathering her things and heading out the door instead of lounging around? It appeared as though she was waiting on me. Like she knew what she had said to me and was waiting for me to come inside and start going off. Well, I was doing exactly as she had suspected, but this time in a different way. I wanted her to *get out*!)

"What are you doing?" I shouted. She stood up quickly as though she knew she had just been busted. She fumbled to put her phone down quickly at her side out of my view and said, "Nothing! I swear!" I continued to yell as she rushed past me out the kitchen and through the den. "You were waiting on me, weren't you?"

Suddenly her demeanor changed, and she strolled very slowly and defiantly before me. She walked tall with her shoulders back. I followed on her heels, and then I realized this wasn't Alexis I was talking to. I became even more livid as I followed her out the door and to her car. All I could see was the back of her and the side of her face. Whatever was working through her kept moving toward leaving, but its body language was very clear to me—"I hear you, I'll do what you say, but you don't scare me."

She paused before opening the door to the car and turned to face me. So angry now, and with the realization that I was dealing with something otherworldly, I looked down around my feet for something to throw at it. Feeling as though I was having an out-of-body experience, the first thing I saw was a rock. I grabbed it. I questioned my choice at first, but then I sensed this was right. For some reason, it entered my mind that this was the right thing to do, because using rocks as weapons was biblical.

I whipped my body back around, drew my arm back, and threw the rock—and *hard*—at it. The rock hit the car, leaving a huge dent. "Never again!" I yelled. "This will never happen again!" She still stood there and looked at me in a haze. I got right up in her face and screamed, "Get out of here!" She turned to grab the car door, got inside, and backed out of the driveway. I watched as she left. I gasped for air, but I stood defensively, as if to say, "You don't want none of this." She pulled out into the road and headed back to Nashville. This would be the last time I saw her, for now.

CHAPTER 31

Or suppose a woman has ten silver coins and loses one. Doesn't she light a lamp, sweep the house and search carefully until she finds it?

—LUKE 15:8

O N THE DAY that would have been Leo's twenty-fourth birthday, his cousin Damien and Damien's dad (Hector) accompanied me to the lot to retrieve Leo's motorcycle. Sal loaned me the $138 to pay the salvage yard. I gave my info to the lady at the window, and then we were escorted by a city worker in a van to the area where the bike was being kept.

Damien automatically knew which bike it was and jumped out of the van's side door before we came to a complete stop. He walked up to the bike, stood it up, walked the bike backward out of the space, and then walked it back to the office building. We followed slowly behind him in the van. I was glad Damien was there with me on this day. It was a hot summer day; he had his shirt off as he pushed the bike with all his might. He needed to do this; it was important that he did.

As I watched Damien in silence, I saw that this was part of his healing. This was more than a bike that he was walking next to.

This was his brother, a fallen soldier; he was valiantly coming to his aid. It was like watching two broken hearts, wounded and defeated but determined to carry on and look out for one another.

When we got to the building, Hector and I jumped out of the van and headed toward the gates and out toward the trailer. Damien stood with his head down, both hands still on the handlebars, trying to catch his breath. His long, black hair fell over his face as his stomach expanded and shrank with each gasp of air he took. His father quickly got in front of him and hurried to find the right key on his chain to open the door to the trailer. Upon opening it, he went inside and extended the ramp.

On the very last stretch, Damien gathered his strength to load the bike. As they secured the bike with straps, I walked into the covered trailer and stood aside to watch. I looked down, and there beside Damien's foot was one tattered and worn penny, tails side up.

━ ━ ━ ━ ━ ━ ━

I now owned this bike, but not by any means or circumstances that I could have ever imagined. Then it hit me. My mind went back to January, when I had gone to *demand* the bike be given over for my possession, and God had said to me, "It's not time." God then put it on my heart that when we do things in God's timing and according to His will and not our own, we don't have to force anything to happen. If we are patient and wait upon the Lord, in due season He will fulfill His promises. He is forever faithful.

God has a plan for everything. Whether you deem it bad or good, it's not up for you to decide. He will work all things for the good of those that have been called according to His purpose. It's usually not how we would do it, but that's where faith comes in. He is the omniscient God. His ways are not our ways; they are past our understanding. To understand His ways would make us equal to Him, which we can never be. That is why we must trust Him, even when things don't go like we think they should. Even if His way hurts or is unpleasant, we must learn to lean on Him and trust His plan. God's Word says, "'For I know the plans I have for you,' declares the LORD, 'plans to prosper you and not to harm you, plans to give you hope and a future'" (Jer. 29:11). Just always remember, it's not about us. We belong to Him.

> And we know that God causes all things to work together for good to those who love God, to those who are called according to His purpose.
>
> —ROMANS 8:28, NAS

CHAPTER 32

The man looked around. "Yes," he said, "I see people, but I can't
see them very clearly. They look like trees walking around."

—MARK 8:24

SAT NEXT TO the bike in a circle with Leo's family, which
included his dad, his mom Donna, his adopted sister, and
his half-sister. As I witnessed to them about my love for God,
they listened on with looks of bewilderment as my eyes filled
up with tears. They couldn't understand how a person who had
been through so much could sit there and profess her love for
God, so much so that it moves her to tears.

His mother was an atheist, so this notion must have been
mind boggling to her. Most atheists have the incorrect idea of
God, viewing Him as a punisher. She watched on with curiosity as I continued to speak. I told them that God wanted a
"new thing" from me in this chapter of my life: new number,
new places, no communication with people from my past. I was
balling at this point. I said to them, "It makes me sad to think
about walking away. I hate to lose you guys."

Donna, trying to comfort me, said, "Well, honey, when you
get done, we'll still be here."

I nodded my head, but for some reason I knew better. Somehow I just knew this wouldn't be the case.

— — — — — — —

The following night, I found myself out at the site where Leo had died. I sat facing the street on the concrete sidewalk, underneath the glow of the street light above. This wasn't a very busy street—only about twenty cars or so passed by in an hour—so it was private enough to spend time alone.

Cash sat next to me on his leash, facing the street. We both sat there in silence as he kept watch around me. I sat and stared at the orange stick figure that had been spray painted by the authorities after they removed Leo's body from the scene. This would be the last time I would come by here, for a while at least. I came to tell Leo my good-byes.

I went to my car and found a large permanent marker I had left in there (for what reason, I can't recall). I put Cash back in the car and promised to be back shortly. I walked back over to the concrete light pole that we had been sitting next to. I felt this was the best place, if any, to leave Leo my official good-bye/love letter. It went something like this:

> God healed a blind man at the pools at Bethsaida. He told him he was to never return to Bethsaida if he wanted to remain healed. I can't stay here and wallow in my grief. I gotta go for now. I dare not waste this life! I long for you. I crave you. I'm so glad I knew you. I'll be seeing you. See you when I get home.
>
> ### JESUS HEALS A BLIND MAN
>
> When they arrived at Bethsaida, some people brought a blind man to Jesus, and they begged him to touch the man and heal him. Jesus took the blind man by the hand and led him

out of the village. Then, spitting on the man's eyes, he laid his hands on him and asked, "Can you see anything now?"

The man looked around. "Yes," he said, "I see people, but I can't see them very clearly. They look like trees walking around."

Then Jesus placed his hands on the man's eyes again, and his eyes were opened. His sight was completely restored, and he could see everything clearly. Jesus sent him away, saying, "Don't go back into the village on your way home."

—MARK 8:22–26, NLT

CHAPTER 33

*Now faith is the substance of things hoped
for, the evidence of things not seen.*

—HEBREWS 11:1, KJV

I HAD NOT SPOKEN to my mother since the day after the funeral. After a couple months of not speaking, I decided to reach out to her, and we went to lunch. Things went well enough, I thought.

A day later, Mom called me. She told me how skinny I was and continued to criticize everything about me that she could. I told her, "Yeah, I'm skinny; I've been dealing with a lot of stress."

Assuming this was the moment I should reach out to someone and let them know what I was dealing with. Things had gotten way out of control; maybe it was time to stop running and just tell someone. Maybe then I could get some help.

"Mom," I said, "I ran out of money."

"You spent all of your father's money?" she screamed.

Taken aback by her reaction, I quickly tried to retract my statement, like it never happened. I said something to the effect of, "Mom why do you talk to me in such a way? This is why I stayed away from you the past couple months. I couldn't take the chance of you doing me this way. I was already in a bad state of mind; I didn't want to add to it. It might have been the trigger to the loaded gun."

I guess she misunderstood what I was saying and took it as a personal attack, although that was not at all my intent. She said, "Nobody talks to me the way you do. Nobody seems to have a problem with me but you. I'm always with people...because people like me. And you're always by yourself because nobody likes you."

Anger suddenly flew over me like a white light heat. I stood to my feet, and my entire body tensed. I stretched my arm down by my side, out as far as I could extend it, and balled up my fist and squeezed it tight. Appalled by her audacity to say such a thing to me, especially at such a time in my life, I was rendered speechless at first. We had not spoken in months. She knew what I had just gone through. And after *all* that and *all* the time we spent apart, she still hadn't learned anything from it? Why did it always seem that I was the only one who thought about things? The one who tried to spend time in self-reflection, to care about my growth as a human being, especially in inter-personal relationships? It always seemed one sided.

"How dare you!" I screamed. I didn't care about being polite anymore; she didn't think much about being polite to me. "This is why! This is why I stay away from you! You have no one to blame for your problems but yourself! I'm done! Don't you dare call me ever again!" At this moment, to me, she was the perfect example of why some people die alone.

I took a few minutes to blow off some steam. I figured a drive would do me some good (after I'd calmed down, of course). I love being on the road, listening to some loud music or a power-packed sermon. I get in the zone, and it really does seem to do the trick, hitting my reset button for my emotional and mental state. So I packed up my animals and a bag for the night and drove down to Murfreesboro. I wanted to be there for church in the morning anyway.

—   —   —   —   —   —   —

After church, I went to my dad's house and got on the lawn mower. I figured doing yard work might help me blow off some steam. Behind the shop, I got the mower stuck sideways in a small ditch. I pushed and I pulled, I huffed and puffed in anger trying to get the darn thing out of the mud. In my spirit I heard, "Are you ready to give up yet?" I grumbled and jumped off the mower, then I threw a tarp over it and left it in the ditch.

Our neighbor, a lifelong friend of my dad's, came walking down the drive toward me. He must have heard all the ruckus and come up with an excuse to stop by to borrow a couple loading ramps that were in Daddy's shop. I didn't feel much like putting on a façade. Barely looking up at him, I scowled and said, "Hey, Jack."

He could probably see steam rising from my forehead. He looked at the screen hanging halfway off the shop window. I had accidently snagged the bottom of it when I got too close trying to mow the small strip of lawn in front of the shop. In months past I would have been more careful not to tear anything up, but when I saw that it was snagged, I didn't stop to lose it—I just kept driving.

"What's that?" Jack asked.

"You ever mowed mad, Jack?" I asked. By this time we were walking up the drive toward the house.

He replied, "You shouldn't mow mad." He gave me a few reassuring pats on the shoulder. I could tell he was at a loss for words.

I threw my hands up in the air and said, "Well, it didn't do me any good being nice!" All he could say was, "Well…"

━ ━ ━ ━ ━ ━ ━

The next morning I was back in Nashville, about to take Cash to the park. We walked out the front door to load up in my car, and I stopped short when I saw nothing but a huge, empty space where my car used to be. My car had been repossessed, I guess sometime during the night. I let out a sigh and walked Cash back into the house. I slammed my keys on top of the bookcase and stormed through the house, down the hall and into my bedroom. "That's it! I'm done! I'm going back to my old ways! I've had enough of this!"

Then suddenly, without any warning, I began to speak in tongues. I had never spoken in tongues before, so it took me a minute to realize what was happening. I always thought if I was to ever speak in tongues, it would happen in a Holy Ghost-thick environment, like at church. But no, it was happening here in my bedroom on a Monday.

My tongue moved up and down and waved with the motions being pushed out with every breath. I wasn't doing this on my own; it was like my tongue was set on autopilot. The sounds that were coming out of me and the way my tongue was moving—I couldn't have made this up if I tried.

Whatever it was that was inside me, trying to make me give up, battled with resistance and did all it could to rebel. "No! No! I'm giving up!" It was as though my inner man was inside of me watching this battle take place. Then, I would speak in tongues again.

Like two forces fighting over a territory, the Holy Spirit fought for me and interceded when something inside of me tried to make me throw in the towel. Yes, the world around me may have been in turmoil; but that didn't mean God had bailed out on me. If He cared that much for me—to step in and not let me give up—I knew that no matter what my circumstances looked like at the moment, it was all part of a bigger plan. I didn't understand what it was yet, or even how He was going to get me out of this mess; I just knew I had to keep going. I was in God's hands now...and there's no better place to be.

> And the Holy Spirit helps us in our weakness. For example, we don't know what God wants us to pray for. But the Holy Spirit prays for us with groanings that cannot be expressed in words.
>
> —ROMANS 8:26, NLT

CHAPTER 34

But when you pray, go away by yourself, shut the door behind you, and pray to your Father in private. Then your Father, who sees everything, will reward you.

—MATTHEW 6:6, NLT

HAD HEARD PASTORS talk about a "prayer closet." *What's that?* I always thought. In my mind I pictured some closet in someone's house specifically designed for that purpose—*Does it have an altar in it? Is it painted gold? Are there offerings of incense and myrrh laid before God in there?*—that is, until I had come to a point in my life where I was desperate to find God. *Can He hear me? Are my prayers getting through?*

This is how I found myself in my small walk-in closet with the door closed, in the dark, on my knees crying out to God. "Why? Why have You brought me this far just to leave me?" The top of my body slumped over. I laid my chest on top of my knees. My head was turned to the side against the cold bamboo floor as I lay there sobbing. Then I heard that still, small voice say to me, "But it got you in here, didn't it?"

I immediately stopped crying. I sat straight up in the darkness and looked from side to side. It was pitch black, so I could see nothing, but "something" was surely aware of me. I stood to my feet and opened the closet door. My eyes squinted as they met with the sun shining through the windows in my bedroom. I blinked like a joey waking up from a nap and peering out from his mama's pouch.

With one hand still on the closet door handle, my eyes went directly toward my digital clock—12:24. Something in me sensed that this was significant, so I dashed out of my room and up to the front of my home to grab my phone. I pulled up Google from the Web and entered "Scripture 12:24" into the search engine. The first result that popped up was Luke 12:24 (NLT): "Look at the ravens. They don't plant or harvest or store food in barns, for God feeds them. And you are far more valuable to him than any birds!"

I smiled big as it became very clear to me: *He was there! He had always been there. And He was going to take care of me. Everything was going to be OK. I just had to trust Him.*

Sometimes God uses our struggles as a "boot camp" to draw us nearer to Him. Even those times that we consider to be our darkest hour God can actually use for our good. God wants an intimate relationship with you. He loves you. He wants what is best for you, even if that means taking things out of your life; things that keep you from *knowing* Him. God is not a mean God. He is not out to punish us. John 3:16 says, "For God so loved the world that he gave his one and only Son, that whoever believes in him shall not perish but have eternal life."

For example, you know how a kid gets sent to his room after he gets in trouble? It's kind of like that. It's a bummer for the kid to be put in a time-out, but the parent ultimately does it in the child's best interest. It's not because the parent doesn't love the child or because the parent wants to be mean to them. Actually, it's the exact opposite: the parent doesn't want their child to keep repeating the same behavior, knowing it's not good for them to do so. By putting the kid in time-out, the parent puts him or her on pause, so to speak, giving the child time to reevaluate, reflect, and finally redirect, exchanging his or her thinking and behavior for something better. God is our *Father*, by the way—the *best* Father there is and ever will be.

> And have you forgotten the encouraging words God spoke
> to you as his children? He said,
> > "My child, don't make light of the LORD's discipline,
> > and don't give up when he corrects you.
> > For the LORD disciplines those he loves,
> > and he punishes each one he accepts as his child."
>
> As you endure this divine discipline, remember that God is treating you as his own children. Who ever heard of a child who is never disciplined by its father? If God doesn't discipline you as he does all of his children, it means that you are illegitimate and are not really his children at all. Since we respected our earthly fathers who disciplined us, shouldn't we submit even more to the discipline of the Father of our spirits, and live forever?
> —HEBREWS 12:5–9, NLT

All I did know for sure was that God was not going to accept mediocrity from me for the second half of my life...and I thank Him for that. I thank Him for holding me back. I thank Him for the times that He said no. If it had not been for Him, I would have completely wasted away my second...well, third...better make it more like ten billionth chance to begin again and get it right—*His* definition of right, not my own. I thank the Lord that He had His hand on me my entire life and never gave up on me. Amen.

CHAPTER 35

So that he does not corrupt his bloodline among his
people, for I am Yahweh who sets him apart.

—LEVITICUS 21:15, HCSB

I FOUND A BOX in my spare bedroom that I'd brought home
from my father's house. I had not opened it yet to see what
was inside. As I dug through it, I found letters my grandmother
had written to my dad years ago.

As I read, my grandmother told my father stories about her
past and the family history. These were stories I had never
heard and would have never known about if she had not put
pen to paper. I was blown away by what I was reading—really
cool stuff from a generation past that survived war, raising families, and just life itself. She spoke in great detail of what it was
like for her and my grandfather to find love, start a family, and
what it was like for them when he was in Europe during World
War II. This was real life, a firsthand account of what that really
looked and felt like. We as a people hear about war, but we don't
realize what it truly consists of. My grandfather was there on
D-Day when the tanks landed on the beach. He survived the

war, was even blown out of five tanks, and came home to have four more children.

With tears in my eyes, I looked up from the pages to look at the contents of the room around me. Leaning against one wall were stacks of framed degrees, doctrines, and honorary awards from when my dad was in school and when he served as a pharmacist at the Pentagon during Vietnam. Suddenly it all became very clear to me: I had lost my father's inheritance (the money), but I had not lost my heritage. I came from good stock—a long line of survivors and champions.

My grandfather came home from war and raised five children on his farm. He and his wife were both beautiful people, inside and out, and loved God and did the best they could to serve Him well with what they had. And what they had was each other. What they had was love. What they had was integrity and two able hands that they used to work hard.

My father was raised on the farm. He and his brothers started driving tractors at the age of five. Can you imagine putting a child on a tractor nowadays? No, I surely can't. But these boys, this is what they knew. They were plowing entire fields that stretched for miles by themselves. They never thought they were being treated unfairly either. The notion never occurred to them that this work was too hard. I think it's awesome. I believe it says a lot about their character and how much the world has declined since those days.

As I sat there on the floor, searching through my history, I finally understood a very important truth. I used to ask people why my stepsiblings acted the way they did after my father died. I didn't understand how they could be so motivated by such greed, with no real concern for anybody but themselves. People would always say, "It's because they didn't come from anything, baby. They've never had anything before."

I used to think that when people said, "they didn't come from anything," they were just talking about money. Now I knew different. That "anything" was a lineage, a background of people, a history with depth.

I thought about my circumstances—a depleted bank account—and then I realized I really hadn't lost what was important at all. What I came from wasn't about the money. My inheritance ran through my veins. That bloodline was something that no one could ever take away from me. If it had not been for this season in my life, a time when I was stripped of what I *thought* was most important, I may have never had this revelation.

To illustrate the point further, Jesus told them this story: "A man had two sons. The younger son told his father, 'I want my share of your estate now before you die.' So his father agreed to divide his wealth between his sons.

"A few days later this younger son packed all his belongings and moved to a distant land, and there he wasted all his money in wild living. About the time his money ran out, a great famine swept over the land, and he began to starve. He persuaded a local farmer to hire him, and the man sent him into his fields to feed the pigs. The young man became so hungry that even the pods he was feeding the pigs looked good to him. But no one gave him anything.

"When he finally came to his senses, he said to himself, 'At home even the hired servants have food enough to spare, and here I am dying of hunger! I will go home to my father and say, "Father, I have sinned against both heaven and you, and I am no longer worthy of being called your son. Please take me on as a hired servant."'

"So he returned home to his father. And while he was still a long way off, his father saw him coming. Filled with love and compassion, he ran to his son, embraced him, and kissed him. His son said to him, 'Father, I have sinned against both heaven and you, and I am no longer worthy of being called your son.'

"But his father said to the servants, 'Quick! Bring the finest robe in the house and put it on him. Get a ring for his finger and sandals for his feet. And kill the calf we have been fattening. We must celebrate with a feast, for this son of mine was dead and has now returned to life. He was lost, but now he is found.' So the party began.

"Meanwhile, the older son was in the fields working. When he returned home, he heard music and dancing in the house, and he asked one of the servants what was going on. 'Your brother is back,' he was told, 'and your father has killed the fattened calf. We are celebrating because of his safe return.'

"The older brother was angry and wouldn't go in. His father came out and begged him, but he replied, 'All these years I've slaved for you and never once refused to do a single thing you told me to. And in all that time you never gave me even one young goat for a feast with my friends. Yet when this son of yours comes back after squandering your money on prostitutes, you celebrate by killing the fattened calf!'

"His father said to him, 'Look, dear son, you have always stayed by me, and everything I have is yours. We had to celebrate this happy day. For your brother was dead and has come back to life! He was lost, but now he is found!'"

—LUKE 15:11–32, NLT

In years past, when I would read the story about the prodigal son, I took it quite literally. The son (being me) returned to his father (my earthly father) after he had squandered his inheritance. And after he came to his senses, he returned to his father to ask for forgiveness and a second chance. But now my eyes had been opened to the true meaning of this story. I now *knew* that this story had nothing to do with my earthly father. The father in the text was used as a metaphor to represent the one and only Father of everything: God, my heavenly Father. Without Him, there would be no inheritance for my earthly father to give. Everything belongs to Him and everything is Him. Without Him there would be nothing to give and nothing available to receive. An inheritance given by any other is worthless; it will surely crumble.

Thank God I "came to myself," repented, and went running back, before I ruined it all. Thank God for revelation and the trials I endured, because now I *know* that He is my provision. He is my supply. My inheritance is in heaven; there is nothing on earth worth more than all of His riches and glory!

CHAPTER 36

IT WAS SEPTEMBER now. I had made a little money here and there from clients coming to the house—just enough to keep my phone on, pay my light bill, and to buy just enough groceries to sustain me and my pets Reese, Bliss, and Cash. I had received five thousand dollars from the estate at the beginning of the month. I paid two months of rent, which totaled $1,600, plus a late fee of $800. I called Ford to see about getting my car back, but by this time the fees that had accrued were just too much for me to pay. I told them to just go ahead and sell the car so they could get their money for it.

On a Saturday, I decided to treat myself and get out of the house. There was festival going on in midtown, so I grabbed a cab and headed that way. I bought eighty dollars' worth of Adderall the day before, and that night I got wasted like the other partakers of the festivities.

The following Tuesday there was a show that I wanted to go to. I started to get dressed before calling a cab. I heard in my spirit, "Check your balance," but tried to ignore it. Knowing better, I sighed and stopped what I was doing to call my bank. God kept giving me a little here, and then a little more, and then He would pull back to see whether I would forget about Him or not when I got back out into the world.

The same principle is used with lions that have spent a lifetime in captivity before they are set free to be on their own in the wild. The trainers will let them out for a short period, and then put them back in their cage. After the lion adapts to each interval of time, the trainer then lets him out for longer periods of time, until the lion has proved that he can be on his own. Then the lion is set free.

I am a lion in a proverbial cage. Prior to this experience, whenever I heard or read the words of God, "Don't forget about Me," I thought it meant just that. Before, I thought I could go out and live however I pleased—as long as Jesus crossed my mind a time or two, then I was good. *Not at all.* Now I was starting to understand what God really meant when He said, "Don't forget about Me."—"Gabriel, don't buy those pills. Did you ask Me before you called a cab and went to Cooper Young? Don't go to bars; don't smoke cigarettes; don't curse; no mixing, no mingling; stay focused on *My* will, not *your* will for your life; don't spend money on whatever you please—ask Me and I'll tell you how to handle your money."

I was in training. God was training me to be ready to step into my destiny. This next half of my life was no longer about me and what I wanted; I was on a kingdom assignment. God needed to know that He could trust me. "From everyone who has been given much, much will be demanded; and from the one who has been entrusted with much, much more will be asked" (Luke 12:48).

God was shifting everything about me from the old ways to the new. I could no longer spend money frivolously like in days past. Any money that came to me belonged to God, not me. So He had to retrain my brain. He was taking me out of the world's system and introducing me to His. Since the money belonged to Him, I had to spend it the way He told me to. "Without vision, there is no provision." God isn't going to fund *your* desires. Sure, He'll bless you with money, but only if it's going to be used to build up His kingdom. My walk with God *finally* started to make sense, as soon as I understood that *it's not about me*! And I think yours will too.

> However, there shall be between you and it a distance of about 2,000 cubits by measure. Do not come near it, that you may know the way by which you shall go, for you have not passed this way before.
> —JOSHUA 3:4, NAS

After checking my bank balance, I found out I had only seven hundred dollars left. I needed way more than that to do things like get my truck out of the shop, pay for the bike, pay bills, eat, survive, etc. So I cancelled my plans, and I sat down and cried. I had planned to tithe five hundred dollars with that money, but I didn't when I first got it in my hands. If I did it now, I would only be left with two hundred dollars. So I kept putting it off.

During that month I ran a 50 percent off special and contacted all of my clients, yet again. Luckily, I was able to accumulate five hundred dollars by the end of the month. By this time, the other seven hundred was already gone. I owed so much money everywhere, with very little coming in, that everything I did obtain quickly left my hands. I hadn't even managed to break even yet. I still had very far to go.

I heard in my spirit over and over again for days that I was to take the five hundred dollars I had left and give it all to God. My rent was almost due, and I had finally collected a decent amount of money. It sounded insane for me to just "get rid of it."

On the twenty-third, I was scheduled to work a big dining event that I had worked two years previously. I made five hundred dollars the last time I worked this event, so I knew making the last three hundred fifty dollars I needed to pay my rent was quite possible. As I toiled with this notion in my mind, weighing out the pros and cons in my head, God told me to go outside behind my house toward the wooded area where He had shown me the obstacle course a couple months earlier. I didn't know what for, so I just put on my rain boots and headed that way.

When I got to the opening in the woods where I had entered the last time, He told me not to go that way because I already knew where it would lead. He said to go past that and keep walking. The path led me up a grassy hill. At the top, it flattened out into a large area with tall weeds and lush green grass that looked like it had never been mowed.

I stopped just before going through this unknown terrain. I didn't know what might be living in that grass, so I turned to look over my shoulder for a better route. To the right of me was a small opening in a densely wooded area. It was the place where Alexis and I had exited after God led us through the woods. I didn't want to go back through what I had just come out of, so I turned to look at what was before me.

God instructed me to go through the tall grass to get to the other side. I looked beyond the blades to the other side, at what looked to be a huge drop-off, like a cliff. "God, I don't know what's living in that grass, and I don't know what's over there on the other side. It looks dangerous. I don't wanna! Can we please go another way?"

Then He said, "Do you think I would tell you to do something that would hurt you?"

"No," I said.

"I am God," He said. "I can see what's ahead of you before you ever do. Trust Me. Now, go."

I picked up my feet, ran in place a little, and looked over into the tall grass. I tried to assess what I was getting into, but I couldn't see through. Not sure what was going to happen next, I braced myself to make a run for it. As I stood there trying to make up my mind about whether I should do this or not, God reassured me by saying, "You have not gone this way before." I smiled as I started to see the purpose in this lesson, and then I took off running to the other side. I made it in no time, without a scratch. Nothing jumped out of the grass and tried to eat me either!

Feeling like a conqueror, I stood proudly and turned to look back at what I had overcome. After I'd gone through and made it to the other side, the tall grass looked less intimidating. The grass seemed sparser from this side; I could see through it better from over here. There was nothing in there that was scary at all. From the other side, the fear of "what if" was the only thing that held me back. The grassy area looked much different to me. I could walk through it now and it didn't bother me at all.

I turned to look at what I had assumed was a cliff from the other side, and what appeared to be a drop-off. Now, from this perspective, it looked like nothing but dense brush. It led straight forward and went down at a gradual slant. This less ominous hill had a fence at the bottom far off into the distance that separated it from an open field that went for miles.

The moral of this story is, there is nothing to fear but fear itself. Trust God. Follow the promptings of His Holy Spirit. Walk it out in blind faith. His instructions and guidance might not make sense at the time, but be obedient. He is omniscient. He can see what's ahead of us way before we ever do. He has a better plan for our lives, far greater than anything we could ever imagine! All we have to do is trust that He will get us there!

I knew what I had to do now. I had to take that money to God. He was about to lead me into my destiny by taking steps, with His guidance, that I had never taken before. I knew the next part of my journey with Him was going to be taken one step at a time, not knowing where the next step would lead, just trusting God for the next step in blind faith; trusting God that with every step, I would eventually find myself exactly where He planned for me to be. Like He said, "You have not gone this way before." It was time for me to put one foot in front of the other, no matter how precarious or uncomfortable it would get. I had to trust—*know*—that it would be worth it once He got me to "the place." He would tell me where it was when I got there.

━ ━ ━ ━ ━ ━ ━

Even still, I continued to hold on to the cash until the nudge to bring it to Him got more persistent. I didn't want to take the chance and not do it if this was really God. Sometimes I blamed these experiences I was having on a wild imagination.

I called Jacob and asked him to take me to the bank where LaShondria had an account for the church in Nashville.

I got to the bank and paced back and forth on the sidewalk. I couldn't make up my mind about what to do. This seemed crazy. Was I crazy? *What am I thinking? I need this money bad!* I texted LaShondria, asking her advice, and then I finally gave up and decided not to do it. I had my friend take me back to the house.

Finally, by 4:30, I knew I had to do this and no later than today. The bank closed at five o'clock, so I ran over to my neighbor's house and begged him to take me before they closed. We made it there by 4:50. I gave the money to the teller and left the bank, telling myself not to question it anymore. It was done.

My neighbor offered to take me to get a pizza before returning home. No money left and starving, I gladly obliged. He had a "buy one get one free" coupon to use. When we ordered the pizzas, the "buy one get one free" deal ended up being too good to be true. By the time we both ordered what we wanted on our pizzas, the price was much more than he had expected. Displeased, he paid for them anyway.

As we waited for them to prepare the pies, he grumbled and complained about spending all that money. I didn't want anybody doing anything for me if it wasn't done gladly. I'd just rather not eat at all. I reassured him that he didn't have to get the food, and told him that he should get his money back. He insisted that it was OK but then continued to grumble.

Without getting his permission first, I stepped up to the counter and asked the girl to cancel our order and refund him his money. She did so, and I handed the money back to my neighbor. Then I heard God say to my spirit, as clear as day, "That's how you made Me feel." I thought to myself, *Uh-oh...I think I'm in trouble.* My neighbor looked at me, dumbfounded.

I turned to walk out the door so we could head back home. I tried to brush it off, hoping that *really* wasn't what God had just said to me. But it was, and I knew it. I would come to understand in the months that followed that, as a result of my behavior—not taking my tithes to God gladly—I had just cursed myself. Thankfully, God is merciful, and He will always give us the strategy to right our wrongs. He will not leave us nor forsake us. But before God shed any light on what I had just done wrong, I had to go through the process of reaping what I had just sown.

I've said it before: our God is not out to punish us, but He *is* God, and we should respect Him and love and care for Him just like we would in any personal and intimate relationship. That's why the Bible talks about having a reverential fear of God.

> All Scripture is inspired by God and is useful for teaching the truth, rebuking error, correcting faults, and giving instruction for right living, so that the person who serves God may be fully qualified and equipped to do every kind of good deed.
> —2 TIMOTHY 3:16–17, GNT

> Don't be impressed with your own wisdom. Instead, fear the LORD and turn away from evil.
> —PROVERBS 3:7, NLT

As soon as I got home, a sadness came over me seemingly out of nowhere. All of a sudden I missed my mom. I wanted to talk to her, and badly. But why now? After being able to go all this time without talking to her, why did I suddenly feel homesick for her? I didn't care about rights or wrongs at this moment. I didn't care about all those reasons I had stayed away from her for so long. All I knew was that I wanted my mama, and now.

I called her, and after two attempts, nothing. I started to panic. What if I had gone all this time not saying a word to her, and I never get another chance to talk to her again? I freaked. When she didn't answer, it reminded me of trying to call Leo's phone after he died—that desperate feeling of wanting to talk to someone so badly but not being able to.

Then my phone rang. It was my mom, and she was crying. She said, "I was trying to call you at the exact same time you were trying to call me!"

I asked, "What's wrong, Mom?" I was extremely concerned now.

She continued, "I cut my foot and it won't stop bleeding...Can we please stop this? I can't stand not talking to each other!"

I said, "Yes, Mom, of course! But first, what are you going to do about your foot? I would take you to the ER, but I don't have a way to get over there!"

"It's OK," she said. "I'm going to drive myself."

I said, "OK, well get going! Make sure you call me after you get there! Let me know you're OK, OK?"

A few minutes passed, and Jacob called to check on me. I told him what just occurred, and he offered to drive me to the ER to go see her. I was ecstatic and jumped at the chance.

We got to the office, and my mom was sitting on the exam table swinging her feet. She had to get stitches, but she was doing fine. It was good to see her—a relief at best.

We followed her back to her house to make sure she was good. Before I left her home, she pulled me into the kitchen and started loading up bags of food from her cupboards and fridge for me. I looked over at Jacob in amazement. I thought this was God answering my prayers. Earlier that day I didn't have food, and now I did. My mom told me that I could use her car that week to go look for a job. *Wow!* I thought. *I didn't have a car, now I have a car! God is so good!*

CHAPTER 37

I SPENT THAT WEEK at my mom's. She picked me and my kids up, and we all loaded up to stay with her for a few days. Everything was turning out lovely! I went out the next day and gave my résumé to every salon I could think of. It was odd being out in the world again. I felt like a fish out of water. I had not driven a car in so long; it was almost intimidating being on the road again. I got callbacks from every salon. I was asked to come in to interview for several the following week.

Everything seemed good between Mom and me—we were excited to be around each other again. Then suddenly, it wasn't. The tables started to slowly turn. Mom became very critical of me and started to lash out in fits of anger. I started to wonder if her niceness was all an act just to woo me back in so she could get her payback.

I remember one night, I went to her room to hug her before she went to bed, and she wouldn't hug me back. It hurt my feelings so badly that I continued to follow her around her room with my arms out, pleading with her, confused as to why she wouldn't hug me. She got into bed, and before rolling over to face away from me, she said, "You didn't talk to me for three months." She turned off the light as I just stood there.

One evening after she returned home from work, we sat on the patio as she drank her wine and I read from my Bible. "Whatcha doin'?" she asked, looking over at the page I was reading. "Studying," I said. She said something critical (I can't remember exactly what) about how strange I was for doing so.

I asked her nicely why she would say such a thing. I even went as far as asking her if she believed in God. I wasn't judging her or trying to be mean, but this ticked her off. She asked me why I would ask her that, and I simply replied, "Because I don't want you to go to hell, mom." She leaned in toward me and snidely replied, "Well, then, what are you going to do about Gloria?"

What? Why would she even go there? That was uncalled for! I darted my eyes up at her as if to say, *How dare you?* I was done with this conversation, so I tried to ignore her, hoping she wouldn't say another word. I looked down and tried to continue what I was reading. "What?" she asked, like what had just come out of her mouth was somehow completely justifiable. "You don't know what it's like for someone to marry your husband."

I couldn't take anymore, so I got up and went inside the house. She had spent the week pointing out to me my every fault, talking bad about my dad and Gloria, and priding herself in the fact that because she had taken us in that week, she had kept me from starving. She tried to take credit for taking care of me even in the past three months. I couldn't take much more. I was very grateful she allowed me to use her car while she was at work, and no doubt grateful for feeding us too, but after what I had just endured the past few months, I couldn't let her take all I had left—my sanity.

She continued to reprimand me about how awful I was because of my current circumstances in life. That was all well and good, but what hurt the most when she said these things was how little she knew about me and my life. Before she said all these things to me, I had been patting myself on the back for making it this far with my life. She hadn't spent any time with me after April 30. She had no idea how close I had come to taking my own life—not just on one occasion, and not just a handful.

Every day after April 30 up until only recently I had to fight the urge to just call it quits. I knew my life was in shambles. I knew the predicament I had gotten myself into. Nobody needed to remind me how hard it was going to be to drag myself out of this massive hole I had fallen into or the many mistakes I had made. It was going to take a lot to get me back on my feet again—I knew this all too well—but the last thing I needed was someone screaming at me every day reminding me I'd screwed up. I did that enough to myself as it was. If I was going to continue to fight to get out of this situation, all I had left was a sound mind and a strong will. And those two things were slipping away quickly since I'd been around her.

I didn't want to go back to my house, truthfully. It sure was nice being there with her—having another person around, not wondering whether or not there would be food to eat the next day—and it was nice being able to use her car so I could get out and look for a job. But if I wanted to get better, I was willing to take my chances and go back to being "on my own" at my house. God had taken care of me this long—why would He stop now, all of a sudden? So I went back home.

— — — — — — —

Every time I felt like giving up, low on hope and faith, not sure if there was a light at the end of this tunnel, I kept hearing a song play over and over in my mind. It was me and Leo's song, "All of Me" by John Legend. Every time I would start to hear the lyrics in my head, I would try to cast it down and make it stop.

Finally, after the song kept popping up over and over again in my weakest moments, I thought back to the days when I would be mowing in my dad's yard and would hear the song "That's What Friends Are For" play over and over in my mind. It was God's way of letting me know that He was with me and that I was a friend of God's. It motivated me on those days I needed a reminder that I wasn't alone. It suddenly became clear to me that this song, "All of Me," was not just popping up in my brain out of nowhere. It was God singing those words to me.

I quickly pulled the song up on my computer and listened to it—only this time, instead of daydreaming about the love I'd lost with Leo, I listened to the words in a whole new light, as if God was sending me a love note. The words go back and forth; one part was my lyrics to God, and the other verses were His promises of His unfailing love for me.

The song used to make me swoon as I listened to it thinking about Leo and I's sordid love, the kind of love that hurts. Now I heard it with new ears and a new heart. It was the same song, but now it felt different. To hear the Almighty God say, "Gabriel, give Me your all, and I'll give you My all" was the sweetest, most beautiful and encouraging thing I could have heard from God. He would never leave me nor forsake me like the world does. He was also answering my prayers by telling me, "There is a way out of your current circumstances, Gabriel. All you have to do is give Me your all; if you will do that, I'll give you My all."

━━ ━━ ━━ ━━ ━━ ━━ ━━

In August, I signed on the dotted line, closing my father's estate. My signature signified, to whom I'm still not sure, that I was pleased with the final outcome. Pleased would be the last word I'd use to describe how I felt inside.

No more returning "home" to my father's house, opening the door and being greeted by the cheer, laughter, sadness, tears, joy, peace, loss, strain, hurt, great news, bad news, "glad to see me," "not thrilled to see me," whatever chapter I would happen to walk into when I entered that space and time of a moment in their lives. No matter what the relationship or hardships I had with those in that house, or around it, I belonged there. Even though most days some people didn't want me there—I'll spare the names—I was a part of something. It was a tie that could never be broken; it was my family.

Friends come and go. People come and go—they forget you; you forget them. But your family is a part of you until your dying day. Actually, it extends further than death. Don't agree? Check ancestery.com. Your family is your legacy, your ancestry, your bloodline, where you inherit things like diseases, a bull-headed personality, your talent, even your curly red hair. No matter what, even if you try your best to erase them or replace them, you are bound to one another. Even if you go as far as changing your name, these people will forever be your kin. I thank God for such a thing.

I'm going to miss walking through my father's house, hearing the TV on in the background as my dad and his wife told me about their latest ventures. "You made soap, Daddy? Well, it's beautiful. It's wonderful! I must say, I'm impressed! Can I have some of it? The fragrance smells so nice. Slice me off a few pieces from that bar that smells like roses." I would look over at him and pause for a moment to take him in. I gently smiled with approval. I felt nothing but love and a sense of pride that he was my father. In a sweet and sincere voice I would say, "You're so smart, Dad," as I helped him wrap each bar of soap in paper and place them carefully in a to-go bag.

Sometimes when I miss him, I try to recreate the comforts of being in his presence by turning on one of his favorite shows.

Sometimes I let them play in the background like comfort food—but it's just not the same. I can't smell him, look over to see his reaction to a scene, or hear him clear his throat. No—I tell ya, it's just not the same. I thought revisiting it would bring joy and at the very least a melancholy ache mixed with a side of peace. Instead, my eyes welled up with tears. All it did was remind me that my daddy isn't here.

━ ━ ━ ━ ━ ━ ━

Things were tricky with my mom now. It was as if she was using the fact that I "didn't have anything" against me. I would go back to my house for a week or so and then find myself weeping and crying over the phone with my mother. She would ask me, "What are you going to do about getting a job? How are you going to eat?" I found myself not knowing how to answer these questions for her, especially since I was asking myself the same things.

She would come at me so angry and mad with her assaults that it caused me to become panicked and confused, making it harder for me to answer. She would barely let me start to answer a question before she was onto the next one. I felt pressured, so I would always give in and go back to her house. I knew within my heart that God told me He was my provision and that He would take care of me, but after talking to my mom, I would just end up feeling confused. I could barely make sense of anything; I wasn't sure which path I was supposed to be on anymore. My focus started to get blurred. My relationship with God was getting diluted. I could barely hear His voice anymore.

My mother told me I was crazy for all this "God stuff," and I was starting to believe her. She would tell me constantly that I needed help and that she was going to take me to a hospital. She talked bad about the church I went to in Murfreesboro. She was wearing me down, and fast. What little confidence I had gotten back recently was now gone. I was embarrassed to be me. I was sure that anybody who even came near me saw what my mother saw. I didn't want to go to church or talk to LaShondria on the phone anymore.

Whoever made up the saying "Sticks and stones can break my bones, but your words can never hurt me" is a fool. With no other weapon used but her words, my mother had beaten me into a puddle of mush on the floor. She continued to tell me that all of her friends were convinced I was the problem too. Now when I went around any of them, or family members, instead of a smile, I hung my head into submission.

I remember returning home after my mom's aunt's birthday party at the nursing home. I thought the day went well, but my mother informed me instead that everybody thought I was so weird. She went on to say, "You don't even act the same anymore." All I remember doing that day was mostly keeping to myself. I spoke when others said hello; I didn't think I appeared standoffish at all. I just didn't have much to say. It wasn't like people were making their way over to me to hold much conversation anyway. After my mother said these words, though, I started to come into agreement with what she said. I didn't think anyone liked me, nor did they have a reason to.

Now that my thinking had been so twisted after being trapped in my mother's bubble of manipulation and mind games, I was no longer able to think clearly. I could barely see my own hand right in front of my face. So I agreed with my mother that I should move in with her. She demanded that I get rid of the dog I had rescued (or the one that rescued me, rather), Cash. I was hoping she might get to know him better and change her mind.

A day later, in one of her rampages, she yelled, "And you have made no attempt to get rid of that dog!" Cash was being good at her home and staying out of her way. I was struck with grief when she still demanded that he had to go. I dropped to my knees where Cash was sitting below me and wrapped my arms around his neck. I lay my head over onto his back, and I couldn't help but weep. If anybody had helped safe my life, it was Cash. If he were taken out of my life, I would be suffering another death. I couldn't imagine just getting rid of him like he meant nothing to me. Plus, I hated to think how sad and lost he would be if one day he looked around and couldn't find me, Bliss, or Reese. I just couldn't do that to him.

I had to go back to my house so I could try to make some sense of all this. I didn't know what to do or whom to call. Then it hit me: Alexis. She and I had made a pact, after April, that if anything should happen to me, she would take care of my animals. I knew we hadn't spoken in a while, and we had our own set of issues—but I knew if anyone would love Cash and take good care of him, it was definitely her.

I was out of options at this point, so I scrolled through one of my old phones to find her number. Not sure how she might respond, I sent her a text to test the water: "Hey! It's Gabriel! I miss you! Give me a shout when you get a sec!"

An hour passed by, and I still hadn't heard back from her. I didn't think much of it—maybe I would have a few months ago, but now I was so used to things not going as planned. I just took it for what it was. Maybe it wasn't what God had in mind. I knew that even if I didn't hear back from her, it would still be OK, because God would have a better plan.

Then, my phone chimed. It was a text from her: "Hey! I'm about to have lunch with my mom and sister. Call you when we get done" OK, well...this was a good sign. I took the fact that she *didn't* tell me where I could "shove it" as a good sign.

Later that afternoon, she called. When I picked up, we both screamed in excitement to hear each other's voice. "Mind if I stop by?" she asked. "I miss you guys so much!" *What a relief,* I thought. "Sure, come over!" I responded.

No matter our history, it sure was nice to talk to an old friend. I was super stoked to see her too. It felt great to talk to someone who "knew me." I hadn't thought of her much at all since I last saw her. Considering what happened the last time she was around, I never questioned whether or not I should ever talk to her again. Now I did. Now I wondered why I hadn't thought of her a lot, because at the end of the day, she had been a really great friend to me.

When she pulled into my empty driveway, she got out to greet me and we hugged each other tight. We squealed like two schoolgirls. We both took a step back to get a better look at each other. I took another step back and then stretched my arms out wide, presenting to her the now empty driveway we both stood in. I gave her the best smile I could, and then said, "I lost everything!" I dropped both my arms and shrugged my shoulders as I looked at her waiting for a response. I wasn't sure how to go about telling her, so I just got it over with as soon as possible.

She smiled at me and gave a reassuring nod, "Yeah? But that's OK. It's OK. You're alive and that's all that matters." Boy it was nice to hear her say that. She was exactly right. I may have lost a bunch of stuff, but that's all it really was—just stuff. I had my life, so I still had a lot. I was glad to know that I wasn't the only one who thought I wasn't all that bad after all.

We were sitting on the front porch catching up a bit when she admitted to me, "I had a dream about you the night before last. I dreamt I ran into your old roommate somewhere and he told me you had killed yourself." Her eyes then welled up with tears. "I woke up in tears and got on Facebook to check your page to see if this was true or not. It scared me. I asked God why He would show me something like that. I told Him that I had done my best to live better. I don't go out anymore. If I'm not at work, the only people I see are my mom and my sister. I was exercising, but I was starting to feel bored and lonely. I said, 'God, You have got to give me something here; I don't know how much more I can take." She paused. "Then...I received a text from you today." She looked up at me and smiled.

"Wow," I said. At this point I wasn't completely blown away by supernatural events. It was awesome, no doubt—but I no longer considered dreams like this to be out of the ordinary or some kind of omen. Nor did it really shock me that she heard from me right after this all happened. I just took it as confirmation that this was supposed to happen and she was supposed to be there. "That's really awesome," I told her. "Well...I'm not dead," I said jokingly, with a smile. "I'm really glad you're here."

She went on to tell me that her mom had paid her car off earlier that day too. Convinced now that this also was no coincidence, she said to me, "So, now *we* have a car. You can use it while I'm at work."

I smiled. "That's super sweet of you...thank you."

━ ━ ━ ━ ━ ━ ━

Alexis and I saw each other every day after that. She would come over after work, we would hang out on her days off, or she would take me with her when she visited her family.

Only a week had gone by when Alexis walked into my house with a look on her face, like she had news to tell. She said, "I'm moving out of my place this month, and my mom is going to pay my deposit and first month's rent after I find a new place to move into. I told her what was going on with you, and...if it would be all right, I could just move in here with you. My mom thought it sounded like a really good idea too, so she said she would pay for the rent you owe from last month and next month's rent too."

"Are you serious?" I asked her as I covered my mouth in disbelief and walked toward her to give her a big hug. "Thank you so much, Alexis! This is unbelievable. Praise God!"

She pulled back from our hug, looked at me, and said, "Don't thank me. I don't want to take any of the credit. God told me to do it." "I know," I said, "but still, *thank you*!" I yelled out in celebration, "Praise God! Thank You, God! You *are* my provision!"

"Wow, God." I said. "Wow. Thank You." I called my mom to tell her the awesome update.

"Are you kidding me?" she asked, also sharing in my joy and disbelief.

I said to her, "See, I told you, Mom. I told you there was nothing to worry about. I knew God was going to work it out somehow!"

Then she said, "I've been praying so hard!"

— — — — — — —

It had been a few weeks since I had seen my mom. I was kind of scared to be around her because I never knew what she would say or do next. I figured some distance might do us some good.

One night I asked Mom if she wanted to have a girl's night, a slumber party of sorts. I suggested that Alexis and I could come over Saturday night with the kids. She loved the idea and asked me if we would like for her to make some chili. "That sounds great, Mom! We'll grab a movie too!" This sounded like so much fun. It was cold out, and there's nothing better than staying cozy in the house and eating yummy food.

The night went well. The food was good, company was great, and so was the conversation. *Ahh…so nice to hang out and not argue.*

The next morning we slept in a bit. It was a lazy Sunday morning, so we all took it slow; we ate some breakfast, read the paper, and watched some TV on the sofa. I could tell something was on the horizon, though. The air seemed tense over where my mom sat. I kept looking over at her, trying to figure out if something was wrong.

Alexis got up to go to the restroom, and my mom got up to go upstairs and make her bed. I followed shortly behind her.

While I helped her, both of us standing on opposite sides of her bed, I asked, "What's wrong, Mom?" Then she laid into me. I still wasn't sure what for, so I kept listening as I helped her make her bed. Out of nowhere she said something about my dad getting me a job at the strip club where I used to work. *Well, that came out of left field!*

I dropped the sheet I was holding in my hand and stopped and looked at her, confused. "No he didn't," I said. "What are you even talking about?"

"Look at you," she said angrily. "No wonder you can't get a job! You probably walked in and they took one look at you and said, *nu*-uh! I mean, look at your hair and those lousy extensions."

Wow. That was a low blow. I didn't feel like I had done anything to deserve to be talked to that way, so I walked out of her room and went downstairs to tell Alexis it was time to leave. We gathered up our things and my kids so we could head back to my house.

My mom came downstairs. She said nothing, but she did that thing people do after they've been crying for a while—she sniffled and caught her breath like she was still crying until we left. Before we left, she went to hand me her credit card, with the most pitiful "poor me" look on her face. I looked at her as if to ask why she was doing this. Between sniffles of what seemed to be a fake cry at this point, she told me to use it to get some groceries.

It felt like a setup, so I paused to think about it before I reached for the card. When my fingers touched the card, she automatically slumped her shoulders and hung her head. She started to cry even harder. Her whining was disturbingly reminiscent to that of a child in a grocery store who doesn't get her way. I quickly let go of the card and looked at her, less than amused. I thought to myself how badly I did, in fact, need groceries. There was no food at my house. I would be a fool to not take the card. *Just take the card, Gabriel. Just take the card, Gabriel.* I paused in complete and utter confusion as to what choice I should make. Then she looked at me and said through tears, "You don't know what it's like to be the *mother* of someone that doesn't have anything!"

This was some next-level kind of mind games. I was so dumbfounded by all this that I was at a loss completely. At this point, I was so confused; I wasn't sure what planet we were on. I said, "Mom, do you want to go back to my house and I'll stay here, and you can see how it feels to *be* the person that doesn't have anything?" She squealed with a loud cry as though I had said something uncompassionate and showed no regard to how she was feeling. I didn't know what to do.

I didn't want to leave there with my mom so upset, but this was *way* over my head. I was at a loss. So I just said nothing. *What could I do to fix this?* I barely knew what was going on. I turned away from her, left the card in her hand as she stood there crying, and walked out the door.

CHAPTER 38

Then, calling the crowd to join his disciples, he said, "If
any of you wants to be my follower, you must turn from
your selfish ways, take up your cross, and follow me."

—MARK 8:34, NLT

I DIDN'T KNOW WHAT to do to get myself back up on my feet
again, but I knew I had to do *something*, and quick. I didn't
know if I could take much more. My life felt like it had become
a proverbial wasteland. I felt like I was being "held back" or "on
pause" on purpose, so to speak, but I couldn't make sense of
why that would be the case.

The next day was Monday. Alexis told me to use her car if I
wanted to go job hunt. I looked at her and sighed from exhaustion. I threw my hand up in the air with my palm open, hoping
an answer might fall into it, and said, "I wouldn't know where to
go even if I did! Girl, this time in my life is so weird. Common
sense would say, 'Yes, Gabriel! What you should do is go get a
job, and stat!' But in my mind, when I try to come up with a
plan of what that might look like, I can't even see past my front
door! I don't know what to do. This is so frustrating!

"I interviewed with some of the best salons here in Nashville. All of them hired me, but each one had some excuse as to why I couldn't start working for them, at least not right now, anyway. One even told me that I had so much to offer but she had nowhere to put me! That has to be God…right? Everything that used to work, or should have worked, just hasn't worked for me at all this time around. Look at my clientele list!"—I picked up a thick stack of papers from my desk—"I mean, look at how many clients I used to have! And now…zilch, zip, nada! I've barely got a handful of people from this entire list that still come to me to get their hair done.

"I don't get it. It just seems like God has shut doors so I can't get out there and do whatever seems to be a good idea *to me* at the time, just because I need a job. And I'm OK with that. I don't feel like I'm supposed to do hair anymore anyway. I don't know what He wants me to do. I wish I knew, because if I did, then I would go do it!"

I was completely at a loss, almost at my wits' end. I plopped down on the chair next to me, dropped my elbows onto the table, and dropped my head down into my hands. I let out an exasperated sigh and a grumble. Then I propped my chin up with both of my fists. I cut my eyes to the right to look over at Alexis and said, "God's been telling me to write a book for months now…actually years. I guess I'll do that and see if that's what He wants. If not, then I'll try something else. Why not? It's worth a try."

So I put my nose to the grindstone, and I committed that day and the next to writing. I still wasn't sure if I had anything to write about that anybody might find interesting, but I wrote the first couple of stories that came to mind to see how I felt after reading them. "OK," I thought, "it's OK. I guess they might be worth reading, to somebody."

On the third day of writing, I pushed through my resistance; I decided to delve deeper and go to those places where I hid stories from my childhood, the ones I'd rather keep there and not revisit, just to see if I would be able to do it. I also wanted to see if my writing made me sound like some sniveling, dumb girl just looking for a pity party so people could feel sorry for her. If I did come off that way, then I wasn't going to write anymore. This would be the one last deciding factor on whether or not I would carry on with writing this book. It sounded like a good enough plan to me. So I wrote. I think I finished four different "stories" that day.

By the end of the day, I started to believe that the emotions that arose from writing just might kill me. Both mentally and emotionally depleted, I placed the pages on top of my dresser and looked at myself in the mirror. I said out loud, "God, this might kill me! I don't know if I can do this. What if I keep digging and it gets to be too much for me, and then I literally go right off the deep end, never to return? I feel like this could be dangerous for me to do right now...What if it's too much for me to handle?"

I kept staring at my face in the mirror, searching for an answer. Then I heard God say, "This is your cross." That was all the confirmation I needed to keep going. I looked down at the pages before me. I picked them up and started to proofread what I had written so far. The writing seemed OK—it might be interesting enough for people to read, I guess—but the places I had to go to dig up the info were places I had done my very best to forget. Some of these things that I unearthed as I continued to dig deeper and deeper into my memory bank were *important* things I had made myself forget.

One of the memories was about my dad, how I used to picture him as he drove back to Murfreesboro from Nashville after dropping me off. I forgot that I used to do that. And that I worried for him so, hoping he wasn't sad or lonely on his own. I suddenly remembered what those days were like for me and how it felt to live them.

Until I had written the words on the page, I had forgotten how much love my dad and I *did* have for each other. I just stuffed it all down. I was twelve when Dad met Gloria. Afterward, his affection for me started to dissipate. I guess in my child mind, it was easier to make myself forget that he ever loved me than to remember the days when he still acted like he did.

It started to make sense to me. I guess it *would* hurt less to pretend like it never happened than to play the memories over and over in my mind, longing for and missing something that wasn't ever going to be there again. All of a sudden, those places where I didn't want to go seemed less scary. They became more like a healing to me. I wasn't sure what I should write about next, so I just kept going.

The following day, Alexis brought me three notebooks and two packs of pens. I filled two of the notebooks up while she was at work the next day. I just kept going, not yet knowing if it was right or wrong, or if it was what God wanted or not. Then I started typing everything I had written down and finished writing the book by typing the rest.

I told God that I needed a way to end the book. I prayed that He would tell me as I got closer to the end. I prayed, "I need a happy ending for my story. People are going to read this and wonder if there's still some girl 'stuck' in her house in Tennessee. Telling my story might make people run instead of wanting to come into a closer relationship with You, God! No offense, Lord, but I want my story to glorify You and the kingdom, not scare people away. I pray, God, for an ending that encourages and inspires those that are lost—an ending that doesn't make it seem, to both unbelievers and believers alike, that all my pain was in vain. I love You so much, God! In spite of it all, I know what You have done for me! I need Your help. How do I make them see that a life with You is better than any other? Amen."

━━ ━━ ━━ ━━ ━━ ━━ ━━

Late one afternoon, God told me to go out into my backyard since I hadn't spent much time with Him outside lately. I grabbed a quilt, and Cash and I headed out the back door. I spread the quilt out over the grass. I lay on my back and looked up at the sky. It was one of my favorite times of day, right as the sun starts to go down.

The sky was beautiful! Every which way I looked, from corner to corner, every inch of the sky was more beautiful than the last. I extended my neck, rolling my head back so I could see parts of the sky behind me. I looked straight ahead again and then from one side to the other, trying to look all around, looking for signs and wonders in the sky. I tried my best to put the shapes of the clouds into something with some kind of meaning, looking for a message from God.

Then God said to me, "Stop looking around for signs and wonders. If I want to show you signs and wonders, you don't have to look hard. If I want you to see it, I will put it in front of you. Now, look directly at the sky above you and focus on that one spot. Don't move your eyes; don't move your head. Just look at one spot and don't move." So I did. Not a minute passed, and there before me in the clouds, directly where I had focused my attention, was a square-shaped rainbow. It seemed to have appeared out of nowhere. I watched as it faded away into the clouds.

Then in my spirit I saw an image of roots under a tree, the tree behind my house in the woods that sat above a dried-up riverbank. (I'd used the roots to crawl up the wall when Alexis and

I were looking for a way out, remember?) God showed me that these roots served a purpose. They kept the dirt from eroding and falling away from the tree, and also kept the tree erect and the embankment intact.

God continued to talk to me about the purpose of some other things that He created. He showed me an apple. He said that the apple had a purpose, and that was to be eaten. If you didn't eat the apple and just let it sit, it would rot, going to waste and serving no purpose at all. He used this illustration as a metaphor for money. He said that if you ate the apple, then took the seeds from the core and put them back into the ground, a tree would grow, thus producing more apples. If you took the seeds from all those apples, they would eventually produce a harvest.

He told me to give the seeds back to Him and not watch the ground to see if the seeds would grow. He said that we should trust that the seeds will produce a harvest because that is how His system works. He wants us to sow the seeds, trust the process, and not worry, asking questions like, "Did you plant the right seeds? Was the seed you planted a dud?" God said that it's just like faith. He wants us to give a portion back and then rest in Him. So go about doing good, and have faith that in His timing, you will reap what you sow. Just as God's Word promises.

—————

A day later, I told Alexis about the stories I was including in the book. I mentioned a few that we both went through before and after Leo died. She said to me, "Remember the dream I had when we first started hanging out in January?" I answered, "No—remind me."

So she continued: "I saw you sitting on a plaid couch. You were bent over crying with your face in both hands. I pleaded, 'God, I don't know what to do for her. You've gotta help me!'

Then He placed a piece of paper on the counter beside me. Written on it was 'John 1:5.' I woke up the next morning and looked up the scripture. It reads, 'The light shines in the darkness, and the darkness has not overcome it.'"

Wow, I thought to myself, *This was it! The answer to my prayer! This is how He would have me finish the book!* Everything made sense now—not just the book...*my life!* It had come full circle. All the trials and misfortunes I had endured could never keep me from being who I really am. I am a child of the Most High God! No matter how the devil tried to snuff me out or to make me curse God, he couldn't do it. I belonged to God, so the dark was not able to overtake me, no matter how hard it tried!

Nevertheless, what I thought then would be an ending to my story would in fact turn out to be just the very beginning...

Job responds to the Lord

Then Job replied to the LORD:
"I know that you can do anything and no one can stop you. You asked, 'Who is this that questions my wisdom with such ignorance?' It is I—and I was talking about things I knew nothing about, things far too wonderful for me. You said, 'Listen and I will speak! I have some questions for you, and you must answer them.' I had only heard about you before, but now I have seen you with my own eyes. I take back everything I said, and I sit in dust and ashes to show my repentance."

Conclusion: The Lord Blesses Job

After the LORD had finished speaking to Job, he said to Eliphaz the Temanite: "I am angry with you and your two friends, for you have not spoken accurately about me, as my servant Job has. So take seven bulls and seven rams and go to my servant Job and offer a burnt offering for yourselves. My servant Job will pray for you, and I will accept his prayer on your behalf. I will not treat you as you deserve, for you have not spoken accurately about me, as my servant Job has." So Eliphaz the Temanite, Bildad the Shuhite, and Zophar the Naamathite did as the LORD commanded them, and the LORD accepted Job's prayer.

When Job prayed for his friends, the LORD restored his fortunes. In fact, the LORD gave him twice as much as before! Then all his brothers, sisters, and former friends came and feasted with him in his home. And they consoled him and comforted him because of all the trials the LORD had brought against him. And each of them brought him a gift of money and a gold ring.

So the LORD blessed Job in the second half of his life even more than in the beginning. For now he had 14,000 sheep, 6,000 camels, 1,000 teams of oxen, and 1,000 female donkeys. He also gave Job seven more sons and three more daughters. He named his first daughter Jemimah, the second Keziah, and the third Keren-happuch. In all the land no women were as lovely as the daughters of Job. And their father put sthem into his will along with their brothers.

Job lived 140 years after that, living to see four generations of his children and grandchildren. Then he died, an old man who had lived a long, full life.

—JOB 42:1–17, NLT

Have you made Jesus Christ your Lord and Savior? Would you like to? Why don't you pray these words with your heart and confess Him as Lord with your mouth by praying this prayer with me?

Lord Jesus, I ask You to come into my life and forgive me of all my sins. I confess my sins before You this day. I denounce Satan and all his works. I confess Jesus as the Lord of my life. Thank You for saving me. I believe with my heart and I confess with my mouth that You rose from the dead. I am saved. Write my name in the Lamb's Book of Life. Today is my God-day with the Lord Jesus! I pray this prayer to the Father in the name of Jesus. Amen.[2]

That if you confess with your mouth the Lord Jesus and believe in your heart that God has raised Him from the dead, you will be saved.

—ROMANS 10:9, NKJV

Jesus answered and said to him, "Most assuredly, I say to you, unless one is born again, he cannot see the kingdom of God."

—JOHN 3:3, NKJV

---

2 Jesse Duplantis Ministries, "Prayer of Salvation," accessed August 20, 2015, http://www.jdm.org/jdmDefault.aspx?tabindex=-1&tabID=50.

Contact the Author

If you would like to contact the author for
general information, interview requests, or speaking
engagements, you can do so by e-mailing:

gabrielisrael@outlook.com

25547909R00215

Made in the USA
San Bernardino, CA
02 November 2015